22-50

ACTIONS AND STRUCTURE

ACTIONS AND STRUCTURE

Research Methods and Social Theory

edited by
Nigel G. Fielding

SAGE Publications
London · Newbury Park · Beverly Hills · New Delhi

Introduction, Conclusion and editorial matter
© Nigel G. Fielding 1988
Chapter 1 © Karin Knorr-Cetina 1988
Chapter 2 © Wes Sharrock and Rod Watson 1988
Chapter 3 © Peter K. Manning 1988
Chapter 4 © Paul Rock 1988
Chapter 5 © Colin Clark and Trevor Pinch 1988
Chapter 6 © John D. Brewer 1988
Chapter 7 © John Scott and Peter Cowley 1988
Chapter 8 © Peter Abell 1988

First published 1988

 SAGE Publications Ltd
28 Banner Street
London EC1Y 8QE

SAGE Publications Inc
2111 West Hillcrest Drive
Newbury Park, California 91320

SAGE Publications Inc
275 South Beverly Drive
Beverly Hills, California 90212

SAGE Publications India Pvt Ltd
32, M-Block Market
Greater Kailash – I
New Delhi 110 048

British Library Cataloguing in Publication data

Actions and structure: research methods
   and social theory.
   1. Sociology. Methodology
   I. Fielding, Nigel
   301′.01′8

   ISBN 0–8039–8147–3

Library of Congress catalog card number 88–060379

Typeset by Fakenham Photosetting Ltd, Fakenham, Norfolk
Printed in Great Britain by J.W. Arrowsmith Ltd, Bristol

Contents

Notes on contributors   vi

Introduction   **Between micro and macro**
Nigel G. Fielding   1

1   **The micro-social order**
Towards a reconception
Karin Knorr-Cetina   20

2   **Autonomy among social theories**
The incarnation of social structures
Wes Sharrock and Rod Watson   54

3   **Semiotics and social theory**
The analysis of organizational beliefs
Peter K. Manning   78

4   **Micro-sociology and power**
A natural history of research on policy-making
Paul Rock   99

5   **Micro-sociology and micro-economics**
Selling by social control
Colin Clark and Trevor Pinch   117

6   **Micro-sociology and the 'duality of structure'**
Former Fascists 'doing' life history
John D. Brewer   142

7   **Individual and social connections**
A perspective from the Q-analysis method
John Scott and Peter Cowley   167

8   **The 'structuration' of action**
Inference and comparative narratives
Peter Abell   185

Conclusion   **Micro-sociology and macro-theory**
Nigel G. Fielding   197

Index   199

Contributors

Peter Abell is Professor of Sociology, Surrey University, with interests in the political economy of industrial democracy, organizational theory, the concept of social action, model-building, and power in social systems.

John D. Brewer is Lecturer in Social Studies, The Queen's University, Belfast, with interests in phenomenology, ethnomethodology, policing and the extreme right.

Colin Clark is Research Fellow in Sociology, York University, and is engaged in a detailed programme of research into market traders.

Peter Cowley was until recently Lecturer in Psychiatry, Leicester University; he is now with Sunnyside Hospital in Christchurch, New Zealand. He has investigated the use of Q-analysis in clinical psychiatry, in defining psychological systems and in developing mental health services.

Nigel G. Fielding is Lecturer in Sociology, Surrey University. He has published books on the extreme right, sociological methodology, and criminal justice, and has theoretical interests in interactionism and in ideology.

Karin Knorr-Cetina is Professor of Sociology, University of Bielefeld, a leading figure in the debate over micro-sociology and social theory, and co-editor of *Advances in Social Theory and Methodology*.

Peter K. Manning is Professor of Sociology, Michigan State University, with wide-ranging research interests, notably policing, and a close concern with discourse and semiotic analysis.

Trevor Pinch is Lecturer in Sociology, York University. His main work has been in the sociology of science and technology, on which he has published several books. His current research is on practical economic reasoning.

Paul Rock is Professor of Social Institutions, London School of Economics, and has published extensively in the fields of interactionism, deviance, and social control.

John Scott is Lecturer in Sociology, Leicester University. His work has concentrated on the analysis of social networks, particularly regarding business and financial power, drawing on mathematical sociology.

Wes Sharrock is Senior Lecturer in Sociology, Manchester University, and a leading ethnomethodologist who has published a number of books in the field.

Rod Watson is Senior Lecturer in Sociology, Manchester University. His interests are ethnomethodology and conversation analysis, the application of analytic philosophy to sociological theory, and the textual and stylistic analysis of sociological writing. He has also published on deviance, education and formal organizations.

Introduction
BETWEEN MICRO AND MACRO

Nigel G. Fielding

Recent years have witnessed a marked increase in research concerning the micro-sociology of everyday life. The work has embraced perspectives from social interactionism to ethnomethodology and conversational analysis. Social scientists have now begun to take stock of these developments, in particular, their implications for the macro-level theory of society. The implications are far-reaching, affecting our understanding of power relations, the manner in which social institutions have, and achieve, structure, and the models of large-scale organizations construed by members and clients.

At issue is the analytic value in regarding macro-scale institutions as systems impinging on the actions of individuals, and whether patterns manifest at the aggregate level should be seen as expressing the system's dynamic or as reflecting the interactions of individuals and groups. The conventional distinction between macro- and micro-sociology has been transected by the shift away from a concern with the functional imperatives and needs of social systems towards a presumption of the importance of conflict and power in the shaping of macro-level institutions and of the knowledgeability and autonomy of social actors in the construction of social reality. That shift is implicit in interactionist and ethnomethodological research and explicit in the onslaught of Marxian and critical theory on structural-functionalism. Even in the analysis of conversation, Giddens has argued that one can no more transcribe meaning in communication by schema that ignore *contextual dependence* than one can grasp it in terms of a *lexicon*. Habermas (1972), following Apel (1967), has attempted to clarify the connection of hermeneutics with other approaches to social analysis. They regard social science as both hermeneutic and nomological, and suggest the need to complement both strands with 'critical theory'. It is a mechanism to connect the 'explication of human action with the properties of social institutions as *structures*' (Giddens, 1976: 69). To Giddens, a distinction is needed between collectivities, consisting of interactions between members, and structures. This leads Giddens to 'structuration' as the locus of explanation in structural analysis. His preoccupation with the conditions which govern the preservation or dissolution of structures necessitates specifying the connections between 'structuration' and 'structure' (1976: 120).

It is to Giddens' credit that he recognizes that the production of 'meaning' is only one element of interaction; 'every interaction is also a *moral* and a *power relation*' (1976: 118). Power is implicated in the production of meaning in interaction. Power is manifest in interaction as resources participants employ in seeking to direct its course. These include the skills by which interaction is made meaningful as well as more obvious sources of influence such as the possession of authority or legitimate force (1976: 112). Giddens argues that the creation of frames of meaning 'occurs as *the mediation of practical activities*' and is marked by differentials of power which actors bring to bear. This at least meets the familiar point that, because it studies micro-level settings, micro-sociology is oblivious to the critical effect of power. Power is apparent at micro-level, despite the 'co-operative' impression one sometimes gets from analyses of actors' 'routine practical accomplishments'. '*The reflexive elaboration of frames of meaning is characteristically imbalanced in relation to the possession of power*, whether this be a result of the superior linguistic or dialectical skills of one person in conversation with another; the possession of relevant types of "technical knowledge", the mobilisation of authority or "force"' (1976: 112).

The empirical problem lies in recognizing the faint echoes of subjects' meaning (known from intensive study of one setting) when the scene is shifted, either 'laterally' or 'vertically'. An instance is the case of occupational culture and situated action in the police. It is argued both that the culture is strong and that discrete features of situation frequently (and unpredictably) determine action (see Chatterton, 1979). If the culture is strong it must generate powerful rules, yet the regularity this implies is subordinate to the officers' situated sense of what is best done in particular cases. As Holdaway asks, 'If a rule is contextualised in a vast range of settings of police work, what is the status of the primary rule? Is it an essential feature of the occupational culture from which its phenomenal use is derived? Or is the essentiality of a rule not clearly formulated in the rank and file mind, being a sort of survival that is so dimly perceived that it hardly warrants the ascription and status of a rule?' (1985). Analyses of the determinants of patrol-officer decision-making have been unable to reconcile these alternatives; decisions either originate in some (analytically derived) world-view or are highly contingent. No linkage between holistic world-view and situated fragment is apparent. Missing is a political economy of police decisions which reveals officers as ciphers neither for culture nor for situation. Giddens' approach takes us away from descriptive analysis of those interactional relations which comprise collectivities towards 'systems of generative rules and resources'. The important emphasis in Giddens is on the *duality* of structure, so that 'social structures are both constituted by human agency, and yet at the same time are the very *medium* of their constitution'. The constitution of action must be studied above the level of interaction *per se*.

Giddens' notion of 'structuration' is not the only attempt to approach reconciliation in the 'agency–structure' debate. That debate has been preoccupied with the concerns raised by Lockwood in his early analysis of system and social interaction (1964). Particularly disputed is the approach taken to the concept of power, where the issue is a question of dualism versus duality (Archer, 1982). For example, Steven Lukes has sought to maintain analytical 'dualism' by separating structural determination from the exercise of power, writing of that point 'where structural determination ends and power begins' (1977: 18). It clearly contradicts Giddens' attempt to transcend the division by defining power as 'transformative capacity'; as Archer notes, this maintains 'duality' by viewing structure as implicated in power relations and power relations as implicated in structure. Lukes does not deny the interconnection but wants to avoid blurring the distinction between responsible and determined action, since the tie between power and responsibility is critical in his approach. Nevertheless, Lukes' conception hardly neglects the interconnection; he puts effort into assessing exactly the boundaries of structural limits on action, 'which delimit the zone in which it is proper (and profitable) to speak of power relations' (Archer, 1982: 481). This is, arguably, a helpful attempt to specify the scope of autonomy and bounds of social determination, that is, 'the degrees of freedom *within which* power can be exercised' (1982: 482).

Margaret Archer has criticized Giddens' neglect of the moves in general systems theory to reunite agency and structure, and of neofunctionalist arguments (Buckley, 1967). Systems theorists are in agreement with Giddens on the processual quality of the interaction between agency and structure, but the process of 'morphogenesis' they describe is opposed to that of structuration in that it has an end-product, structural elaboration, whereas Giddens' social system manifests simply as a 'visible pattern'. Unlike Giddens, the systems theorists see the elaborated structure as having properties which cannot be reduced to recurrent social practices alone. This approach emphasizes the discontinuity between initial interactions and their product (the complex system). This position insists on analytical dualism with regard to structure and action because of the implication of sequentiality intrinsic in arguing that all subsequent interaction will differ from earlier action because it is informed by the structural results of the earlier action. '(T)he morphogenetic perspective is not only dualistic but sequential, dealing in endless cycles of structural conditioning/social interaction/structural elaboration – thus unravelling the dialectical interplay between structure and action. "Structuration", by contrast, treats the ligatures binding structure, practice and system as indissoluble, hence the necessity of *duality* and the need to gain a more indirect analytical purchase on the elements involved' (Archer, 1982: 458).

Archer identifies three principal advantages that analytic dualism has over the duality of structure in relation to the dichotomies generated by considerations of action and structure. First, the systems-theory emphasis on specifying the extent of autonomy and constraint facilitates theorizing about the variations in voluntarism and determinism. In contrast, Giddens' insistence on 'the simultaneity of transformative capacity and chronic recursiveness' (Archer, 1982: 477) implicitly rules out theorization of the conditions under which one or the other will achieve dominance. Secondly, despite Giddens' recognition of the theoretical importance of space and time, theorizing about temporal structuring and restructuring is blocked by his argument that the conceptual bonding of the synchronic and diachronic produces 'a seamless web of "instantiations"'. In the morphogenesis approach the analytic separation of structure and interaction over time facilitates such theorizing. Thirdly, it is apparent that maintaining the analytic distinction between subject and object over time permits theorizing about the influence of individuals on society and society on individuals; by contrast, the duality-of-structure approach tends either to the incorporation of 'society' into 'man' or to the 'dubious imputation of "principles" articulating the two' (1982).

Archer argues that an approach based on 'morphogenesis' is more resilient than 'structuration' and, as Dandeker notes, this is particularly so in the case of producing testable theoretical propositions about when and how much freedom is available to social actors (1986). That this debate is at the heart of the division of labour between disciplines that concern themselves with social behaviour is apparent from Jeffery Alexander's recent attempt to identify how interactionist and phenomenological sociologies have enriched structuralist accounts of social order (1985). He argues that basing theory on the presupposition that social structures are comprised of individuals inevitably leads to a fragmented, anarchistic model of society, and he reminds us of the efforts of Husserl and Mead to reveal the dialectic between the efforts of individuals to construct social reality and the collective resources employed in so doing.

To Alexander, recent standard-bearers such as Garfinkel and

Blumer have tended towards 'radically individualist accounts of social order' which have driven apart the poles of debate between
'subjective and objective idealists'. It is, inevitably, a matter of
interpretation, but the important point is that the grounds of debate
are agreed. For example, Johnson and Picou (1985) have criticized
the recent emphasis on the 'objectivist' and social realist theme in
Mead, and the characterization of Blumer's theoretical thrust as
individualist, but despite this they too speak of a transcendence
between nominalism and realism (in this case, by endorsing lines of
argument in James and Mead). This convergence on the issue of the
mechanism of translation between action and structure is particularly
important in light of the considerable increase in research informed
by micro-sociological traditions. It is a change from the position
prevailing during the rise of ethnomethodology, when the tendency
was to regard such subdisciplines as self-contained and largely independent, if not actually subversive, of the wider agenda of social
theory (Atkinson, 1985).

But this debate is not merely motivated by the concerns of subdisciplines and schools of thought. There is a strong argument that,
latterly, social scientists' range of inquiry has been considerably
reduced and partly superseded by a 'research enterprise defined by
the agenda of "clients"' (Wardell and Turner, 1986: 165). While the
prevailing harsh climate towards social science in North America and
Britain has much to do with this, Wardell and Turner locate a
measure of blame in the divergence of theoretical and practical study
which has been tolerated during a time of increasing specialization.
Classical sociology hardly separated the two. While sociologists can
do little directly to affect the wider political problem they can at least
re-establish connection between empirical study, social theory, and
the dimensions of analysis which inform political criticism. This
orientation to the wider implications of empirical research again
leads to the core theoretical arguments over action and structure, but
with a political focus sharpened by social scientists' own (albeit
relative) experience of disprivilege. In some analyses this leads to
attempts to transcend the bipolar disputes between structuralism and
what Hindess terms 'theoretical humanism' by means of an anti-
reductionist stance (see Hindess, 1986).

An instance of these developments is the major shift since the early
sixties in the study of law, deviance, and social control. The processes
by which rules are created, enforced, and transformed are obviously
critical here, and reflect our general understanding of the extent to
which control is truly 'social'. Even in American criminology it has
become acceptable to argue that the once-pervasive conception of
social control as cornerstone of social order and expression of inte-

grating, shared and consensual needs is obsolete. The relationship between 'society' and 'control' has become a problem, not a given, and a matter of contingency (Black, 1984). As Spitzer and Scull note, 'instead of assuming that laws, regulations and other socially-organised sanctions are embedded in the immediate and informal arenas of "role-taking" (Mead, 1925), the "complementarity of expectations" (Parsons, 1951), "voluntary associations" (Park and Burgess, 1924; Ross, 1901) or "community" (Davis and Anderson, 1983), recent scholarship has insisted on exploring control's darker and less conspicuous side' (Spitzer and Scull, 1985: 2). The coercive dimensions of order have been highlighted, and instead of order being a natural emanation of society in equilibrium it is seen as the conscious product of definable groups and classes, with the State a principal actor.

In the shift from an organic to a critical conception of social order, a corollary has been the idea that the 'social' character of control is more likely to be determined by the bureaucratic and rationalized institutions of the State than by the 'organic' institutions in the traditional conception of 'society'. 'While the old definition of social control saw control as embedded in and reflective of the "social", the new perspective sees "the social" as an expression of and vehicle for the agendas of control. Only by turning the traditional conception of social control on its head is it possible to appreciate how new understandings of the relationship between law, deviance and social control have emerged – understandings which stress the significance of conflict, hierarchy and ideology in the ordering and regulation of social life' (1985: 2–3).

So what has emerged is an inversion of past assumptions. Where it was formerly argued that 'order' suffused local relations and permeated up from small, co-operative relations through law-making institutions to the relations of the State with its citizens in an organic order, it is now argued that a State concerned to maintain its grip, and itself a prize in a continual struggle of competing interests, manipulates its agencies and institutions, and semi-autonomous institutions such as family and local community, by means of physical and mental resources (ideology). Yet the previous conception was well supported by empirical research, as even the few citations above suggest. It is not empirical studies that have led to this shift. It is arguable that the impetus came from the politicization of social scientists during the sixties, particularly in the USA. Nor is it empirical research that will establish this version as finally compelling, if it ever is. That is because of the fitful way in which research is done and knowledge emerges.

The susceptibility to dramatic 'paradigm shifts' suggests the necessity, in theoretical analyses of empirical phenomena, to make explicit the articulation between action and structure, phenomena observed in micro and their impact at macro-level, and vice versa. For example one may take the argument over the 'universality' of criminological theory and the need for comparative studies of crime. Refuting the case for separate theoretical discourse for each 'region' of the world, Birkbeck has argued that a more fruitful basis for comparative theory in criminology is to specify the 'testable domains' outlined by any theory. Applying this criterion to regionally specific theory, he argues that this will establish how much understanding is gained by region-specific theory and that rather than adopting regional distinctions a priori, the regional specificity of any crime phenomenon be tested rather than assumed. This will obviate the veracity of alleged 'Latin American' patterns of victimization or 'Oriental' police systems in the absence of empirical proof (Birkbeck, 1985). Like the argument in social theory, the shift in criminological theory proclaims the need to ensure that, when a phenomenon at local level is held to have wider consequences, or when a supposedly universal phenomenon is said to cause things locally, the linkages be made explicit and each element rigorously sustained empirically.

Methodology and the theoretical debate

A concern with 'meaning' and subjective experience is characteristic of qualitative sociology. The stance is demanding, for it requires us to convince others that all analysis is partial, but that our own is compelling. What counts as 'knowledge' in phenomenology is distinctive. The concern with subjective experience leads to a preoccupation with 'world-view' and a holistic analytic stance, which can never be achieved in a final sense, since the methodology is replete with warnings against merging with the subjects of research (see Glassner, 1980: 42). It is apparent that the range of utility of knowledge derived in this fashion is limited. Strictly applied, approaches based on subjective experience are severely limited. This is not to argue that they are not illuminating, only that the range of application cannot be established without the use of other sources of data and by the presentation of an analysis which spells out links in pursuing the most general possible application of the data (see Fielding and Fielding, 1986).

In the relatively rare cases where qualitative data are employed in a causal analysis, the line of argument corresponds to analytic induction's procedure of defining the phenomenon and a hypothetical explanation of it (Znaniecki, 1934). One case is then studied to see whether the hypothesis relates to it. If not the hypothesis is reformulated (or the phenomenon redefined to exclude the case). While a small number of cases support 'practical certainty', negative cases disprove the explanation, which is then reformulated. Examination of cases, redefinition of the phenomenon and reformulation of hypotheses is repeated until a universal relationship is shown. The obvious problem of this approach is the matter of universal propositions, whose applicability one must question in relation to all case studies.

The problem is not solved by Glaser and Strauss' 'grounded theory' approach. Unlike analytic induction, their 'constant comparative' method is designed to generate and develop categories, properties and hypotheses, not to test them. Incidents are compared which apply to each category by coding the data and comparing them with previous data. Then the categories and their properties are integrated. The theory is then delimited or reduced, and the 'saturation' of the categories is delimited. Glaser and Strauss' dismissal of the need for testing or refining hypotheses has been widely criticized. Further, they have a rather naïve impression of the field-worker's ability to ignore prior conceptualizations, including their own common-sense understandings (Brewer, 1979). Others have criticized their characterization of 'theory'; Williams suggests that by theory they simply mean 'properties, categories and hypotheses' (1976). In fact, 'grounded theory' does not much resemble the prevalent analytic activity in qualitative research: the treatment of detailed ethnographic description as illustrating only certain elements of some theory. The difference between descriptive and analytic accounts is seen by Ditton as a transfer of interest from the full ethnography to general social processes associated with the phenomenon (1979). In the 'theorized ethnography' the theoretical formulation appears to emanate from mysterious *ad hoc* choices as much as from systematic procedures accessible to *ex post facto* reinterpretation.

There are limitations on the validity of the generalizations of qualitative research and its strength as a basis of causal explanation. Data to enable a particular interpretation to be checked may not have been gathered, or the 'typicality' of crucial items of data may not have been assessed, or comparative cases to enable testing of an emergent theory may not have been explored. We should also implicate how qualitative researchers confirm the validity of their findings. It is a clear requirement of an approach emphasizing the articulation of micro- and macro-analysis that no source of data be accorded priority as a given, a claim sometimes made of data gathered by subjective experience. However, many qualitative researchers share with others a concern with validation and reliability, but can be as slippery as others in making a virtue of necessity when it comes to the characteristic weaknesses of their position.

Of course there are also legitimate objections to the assumptions made by researchers using large-scale data sets, particularly concerning procedures at the point of data collection; quantitative researchers can hardly expect to escape the charges they have often brought against qualitative research. Harré has explored the points of ambiguity in questionnaire/interview schedule response. He cites the fact that by asking a question one invites the use of the answering to perform an act of self-presentation. A second criticism is the context-dependence of the interpretation of even quite direct questions. It raises the vexed relation of beliefs and action. A third problem is that what are presented as empirical generalizations may actually be 'necessary truths' which reflect a conceptual relation. 'Some recent studies of the social conditions that engender personal popularity have been shown to be seriously confused, setting about empirical studies to verify statements that simply define "popularity"' (Harré, 1981; see also Gilbert, 1979).

It is conventional for positivist researchers to commend qualitative work in the limited role of pilot work or hypothesis formulation. The reason for this is a quite fundamental epistemological distinction, rather than ignorance, convenience, or preference for established procedures. The matter cannot be resolved merely by commending mutual orientation to more rigorous standards of data 'quality control'. As Giddens notes, 'self-consciousness has always been regarded, in positivistically-inclined schools of social theory, as a nuisance to be minimized; these schools endeavour to substitute external observation for "introspection". The specific "unreliability" of the "interpretation of consciousness", indeed, whether by the self or by an observer, has always been the principal rationale for the rejection of *verstehen* by such schools' (Giddens, 1976: 19). They see the empathic apprehension of consciousness merely as a possible source of hypotheses. Yet, as Knorr-Cetina has argued, 'short of sufficient knowledge of *how* data, records and reports are generated interactionally and organizationally, we have no basis for unequivocally assessing the meaning of these outcomes, much less for assessing their validity', and if we are to achieve a macro-sociology that is empirically grounded she argues that the project must be to study the 'situated social production of data and records microscopically across different types of organizations' (1981: 14).

Qualitative researchers have also pursued a reductionist stance on the need to dismantle what they regard as the overly condensed character of the variables used in quantitative research. For example, Collins has asserted that only time, space, and number of combinations of micro-situations can be admitted as 'pure macro-variables' (1981a). All other sociological variables and concepts can be translated into people's experience in micro-situations, a stance which argues that there are 'pure micro-principles' and that these should be at the core of all empirically causal explanations (1981b: 101). Whether this is genuinely in prospect is best assessed by considering the macro-sociologists' view of the current achievements of micro-sociology.

An ironic statement of the macro-sociologists' position on micro-sociology is suggested by Cicourel, speaking of the seemingly ahistorical and limited character of the fragments of interaction treated by micro-sociologists. To macro-sociology, the problem is the way 'a few fragments of a conversation or even several pages of discourse can presume to stand for the complex social structures identified in macro-theory, such as large-scale political, economic, demographic and stratificational patterns' (1981: 54). The problem lies in the assertion that the extracted fragments can sustain claims to recurrence, as being expressions of systematic patterns. Cicourel notes the criticisms that conversation analysis has focused on exchanges that involve spontaneous encounters between friends, members of therapy groups, and so on. This may be why the 'ethnographic or organizational context' is seldom treated as an explicit source of information. If there are limits for the macro-sociological project here, the same applies to participant observation; there would be a need to demonstrate the applicability of data found *in micro* to a wider context. Cicourel's point is that many of the criticisms cut both ways. In the 'labour intensive' understanding of their materials qualitative researchers gain, for example, by listening to tapes repeatedly while 'fixated on the transcript' and thus refining the transcript, the procedure is seldom directly signed for the reader as background to some analytic point. But the same can be said of survey researchers experiencing pre-tests in the field. They give unreported inferences and background to interpret aggregated findings, but a systematic grasp of the context is unlikely to come from visits to the field sites.

Part of the problem is the procedure for aggregating data and building analysis (or 'summaries'). Interaction between levels of analysis can be obscured by survey work. 'When we aggregate across individual responses to items of a questionnaire we are forced to restrict severely if not eliminate the local and larger contextual conditions that could clarify the respondent's perspective. The aggregation is a summarization process that obscures our thinking of the way local context and individual responses contributed to the larger picture' (1981: 64). What is achieved is a 'constructed account of a collective or group or class response'. The relevance of individual differences, and the interrelation of response with the groups in which choice occurs in practice, is not part of the apparatus of quantitative work. Instead, the aggregated responses 'provide their own collective reality by the choice of variables for creating classes or "groups" ' (1981: 65). The analytic categories thus devised are potentially mere artefacts of the analytic procedure itself, creating collective entities out of distributions by income, class, education, or occupation regardless of their actual existence.

Conventional assumptions about appropriate data can obstruct understanding. For instance, too often the treatment of 'structure' seems to be done quantitatively while that of 'culture' is done qualitatively. Culture is dismissed as the ephemeral world of thoughts and feelings, and whether it is manifest as behaviour is often challenged. Thus studies try to relate 'subjective' perceptions to 'objective' circumstances; 'attitudes to behaviour, opinions to voting, ideology to revolution, class consciousness to class, alienation to inequality, and so on' (Wuthnow, 1984: 5). As Wuthnow remarks, the object has been more to explain culture away than to understand it, to regard patterns of observable ('objective') behaviour as the real source of ideas. The reductionist assumption is that culture can only be understood by relating it to social structure.

Thus, the roots of ideology are sought in vested politico-economic interests and not within its own terms. Wuthnow notes that 'there is value in this approach for certain purposes, just as there is value in reducing human behaviour to the functioning of chemical impulses. But social scientists have generally resisted such attempts as far as social structure is concerned on the grounds that much of value is overlooked. They have been less conscientious in dealing with culture' (1984: 5-6). Culture has generally been studied as an attribute of individuals, and attitude research has had a stake in this not because of the difficulty of operationalizing measures sensitive to intersubjectivity, but because of the initial assumption that the only logical course of inquiry into culture is to probe the subjective consciousness of individuals. 'Thus, for all the research that has been made possible by survey techniques and quantitative analysis, little has been learned about cultural patterns ... Cultural analysis has been inhibited, not so much by a simple failure to specify testable propositions or to employ rigorous methods, but by deeper assumptions about the nature of culture itself' (1984: 6-7). Cultural analysis could be amenable to quantitative work, provided effort is made to specify its elements and indicators, and to determine its relation to social structure.

Having an idea of the shared problems of quantitative and qualitative research, as well as their points of difference, puts us in a more informed position to consider the issues raised by attempting to achieve a working convergence of methods in relation to substantive problems. It was apparent at the symposium from which this collection emerged that none of us felt the 'dissolution of the micro–macro dimension' (Cicourel, 1981) was realistically in prospect. But no one denied that the flurry of work in micro-sociology now calls for a change in the way the micro–macro problem is argued. It has transformed our understanding of the distinctions between individual and collectivity, action and structure, and, especially, the association of the micro-level with powerlessness and the macro-level with power. An important instance is the effect of new research on our concept of action. In Weber's formulation, action includes all behaviour 'when and insofar as the acting individual attaches a subjective meaning to it' (1957: 88). We have already noted the tendency to replace notions of individually meaningful social action with situated interaction. The effect of this is to declare individual purposive action a derivative rather than the constituent element of the larger structures of interaction. The emergence of 'methodological situationalism', that is, a concentration on the *episode* of situated interaction as unit of social analysis, challenges the merely dichotomic notion of action and structure. But the need to reformulate conventional distinctions is more encouraging than the dismissal of 'big' issues altogether on the grounds that empirically warranted answers are by definition 'unknowable'.

It is on such grounds that the methodologically very demanding proposals for the qualitative study of macro-level problems can be welcomed. One formulation is the 'aggregation hypothesis' advanced by Collins, that macro-phenomena comprise aggregations and repetitions of numerous similar micro-episodes (1981a, 1981b). The episodes are situated social encounters which are partly structured by past definitions and yet always contingent on reinterpretation. Since all our experience of the social world is in such situations, all our direct evidence regarding macro-level phenomena is aggregated from micro-level experience. The macro-level approach to social class, seen as a collective phenomenon signified by tables of socioeconomic status, and the micro-sociological approach to it as, for example, an attribute of individuals surveyed in social research (1981b), may thus be reconciled. 'If class relations are seen to consist of a multitude of situations in which those who dispose of the means of production confront and exploit those who do not, a social class can presumably be defined in accordance with the aggregation hypothesis as the sum total of individuals who engage in their working-life situations in similar relations of this kind' (1981b: 26). The macro-phenomena are manifest taxonomically, that is, as 'societal' properties derived from the formation of similarity classes based on identified membership criteria. While phenomena such as social strata or mobility rates may be spoken of as characteristic of social structure, they may be seen as referring to aggregate sets of similar episodes.

A theoretical alternative more in keeping with the conventional concerns of macro-sociology pursues the interrelation of situated social events or the linkage between events in diverse micro-situations. Examples of this focus in established social theory include analyses of the exchange of goods and services, or of functional interdependence and role differentiation. Bourdieu's notion of the 'field' as locus of competition among actors for a monopoly of symbolic capital sees the fields of, for example, scientific disciplines, as the battleground on which scientists become interrelated by competition (1975). The incorporation of mechanisms for the interrelation of actors and situations in macro-social theory is an obvious requirement of theories which have conventionally worked from statistical data of a high order of generality. It is part of their attempt to warrant the application of such data to 'real life' situations. Similarly, efforts are needed to address interrelations between micro-social situations. Such a project is Duster's study of the operationalization of laws for screening inherited disorders, which draws attention to the transformations which occur when a law emerges from the legal context to its spheres of application (1981). Such work cannot be restricted to the study of one particular setting.

Another alternative, if one wishes to see macro-level phenomena neither as the sum of unintended consequences of micro-episodes, nor as their aggregate, nor their network of interrelations, is to see them as summary 'representations' which are actively constructed and oriented to by people in micro-episodes. The macro need not appear as a 'layer' of social reality *on top* of micro-episodes. Rather, it is lodged within micro-episodes and results from the *structuring practices* of agents. 'The outcome of these practices are representations which thrive upon an alleged correspondence to that which they represent, but which at the same time can be seen as highly situated constructions which involve several levels of interpretation and selection' (Knorr-Cetina, 1981: 34). As has been noted, there is keen interest in this both in social theory and general systems theory.

The collection

In 1986 a symposium was convened at the University of Surrey to address the debate over micro-research and macro-theory. The resulting collection is divided into chapters taking a theoretical approach to action and structure, and substantive applications and illustrations of different methods sensitive to this theoretical issue. In the opening chapter Knorr-Cetina argues that the 'gap' between micro-sociological analyses of everyday interactional practices and certain conceptions of macro-social structures reveals not just failure on the part of sociologists to deal adequately with micro–macro relations. Rather, the gap constitutes but one expression of the relative autonomy of these levels in social reality. There exists no 1 : 1 relationship of correspondence, or translation or summarization between action and structure. The chapter develops Knorr-Cetina's conception of the *double production* of social reality in terms of processes of everyday interaction which create *and* deliberately counteract disembodied principles of stucturation (including the sociologists' 'structures') on the one hand, and in terms of structural features which act as reference points invoked by participants in social practice on the other.

The interstitial area between the micro and macro is at issue in the debate between Giddens and Archer, and Knorr-Cetina's analysis is distinctive. This is also the point of connection to Sharrock and Watson's argument. They start from the position that *the* micro–macro distinction involves a separation of action and setting in a way which ethnomethodology (and, arguably, interactionism) cannot accept, because it necessarily regards social action as action-in-a-social-setting and sees social settings as settings-rendered-observable-in-the-routine-actions of members. Sharrock and Watson want to rebut the common charge that ethnomethodology evades the problem posed by environing social structures. While their conception differs, the impetus is the same as Giddens' 'structuration'; action inheres in structure and vice versa, and, with this parallel in mind, it may be more fruitful than destructive to entertain their assertion that this position at the heart of ethnomethodology requires us to dispense with many of the dualisms and oppositions which define sociology's established framework of problems, including the micro–macro distinction.

The dispute over the status of 'structural' or macro-level influences on action in organizations relative to contextually situated inter-action focuses attention on the orientation to external, 'structural' constraints on the part of members engaged in producing organizational action. Members' beliefs about such influences affect the action produced. Manning seeks to demonstrate the utility of discourse analysis as a means of mapping the 'internal structure' of the organization, conceived as the members' rendering of the external environment in terms which resolve its importance for the production of action. The role of 'beliefs' is accentuated in his analysis because the empirical case he treats, safety in the nuclear-power industry, is one in which high levels of uncertainty apply to the information on the basis of which external constraints (resources) are determined.

The symposium was particularly concerned to establish ground for this theoretical debate in concrete examples of empirical research, and subsequent chapters, like Manning's, address the issue by means of research where issues of micro–macro relationships have been analytically significant or where research has evaluated one of the principal theoretical formulations. Thus, Paul Rock illustrates the utility of ethnographic research in an interactionist tradition in understanding the relationship between power in large bureaucracies and the manifestations of its routine workings in the organization. It is, of course, a province which those more comfortable with macro-level data have customarily regarded as inaccessible to micro-sociologies such as symbolic interactionism. The chapter describes the emergence of analysis and data pertinent to the reconstruction of bureaucratic life-worlds, those shifting symbolic habitats occupied by officials, that are composed of organizationally prominent and familiar figures, processes, strategies and eventualities. It does so in relation to a particular policy initiative, which is treated as an evolving exchange between frameworks and purposes in a metaphor for the emergence of policy in general.

In a novel and intriguing chapter, Clark and Pinch show how some of the most basic and universal axioms of economic behaviour are challenged by micro-sociological analysis of trading relationships among market traders and customers. They suggest that buying and selling can be better understood as an interactional, social accomplishment rather than as an economic one. In doing so they illustrate how micro-sociology not only can test the applicability of macro-level theory but impels a recognition of the situated, contextual character of apparently universal phenomena. They argue that rules of micro-economic behaviour can only be understood in terms of the exploitation of culturally held social conventions, but that rules and systematic practices must be analytically formulated within localized contexts.

John Brewer's intensive research with former members of a British Fascist organization led him to ponder the theoretical significance of their reflections on their reasons for membership. In particular, he realized that these data pertained to the duality-of-structure concept central to Giddens' theory of 'structuration'. The recursive element of Giddens' conception was especially appealing, and Brewer analyses the 'doing' of life history by the ex-Fascists as a recursive achievement, demonstrating the duality that is said to exist in this view of structure, and the use of time and space by these knowledgeable agents as dynamic elements in structuration. The exercise provokes some new, critical insights into Giddens' formulation.

Like the other substantive chapters noted so far, Brewer's data are derived from intensive study of a relatively small number of cases. However, the final chapters offer the promise of extending a firmly grounded analysis to the macro-level, but by very different means. The preceding section of this chapter closed with a discussion of various constructions of macro-level social phenomena. The strategies reviewed there broadly share the view that in the present state of our knowledge, our grasp of events at the interactional level is the strongest. The various approaches that were noted sought to work 'upwards' from this, by different means; for example, by way of applying the 'aggregation hypothesis'. In large measure the contributions to this volume share this project. However, the two final chapters approach the matter quite differently from the previous chapters and from each other. Both represent innovative, distinctive, and promising alternative procedures.

Peter Cowley and John Scott use two important empirical examples to illustrate how the technique of Q-analysis can handle data relating to large-scale social structures as well as personal mental constructs. Scott's development of novel techniques of network analysis with which to explore the constellation of interests at the heart of modern capitalism has attracted considerable attention in sociology, where the examination of controlling shareholdings and their interconnections have exposed the primary features of corporate financial power. To make their case for the wide range of utility of Q-analysis, Cowley and Scott illustrate its application to the investigation of psychiatric symptoms in patients and intercorporate shareholdings in Japan. In assessing the promise of this method it is important to note the position Cowley and Scott take towards structure. They see structure as *constraining* in a way that conflicts with the other contributions. One should also note that their perspective, whose reach is the furthest 'upward' of the chapters, necessarily takes us the greatest distance from the interactional level. The compelling issue on which Cowley and Scott need to reassure us is that the point at which data are collected from 'individual units' is reliable and valid. For example, we must satisfy ourselves that the psychiatric symptoms are intersubjectively consistent. After that, the network procedure affords a secure means of handling the relational data.

The strength of the technique, and its connection to the micro–macro debate, lies in its concern with defining the interrelationships within a data set, and in its holistic approach, which allows accurate representation of complex situations. It is an approach in sympathy with Peter Abell's method of comparative narratives. In his chapter

Abell interprets the micro–macro distinction restrictively as the problem of moving from statements about the action of individuals to statements about the action of collectivities (for example, an organization). In the comparative-narrative approach the problem reduces to one of making suitable translations (homomorphisms) from narratives at the individual to the collective level. The empirical focus in the chapter is the problem of divining the objective or goal of an organization from the organizational activity of individuals. Once again, Abell's formalization of the notion of narrative involves a departure from the conventional means by which such qualitative data are analysed. At issue here is just how much detail may be discarded while preserving the core narrative. It confronts us with the need to clarify what it is that we draw on in analysing qualitative data, and whether the distinctive detail or the core abstractions afford our best analytic sense.

The micro–macro distinction, some have asserted, is dead. It is the force of argument in this volume, even from a divergence of perspectives, that the assertion is misconceived. What is obsolete is the rigid separation, the dualism or opposition, between the micro and the macro. But even as this is recognized, we acknowledge the utility of a language which has these concepts, for teasing out the signs of the external in the interaction and the symbolic meaning of action in the institutional environment. In that sense, the new province is all a middle ground.

References

Alexander, J.C. (1985) 'The "Individualist Dilemma" in Phenomenology and Interactionism', pp. 25–57 in S.N. Eisenstadt and H.J. Helle (eds), *Macro-sociological Theory: Perspectives on Sociological Theory*, vol. I. London: Sage.

Apel, K.-O. (1967) *Analytic Philosophy of Language and the Geisteswissenschaften*. New York: Reidel.

Archer, M.S. (1982) 'Morphogenesis versus Structuration: On Combining Structure and Action', *British Journal of Sociology*, 33(4): 455–83.

Atkinson, P. (1985) 'Talk and Identity: Some Convergences in Micro-sociology', pp. 117–32 in H.J. Helle and S.N. Eisenstadt (eds). *Micro-sociological Theory: Perspectives on Sociological Theory*, vol. II. London: Sage.

Birkbeck, C.H. (1985) 'Understanding Crime and Social Control Elsewhere: A Geographical Perspective on Theory in Criminology', pp. 215–47 in S. Spitzer and A. Scull (eds), *Research in Law, Deviance and Social Control*, vol. 7. Greenwich: JAI.

Black, D. (ed.) (1984) *Toward a General Theory of Social Control*, vols 1 and 2. New York: Academic Press.

Bourdieu, P. (1975) 'The Specificity of the Scientific Field and the Social Conditions of the Progress of Reason', *Social Science Information*, 14(6): 19–47.

Brewer, M. (1979) 'Concepts in the Analysis of Qualitative Data', *Sociological Review*, 27(4): 651–77.

Buckley, W. (1967) *Sociology and Modern Systems Theory*. Englewood Cliffs, NJ: Prentice-Hall.

Chatterton, M.E. (1979) 'The Supervision of Patrol Work under the Fixed Points System', in S. Holdaway (ed.), *The British Police*. London: Edward Arnold.

Cicourel, A.V. (1981) 'Notes on the Integration of Micro- and Macro-levels of Analysis', in K. Knorr-Cetina and A.V. Cicourel (eds), *Advances in Social Theory and Methodology*. London: Routledge & Kegan Paul.

Collins, R. (1981a) 'On the Microfoundations of Macro-sociology, *American Journal of Sociology*, 86(5): 984–1014.

Collins, R. (1981b) 'Micro Translation as a Theory-building Strategy,' pp. 81–108 in K. Knorr-Cetina and A.V. Cicourel (eds), *Advances in Social Theory and Methodology*. London: Routledge & Kegan Paul.

Dandeker, C. (1986) 'Social Theory', *Network*, 35 (May): 15–16.

Davis, N.J. and Anderson, B. (1983) *Social Control: The Production of Deviance in the Modern State*. New York: Irvington.

Ditton, J. (1979) *Part-time Crime: An Ethnography of Fiddling and Pilferage*. London: Macmillan.

Duster, T. (1981) 'Intermediate Steps between Micro and Macro Integration: The Case of Screening for Inherited Disorder', pp. 109–36 in K. Knorr-Cetina and A.V. Cicourel (eds), *Advances in Social Theory and Methodology*. London: Routledge & Kegan Paul.

Fielding, N.G. and Fielding, J.L. (1986) *Linking Data*. London: Sage.

Giddens, A. (1976) *New Rules of Sociological Method*. London: Hutchinson.

Gilbert, M. (1979) 'On Being Categorized by Others', in R. Harré (ed.), *Life Sentences*. Chichester: Wiley.

Glaser, B. and Strauss, A.L. (1967) *The Discovery of Grounded Theory*. Chicago: Aldine.

Glassner, B. (1980) *Essential Interactionism*. London: Routledge & Kegan Paul.

Habermas, J.C. (1972) *Knowledge and Human Interests*. London: Heinemann.

Harré, R. (1981) 'Philosophical Aspects of the Macro–micro Problem', pp. 139–60 in K. Knorr-Cetina and A.V. Cicourel (eds), *Advances in Social Theory and Methodology*. London: Routledge & Kegan Paul.

Hindess, B. (1986) 'Actors and Social Relations', pp. 113–26 in M. Wardell and S. Turner (eds), *Sociological Theory in Transition*. London: Allen & Unwin.

Holdaway, S. (1985) 'Discovering Structure: Studies of the British Police Occupational Culture', in B. Irving and M. Weatheritt (eds), *Contemporary Police Research*. London: Croom Helm.

Johnson, G.D. and Picou, J.S. (1985) 'The Foundation of Symbolic Interactionism Reconsidered', pp. 54–70 in H.J. Helle and S.N. Eisenstadt (eds), *Microsociological Theory: Perspectives on Sociological Theory*, vol. II. London: Sage.

Knorr-Cetina, K. (1981) 'The Micro-sociological Challenge of Macro-sociology', in K. Knorr-Cetina and A.V. Cicourel (eds), *Advances in Social Theory and Methodology*. London: Routledge & Kegan Paul.

Knorr-Cetina, K. and Cicourel, A.V. (eds), (1981) *Advances in Social Theory and Methodology: Toward an Integration of Micro and Macro-Sociologies*. London: Routledge & Kegan Paul.

Lockwood, D. (1964) 'Social Integration and Systems Integration', in G.K. Zollscham and H.W. Hirsch, *Explorations in Social Change*. Boston: Houghton Mifflin.

Lukes, S. (1977) *Essays in Social Theory*. London: Macmillan.

Mead, G.H. (1925) 'The Genesis of Self and Social Control', *International Journal of Ethics*, 35: 251–89.

Park, R.E. and Burgess, E.W. (1924) *Introduction to the Science of Society*. Chicago: University of Chicago Press.

Parsons, T. (1951) *The Social System*. New York: Free Press.

Ross, E.A. (1901) *Social Control: A Survey of the Foundations of Order*. New York: Macmillan.

Spitzer, S. and Scull, A. (eds) (1985) (Editorial introduction) *Research in Law, Deviance and Social Control*, vol. 7. Greenwich: JAI.

Wardell, M. and Turner, S. (1986) 'Epilog', pp. 161–5 in M. Wardell and S. Turner (eds), *Sociological Theory and Transition*. London: Allen & Unwin.

Weber, M (1957) *The Theory of Social and Economic Organisation*. Glencoe, Ill.: Free Press.

Williams, R. (1976) 'Symbolic Interactionism: The Fusion of Theory and Research', pp. 115–38 in D.C. Thorns (ed.), *New Directions in Sociology*. Newton Abbot: David and Charles.

Wuthnow, R. et al. (1984) *Cultural Analysis*. London: Routledge & Kegan Paul.

Znaniecki, F. (1934) *The Method of Sociology*. New York: Farrar & Rinehart.

1
THE MICRO-SOCIAL ORDER

Some highly engaging speculations have been inspired by recent attempts to explore the area of interrelation between micro-social and macro-social processes. Karin Knorr-Cetina has been centrally involved in the debate over recursiveness, structuration and the discreteness or ambiguity of given levels of social reality. She has evolved a conception of the 'double production' of social reality, which she elaborates in this chapter. The argument is that elements of the presumed structural level inhere in the orientations to them by persons in interaction, and that interaction so informed affects the reality of presumed structure.

This stance squarely challenges the conventional dichotomy of the individual and the collective, or action and structure. It derives from the tradition of 'methodological situationalism', in which the starting-point for the analysis of the macro-social is the social situation rather than the individual or the collective *per se*. Knorr-Cetina's assessment of current attempts to put macro-social issues on a micro-sociological foundation leads her to the notion of the 'representation hypothesis' of macro-social order, a distinct alternative to prevailing interpretations.

In our present state our soundest knowledge is of the interactional level, but fiction or fact, structure is too important to discount, even if the clearest sign of it is in its micro-level manifestation.

The micro-social order
Towards a reconception

Karin Knorr-Cetina

There is a venerable tradition in sociology which argues that social analysis is divided between individualism and collectivism, or between action perspectives and structuralist views, and that one or the other (depending on the writer's preference) arbitrarily reduces social phenomena to one level of reality. In 1939, an article in the *American Journal of Sociology* argued that the main stream of sociological thought had forgotten the question whether individuals or structures are the ultimate units of social reality, and analysed social phenomena in terms of the meaningfully oriented actions of persons reciprocally related to each other (Wirth, 1939: 966). In the eighties, the issue is vigorously alive, with theorists like Parsons sometimes assigned to the individualist and sometimes to the structuralist creed (Mayhew, 1980, 1981; Ditomaso, 1982). Some reject the idea of a dichotomous choice between these doctrines, and consider the problem to be the linkage between voluntary action and social restraints. Within these terms, Bhaskar (1979), Giddens (1979, 1981) and Alexander (1982) have attempted afresh to bridge the gap between agency and structure.

This chapter presents another analysis of the puzzle, but one which builds upon a different tradition. I try to follow a line of sociological thought which dates back at least to Simmel, but one which the confrontations between individualism and collectivism tend to forget – the tradition of 'methodological situationalism'. Three attempts have recently been made to put macro-social issues on a micro-sociological foundation, taking as a starting-point the social situation (Cicourel, 1981; Collins, 1981a, 1981b; Harré, 1980, 1981; Knorr-Cetina, 1981a). In the following, I will first present the case for methodological situationalism and then review these attempts. My object in this chapter is to elaborate in some detail the 'representation hypothesis' of macro-social order as an alternative to the above conceptions. The elements of this hypothesis are familiar to sociologists. I want to develop a synthesis of these elements.

Methodological situationalism

For over twenty years, micro-social reseach has been founded on the assumption that 'the only valid and reliable (or hard, scientific) evidence concerning socially meaningful phenomena we can possibly have is that based ultimately on systematic observation and analysis of everyday life' (Douglas, 1970: 12). The first object of social analysis ought, thinks Goffman, to be ordinary, actual behaviour (1974: 564). Actual behaviour is behaviour in social situations. The sequence of social situations within which we live determines our experience. This sequence is uninterrupted, since the life-world of everyday experience is essentially a social world.[1] To understand social life, we must find our feet in what people do and say in actual social situations. Radical micro-sociology implies that social objects, and particularly macro-social phenomena, are unknown and unknowable unless they can be grounded in knowledge derived from the analysis of micro-social situations.

I shall call methodological situationalism the principle which demands that descriptively adequate accounts of large-scale social phenomena be grounded in statements about actual social behaviour in concrete situations. This principle assumes that large-scale social phenomena such as 'the direction of price changes in an industry' ultimately come about through mundane transactions of people in micro-social situations. In other words, it is rooted in certain beliefs about the ontological make-up and causation of social phenomena. It does not rule out the study of the formal properties or behaviour of macro-variables from an instrumentalist point of view. We may wish to predict the impact of changes in one economic indicator upon others, knowing that the neo-classical model by which we make these predictions is not descriptively adequate.[2] According to the same logic we develop computers that perform reasonably well at playing chess like humans, but do not mimic the mechanisms of the human brain. Nor does the above principle prevent the study of the anatomy of social bodies, for example of the relationships implied by an institution design. After all, we have learned from formal analyses of conversations even though, as Birdwhistell argues, typed transcripts of conversations are in fact only 'the cadaver of speech' (1971).

Methodological situationalism is reductionist with a view to the constitution of macro-social reality in the following sense: it assumes that notions such as 'the State' ultimately refer to micro-scale transactions, for example to the transactions of government officials. This form of reductionism is compatible with the Marxist principle that 'men make their own history ...', though they may not make it accidentally nor under conditions of free choice – it leaves entirely open questions of the existence and efficacy of 'constraints' imposed upon human action.[3] Reductionism of this kind is commonly presupposed in empirical inquiry. Sociologists, when they study a political administration, are likely to launch an inquiry into the words and deeds and situations of those who constitute this 'administration'. But what if somebody claims that aggregate social and economic indicators may give a better global picture of this administration's activities than descriptions of concrete micro-transactions?

Common-sense reductionism, as we might call the above assumption, is an argument about the referent of certain sociologically important macro-concepts. 'Class relations' refer to transactions between people who, in their daily encounters, bring about these relations. Now assume that these encounters proceeded similarly in the entire population, and could be recorded in comparable ways across different situations. Surely in this case there would be no reason to reject an appropriate aggregate measure of 'class relations'. Situationalists have charged that we do not possess an empirically substantiated model of micro-social transactions that would allow us to adopt without serious hesitations the assumptions of similarity and comparability upon which aggregate measures are built.

Methodological situationalism is reductionist in a second sense by virtue of the argument that the data-points from which macro-measures are aggregated are themselves socially accomplished in particular measurement situations. This has been spelled out most comprehensively by Aaron Cicourel (1964). Cicourel challenged the assumption of traditional sociological methodology that data collected in interviews, official statistics, or other records can be taken at face value, and that measurement error in so far as it exists can be coped with through statistical procedure. In contrast, micro-sociological research sees such data as unspecified collaborative products created in social situations in accordance with the practical procedures and background assumptions of participants.[4] Since we cannot assume the working perspectives, methodical procedures, or negotiated definitions of the situation to be comparable across different occasions, we have no basis for assessing the meaning or validity of aggregate data outcomes. Methodological reductionism, as one might call this argument to distinguish it from common-sense reductionism, asserts that short of sufficient knowledge about how data, records, and reports are generated in different micro-social situations and across different organizations, the resulting constructs cannot be accepted as unproblematic indicators of (aggregate) social life.

None of this, it should be noted, entails methodological individualism, the doctrine that social phenomena must be explainable in terms of particular acts of individual persons (O'Neill, 1973; Watkins, 1955,

1957; see also Lemert, 1979). To expound the difference between methodological situationalism and individualism, I shall draw upon two arguments: first, the dissolution of the individual person as a natural unit of social analysis; and, secondly, the rebuttal of the Weberian explication of social action.

Methodological individualists appear to consider the individual as a stable and unproblematic source of social action: individuals are causal agents who produce, mediated by their dispositions and beliefs, a steady flow of social phenomena. Yet research into the nature of individual persons consistently shows that human beings are not simple, coherent, stable entities throughout all their encounters. Obviously, nothing is gained in social analysis from a conflation of the biological organism with the sociologically relevant person. To begin with, this person is not a perceptual unit; it can be observed only through a series of actions and behaviours (Warriner, 1956: 552). In these actions, the person manifests a multiplicity of personas which have been linked to social roles, to the management of the self, or simply to different situations. Simmel provides an early and eloquent statement of this 'fragmentation' of the person:

> All of us are fragments, not only of general man, but also of ourselves. We are outlines not only of the types 'man', 'good', 'bad', and the like, but also of the individuality and uniqueness of ourselves. Although this individuality cannot, on principle, be identified by any name, it surrounds our perceptible reality as if traced in ideal lines. It is supplemented by the other's view of us, which results in something that we never are purely and wholly. It is impossible for this view to see anything but juxtaposed fragments, *which nevertheless are all that really exists*. However, just as we compensate for a blind spot in our field of vision so that we are no longer aware of it, so a fragmentary structure is transformed by another's view into the completeness of an individuality. (1971: 23; emphasis added)

But the locus classicus of the dissolution of the person as a natural unit is George Herbert Mead. Mead, as we know, finds the person (the self) arises out of an organism in communicative relations to others, through a process of taking the attitude of others, assuming the role of others, and regarding oneself from their perspective (1974). Similarly, many others have argued that becoming a self means becoming an object to oneself, a process which is inferential and emerges from a backward-looking glance upon 'oneself' from the standpoint of others (for example, Dewey, 1910; Gurwitsch, 1941; Schutz, 1973: 167ff). Mead sees thought itself as a form of internal dialogue which involves interior audiences and internalized reference groups. Thus the others are found within the person. Yet while this happens, the person all the time extends beyond the individual organism:

> If mind is socially constituted, then the field or locus of any given individual must extend as far as the social activity or apparatus of social relations which constitutes it extends; and hence the field cannot be bounded by the skin of the individual organism to which it belongs. (1972: 242f)

Goffman, referring to the relationship between persons and roles, considers this relationship to 'answer to the interactive system . . . in which the role is performed and the self of the performer is glimpsed'. Thus the person enacting a role becomes a function of the respective occasion:

> Self, then, is not an entity half-concealed behind events, but a changeable formula for managing oneself during them. Just as the current situation prescribes the official guise behind which we will conceal ourselves, so it provides for where and how we will show through . . . (1974: 573f)

In sum, then, this research illustrates that the self is not the content or essence of the sociologically relevant part of a biological organism (McKinney, 1970: 237). Rather, it displays the person as existing only in and through communication and typification and not as initially given (a); as (discursively) extending beyond the individual organism and incorporating others within it, hence as not bounded by its biological skin (b); as consisting of a multitude of personas which vary with the occasion in which 'the person' is glimpsed (c); and as observable only in its fragmentation through a series of actions and behaviours (d). When conceived of with respect to its social and psychological functioning, the individual appears as a set of multiple identities which are insulated rather than functionally integrated into just one set of dispositions and beliefs which make up just one individuality. Methodological situationalism takes the fundamental datum of the analysis of human conduct to be transactions-in-context not decomposed into individual actors.

But there is a second argument that needs to be considered. For one might hold that the dissolution of the individual as an alleged unity of dispositions and beliefs is not what matters: the basic micro-elements of social life are individuals' purposive actions, not the subjects themselves. Methodological individualism is sometimes explicated as just this: the demand that macro-social phenomena be treated as solely resulting from subjectively meaningful acts. As Miller (1978) has argued, this version of individualism is non-trivial; it amounts to the Weberian definition of sociology as the explanation of human conduct in terms of the subjective meanings that agents attach to their actions. Subjective meanings are subjects' reasons for acting as they do (1978: 392). But what are subjective reasons? Can they be defined and treated as causally efficacious independent of other agents and the situation?

Schutz has criticized Weber for lumping together the in-order-to of the action, that is, its orientation to a future event (the goal), and its genuine 'because-motive', which is its relation to past lived experience. Both function as subjective reasons which agents attach to their actions. But the former is lived through as a discrete, phenomenal experience, while the latter arises from the agent's investigating the origin of his or her present projects through an act of self-interpretation (1967: 86ff, 95). Lived through in-order-to reasons always answer to the presence of others in the face-to-face situation, and take account of those who are absent from but felt to be relevant to a situation. Again, it was Simmel who provided one of the first statements of the interactive nature of social conduct:

> Society exists where a number of individuals enter into interaction. This interaction always arises on the basis of certain drives or for the sake of certain purposes. Erotic, religious, or merely associative impulses; and purposes of defense, attack, play, gain, aid or instruction – these and countless others cause men to live with other men, to act for them, with them, against them, and thus to correlate his condition with theirs. In brief, he influences and is influenced by them. (1971: 23)

Now Simmel's formulation appears to be compatible with an action–reaction model of conduct according to which subjective meanings are discrete and identifiable entities that change as they are influenced by the meaning of other participants. However, if we look more closely at the face-to-face situation, it appears that social action arises from an *interlocking of intentionalities* in which subjective in-order-to motives are themselves contingent upon the conduct of others. Consider Schutz' analysis of social interaction as a form of relationship in which each participant becomes aware of and takes into account much more than the other is trying to communicate:

> As I watch you, I shall see that you are oriented to me, that you are seeking the subjective meaning of my words, my actions, and what I have in mind in so far as you are concerned. And I will in turn take account of the fact that you are thus oriented to me, and this will influence both *my intentions* with respect to you and *how I act toward you*. This again you will see, I will see that you have seen it, and so on. This interlocking of glances, this *thousand-faceted mirroring of each other*, is one of the unique features of the face-to-face situation. We may say that it is a constitutive characteristic of this particular social relationship. (1967: 169f; emphasis added)

Schutz concluded from this that participants in an interaction are incomparably better attuned to other participants than they are to themselves. It is this *reciprocity* which creates the unity and analytical priority of the situation:

The many different mirror images of self within self are not therefore caught sight of one by one but are experienced as a continuum within a single experience. Within the unity of this experience I can be aware simultaneously of what is going on in my mind and in yours, *living through* the two series of experiences as one series – what we are experiencing together. (1967: 170)

As a form of experience the meaning-giving unity of the *we*-relationship is constitutive of the face-to-face situation. But even if others are not present, subjective meanings can be seen as socially accomplished in context. The phenomena of internal dialogues, of internal audiences and 'Monodramas' (Evreinow), and of individuals taking the perspective of others, suggest that 'subjective' goals continuously depend upon others for their conception and articulation. The same holds for subjective reasons that are genuine because-motives. These make reference to past experience which agents hold responsible for their present undertaking. For example, we tend to 'explain' a particular activity by reference to dispositions acquired in childhood situations. This type of meaning is not lived through in encounters with others but consists of *post hoc* interpretations. However, it is nevertheless contingent upon the situation. As Schutz has emphasized, every such interpretation 'is determined by the Here and Now from which it is made'. Which past experiences are selected as genuine reasons for an action and how they are highlighted and put into perspective is a function of the specific situation out of which they are recalled. Genuine because-motives can only be reconstructed; they have 'no existence as discrete experiences as long as the ego lived in them' (1967: 95).

Social reality as a local accomplishment

My argument so far has been that we have good reason not to reduce micro-social situations to the psychologies of participants or to subjectively meaningful individual action. Neither individual psychologies nor subjective intentions are elementary constituents of social reality. But there is another argument which is not built upon the derivative and contingent articulation of subjectivity. This is the claim that social situations constitute a reality *sui generis*. They display a dynamic and organization of their own which we cannot predict from knowing the attributes of participating agents. Thus even if individuals or their subjective reasons could be regarded as the primordial stuff out of which society was made, they would not provide the key to understanding its processes and regulations. As Goffman pointed out in regard to much social research, the source of its trouble might be its neglect of the social situations: the neglect of the setting in which speakers perform their gestures, and the neglect of the social occasion when bearers of particular social attributes become accessible to each other. Situations make 'little systems' of activities which furnish their own ways of organization. They do not 'merely mark, as it were, the geometric intersection' of participants defined by age, sex, and other attributes of social structure (1972: 62f). What is hinted at somewhat obliquely in these remarks and related writings as the reality *sui generis* of the situation are the following properties of ordinary social action.

First, to describe human behaviour, let alone *uncover its meaning*, we have to make reference to the *human and physical environment* in which it occurs. For example, there is a sense in which the *loudness* of a statement can only be assessed by knowing the *distance* between the speaker and the hearer (Goffman, 1963: 62). Similarly, as work in the pragmatics of communication indicates, the *content*, *intonation* and *organization* of speech acts, not to mention other features, depend on whether the speaker is talking to the same or opposite sex, to a peer or to someone older or younger than she/he, to a superior or subordinate, whether she/he is speaking in court or at the street corner, at a formal or informal occasion, and so on.

Traditional sociological wisdom is of course aware of the influence the immediate environment has on social action, and takes care of this influence by introducing 'background' variables. Is the behaviour observed in public or private places? In a rural or urban environment? In industry or a university setting? In a chemistry lab or a history department? The sophisticated social researcher will always measure and ultimately control for variables judged relevant to the behaviour in question. Of course, the grid of the typologies commonly used is mostly not fine enough to account for the distinctive features of micro-social situations. But they can be refined, as shown by students of face-to-face situations.[5] What complicates the picture are interaction effects between descriptions of settings on various levels and these and other variables which mark the situation. For example, a black woman who has attained a high occupational status may find her sex and race add to her social position in metropolitan academic circles, but diminish this position in a homespun rural environment. As the fineness of the grid and the number of relevant attributes increases, we are less likely to guess what the outcome of each arrangement of attributes that marks a social situation will be. This is one way in which we can make sense of the definitive role and the unpredictable dynamics of the situation.

Along with this sense goes a second. Consider the following banal episode reported by Fleck (1979: 120ff). At a meeting of medical historians, the discussion revolved around the possibility of making a modern diagnosis of a disease described in an ancient historical text. One member claimed this would be impossible, because the methods of examination had changed considerably. Another argued that such a diagnosis was always possible, since the diseases themselves remained unchanged. The first granted that the diseases certainly remained unchanged, but our training did not. The ancient texts accurately describe a patient's odour, excretion, perspiration and even his or her cries of anguish. But we cannot even find out whether the patient had a fever or not. The discussion continued for more than one hour, during which the basic claim that diseases remained unchanged was upheld. However, as Fleck, a physician, a microbiologist and historian of science confirms, this claim was 'a kind of lapse' by the second speaker, who admitted the point afterwards.' This lapse became reinforced when the second speaker confirmed it rather offhandedly, and thereafter turned it into an axiom of the discussion. Yet all participants 'knew' the claim was untenable; and nobody was prepared to take responsibility for it when the discussion was over. Fleck concludes that there is often no author of an idea which 'emerges' in a situation, changes its meaning several times, and acquires the status of an axiom presupposed in further discussions. Why do participants 'lapse' into saying or doing things for which they do not wish to be responsible at a later point in time? How do we account for these 'emergent' properties of the situation? It is hardly possible to blame them all on interaction effects of the kind outlined.

Conceivably, at least some of the events which obscurely 'emerge' in a situation are unleashed by features of organization which accommodate the occasion. Situations, we have heard, are little systems of organized activities that furnish their own processes and regulations. Just what these processes and regulations are is not very clear at this point; hence the oblique reference to the 'dynamics' of the situation. However, some candidates for the organizing properties of social episodes have been proposed by ethnographers of speaking, ethnomethodologists, and other students of small encounters (for example Cicourel, 1970; Frake, 1964; Garfinkel and Sacks, 1970; Goffman, 1963; Gumpertz and Hymes, 1972; Schegloff, 1968). Best known among these are the results of studies of turn-taking in conversation. They provide a wealth of information on the sequential organization of encounters in terms of openings and closings, of topic formulation and focus stability, of cues for requesting a turn and giving it up, for managing overlaps and pauses, for selecting the next speaker, or for keying the talk through gestural work. Of course, to accommodate emergent features of the situation such as those illustrated by Fleck we would need to know more about other features of conversations, for example about patterns of argumentation. But the

general point should be clear: 'unauthored' and 'unintended' occurrences in situations possibly arise from interaction routines which
organize the occasion. These locally organizing features of activities
furnish a second sense in which one can talk about the reality in its
own right of the situation.

There is, however, a third sense. The outcome of social episodes
depends not so much on the pattern of rules and social attributes
which 'structure' the situation, but on the values participants place on
these structural variables as they are represented and interpreted in
the situation.[6] We have heard that participants constantly engage in
behaviour the sense of which is, in Wieder's formulation, relative to
an 'indefinitely extendable collection' of contextual matters: it
answers to the place in which the behaviour occurs, what participants
know about each other and presume to be known in the situation,
how they define the occasion, and so on. Now one might argue that it
is precisely the role of rules and structural variables to reduce these
indefinitely extendable contextual matters to manageable size.
Behaviour-in-context is behaviour governed by rules and structures
whose applicability alone depends on the context; that is, it depends
on certain initial conditions whose presence-as-context triggers suitable behaviour. The obvious problem with this conception is that
neither the meaning nor the applicability of these ideal objects can
apparently be settled concretely in advance. It cannot be settled, that
is, *without* reference to contextual matters. As Wittgenstein says:
'What is it "to learn a rule"? – That. What is it "to make a mistake in
its application"? – That. And what is being pointed to here is something indefinite' (1968: 28).

It is this 'essential incompleteness' (Mehan and Wood, 1975: 78) of
ideal objects which practical circumstances round off as they are
acknowledged by participants at concrete occasions. As micro-
sociological research has illustrated, rules and structural variables do
not normally specify a unique course of action, but are interpreted in
practice against a background of situational features (Berger and
Luckman, 1967; Cicourel, 1964, 1968; Garfinkel, 1967; Mehan and
Wood, 1975; Wieder, 1973; Zimmerman 1970). Rather than having a
stable meaning across circumstances, ideal objects 'are matched
against cases by elaborating the sense of the (ideals) or the case to
encompass the particular occurrences' of the situation (Wieder 1970:
128). Which rule applies, what it actually prescribes, what counts as
violation or compliance with the rule, what consequences are en-
tailed, appears to be worked out on a case-by-case basis in accordance with 'the requirements of the situation'. Even whether an arguably applicable rule can be invoked to support one's case must be
decided in the situation. Frequently, participants prefer to forgo

arguable rights in order not to damage their social relations. It is also clear that rules which fit the case may be made up 'as we go along', a practice corresponding to the inconsistent and oscillating use of rules over a course of behaviour. Typically, more than one rule or structural variable can be seen to fit an occasion and these objects may not be consistent with each other. Thus, some structures may be called upon to explain a course of events, while others contradicting the match may be ignored at the occasion.

But what about this occasion? Quite obviously, a context or a situation is not given to us but must be correctly read; hence we cannot unproblematically rely on the context to repair the indexicalities of rule application. In particular, participants may have to draw upon a normative order of rules and structures to uncover the meaning of the situation. Thus, as most of the above authors have argued in one form or another, the snake bites its tail; the relation between situation and structure (rule) is reflexive in that each is identified and elaborated in terms of the other, and the meaning of each becomes modified in the process of identification/elaboration.

This argument does not establish, I think, some circularity of practical reasoning, for we may identify a situation in terms of criteria (rules, structures) which are not the same as those whose negotiation forms the topic of a social episode. Instead it makes reference to the in-principle infinite regress of background assumptions which inform social behaviour. None of these assumptions (theories) is fully interpreted, that is, can be rewritten into statements whose truth is context-independent (does not require further interpretations). Yet to get on with one's business, some of these assumptions must always be taken at face value and 'held constant' in the process of interpretation. Thus there are no fully interpreted rules, criteria or structural variables which foreclose further interpretation-in-context. Yet to achieve interpretation-in-context, the 'situation' and its 'requirements' must be defined on the basis of further assumptions which are taken for granted for the time being. In practice, says Quine, we terminate the regress of background assumptions 'by acquiescing in our mother tongue and taking its words at face value' (1969: 49). But words, just like rules, structures, and other symbolic objects, remain indefinite (in principle defeasible), as long as they are considered as objects of general agreement. They take on definite value only as they are acknowledged (acted upon with variable consequences) in concrete situations.

The claim about the analytical primacy of the situation amounts to just this: recognition of the invariably local accomplishment of general structures and regulations of behaviour, and recognition of the ordering properties which locally organize this accomplishment.

Commitment to the locally accomplished nature of social life has led several authors to reconsider what it might mean to speak about macro-social reality. In the following, I will review several outcomes of this reconsideration.

The macro-order: aggregate or unintended consequence of the micro?

Assume, then, that we have reason to consider the micro-reality of locally accomplished transactions in social situations as a kind of paramount reality inescapably implicated in sociological investigation. By definition, we cannot ever leave these micro-situations. Arguably, they should not be reduced to individual psychology or subjective motivations. Apparently, rules and general regulations depend for their interpretation on concrete situations. Finally, micro-social episodes seem to follow their own principles of organization. All of this establishes the sense in which ordinary social trans-actions-in-context furnish 'the stuff of social structure' (Brittan), and an ultimate focus of social-science investigation. But once this is recognized, what do we make of macro-social phenomena? Commitment to the micro-scale study of social life often implies a commitment to phenomena and their nature, that is, to preserving the everyday meaningfulness and organization of conduct and experience through social-science description. This means it implies a preference for a brand of methodological naturalism and perhaps phenomenalism. How can we make sense of the notion of macro-social order on the basis of such a preference?

Several authors have recently confronted this question from the vantage point of a micro-sociological conception. I shall summarize the discussion by referring to an Aggregation Hypothesis (Collins, 1981a, 1981b; Giddens, 1981), a Hypothesis of Unintended Con-sequences (Giddens, 1981; Harré, 1981), and a Representation Hypothesis of macro-social phenomena (Cicourel, 1981; Knorr-Cetina, 1981a). The ideas upon which these versions are built are not altogether new. My concern is to draw out and compare some of their implications.

The most straightforward way to handle the macro-world from a micro-sociological perspective is to consider it as the sum total of micro-events. This is the core of the Aggregation Hypothesis advanced by Randall Collins (1981a, 1981b), and, to some extent, Aaron Cicourel (1981). In essence it says that 'macro-phenomena are made up of aggregations and repetitions of many similar micro-events' (Collins, 1981a: 265). Everyone's life, says Collins, is experienced as a sequence of micro-situations, and the sum total of all sequences of individual experiences in the world constitutes all the possible sociological data there is. Consequently, all macro-evidence must be aggregated from such micro-experiences. Collins emphasizes that there are no such things as 'states and economies', 'cultures and social classes'. 'There are only collections of individual people, acting in particular kinds of micro-situations.' While it is strategically impossible for sociology to do without the shorthand notions by which we refer to these collections of micro-situations, these concepts 'can be made fully empirical only by grounding them in a sample of the typical micro-events that make them up' (1981a: 264f). Collins suggests that we translate macro-sociological concepts into aggregates of micro-phenomena to test their empirical validity. However, he admits to three 'pure macrovariables': time, space, and number. The only irreducible macro-concepts are temporal, numerical, and spatial aggregations of micro-experiences (1981b: 98f). For example, a term such as 'centralization of authority' relies on the number of links in the chain of command, that is, on 'the number of situations involving different combinations of people, either passing along or giving orders'.

In sum, then, the Aggregation Hypothesis suggested by the above work says that (a) empirically, structural patterns, macro-institutions and other macro-phenomena are made up of aggregates of micro-situations; (b) macro-concepts are shorthand summaries of these micro-episodes; and (c) time, space, and number are the only true (irreducible) 'macro-variables' needed in sociology. The plausibility of this hypothesis depends, I think, on the definition of the elementary particles which are aggregated into macro-phenomena. To speak about an 'aggregation', a 'sum total' or a 'collection' of ingredients typically means that the whole is seen to come about through a procedure of addition; it is neither more nor less than the added sum of the parts. Consequently, all depends on the parts. If these are defined as social situations which include *inter*action, relationships, internal environments, indexical interpretations, power, and so on – in a sense *all* sociologically interesting phenomena – it would seem that macro-phenomena can be logically derived from micro-situations.

It is some such definition of the micro-units of social life as internally complex interaction environments upon which the Aggregation Hypothesis is built. Consider it as a hypothesis which sees structure as something internal to society's constitutive elements rather than as the interrelated pattern of these elements. And consider it as a recommendation to characterize society by the (aggregated) properties of situation–internal action structures. Understood in these terms, the Aggregation Hypothesis draws the micro-sociological revolution to what is perhaps its most radical conclusion.

But these are open questions. Macro-sociology recognizes not only aggregate properties of populations derived by simple addition from the characteristics of individual population elements (for example, the variable population size). It also recognizes 'emergent' properties of social units. In fact, macro-sociology and social structuralism appear to be consistently defined as the study of those 'emergent' properties which macro-scale units are seen to possess 'above and beyond' those of micro-scale units (for example, Etzioni, 1970: 71; Marx, 1939: 1976; Mayhew, 1980: 338). One way to think of these properties is by reference to the *unintended* consequences (latent functions) in addition to the intended consequences (sustained goals) of micro-social transactions (for example, Giddens, 1981; Merton, 1957). Several writers have recently reconsidered this view from a micro-sociological perspective. I want to call their conception of the macro-order the Hypothesis of Unintended Consequences (Giddens, 1981; Harré, 1980, 1981).

Harré begins with supra-individual entities in the physical and biological sciences. These are accustomed to the idea of emergent properties manifested by a whole but not by its parts when these parts are considered independently. They explain emergent properties almost invariably by structure, that is, by the relationships which obtain between particles (such as molecules) and individuate the whole (such as the key formed by iron molecules). Now apply this to collective phenomena in the social sciences. Talk about macro-collectives makes sense in so far as these display structure, that is, internal relationships between parts. If in addition they have causal powers distinct from those of their members we may call these collectives supra-individuals (for example, a committee). However, Harré argues, such structures as can be unproblematically identified in social life are relatively small – for example a family, a firm, or a modest institution. Their ontological status is indubitable, and they can be studied by micro-social methods. In contrast, the very large-scale groupings such as a nation or a social class are better understood as taxonomic collectivities, that is, as constructs which exist only in the mind of the classifier and have no empirical referent (as an ordered system in addition to the parts).[7]

However, this does not establish that there *can be* no emergent properties on a macro-level by virtue of some structural features of the total flux of interpersonal actions. Indeed, Collins (1981b) and Cicourel (1981) propose that repeated sampling over time of a large number of micro-social situations might generate a comparative data base from which to aggregate such macro-properties. Harré's objection to this procedure is that it is ramifying systems of unintended consequences which, according to the central doctrine of the macro-approach, are constitutive of macro-orders. The social sciences are methodologically bound to draw upon members' knowledge and accounts; yet ramifications of unintended consequences by definition cannot be part of social knowledge. Hence there can be no question of any empirical claims about the nature of a macro-social order that results from the total flux of intended and unintended consequences of social interrelations (1981: 153, 156ff).

However, these consequences may nevertheless exert a diffuse but significant influence upon the course of daily life. Harré considers their significance to be that they constitute system properties which confront us as selection environments of future actions. For example, these environments determine, analogous to biological evolution, which mutations occurring in micro-social practices will 'take' and persist to create actual social change. Along similar lines Giddens argues that the long-term formation and transformation of social institutions must be seen in the light of the unintended consequences of social action through which the capability and knowledgeability of social actors is always bounded. These unintended consequences of social action work behind our back and implicate transformations which we have to distinguish from the continual and contingent reproduction of institutions in everyday life. Giddens holds that unintended consequences *condition* social reproduction and hence fundamentally determine the process of structuration through which systems are maintained and change over time. Social systems appear to exist and to be structured only 'in and through' their reproduction in micro-social interactions, which are in turn limited and modalized through the unintended consequences of previous and parallel social action.

The Hypothesis of Unintended Consequences transcends the purely micro-sociological perspective promoted by the Aggregation Hypothesis by acknowledging influences which operate behind the back of agents, and which therefore *cannot be found in* micro-situations. Nevertheless, the hypothesis is micro-sociological at root: it concludes that these macro-influences cannot be known through direct evidence, and that we can, at best, derive a proof of their existence from simplified conditions. The micro-sociological recon-struction of macro-phenomena remains consistent in itself: to the degree to which it recognizes a residuum of macro-properties beyond the micro-level it declares these properties unknown and unknow-able.

The Representation Hypothesis

All of this, I think, still avoids the serious sense in which structure can be seen as a phenomenon of interrelation above and beyond the micro-units of social life. Consider the notion of structure invoked by Harré. This is the notion of a structured group, of an ordered set of relations between individuals exemplified by moderate forms of organization. Unpacked, such 'relations' amount to repeated trans-actions (or the possibility thereof) between designated individuals under specific circumstances. A specific relationship exists when certain transactions-in-context can potentially be (re-)activated as essentially the same. This is compatible with the Aggregation Hypothesis: 'structure' consists of the (actual or potential) repetition of *internally* patterned micro-social situations.

Yet this ignores the sense in which micro-situations are themselves interrelated, in which the happenings of diverse social episodes tie into each other. This is the sense in which functionalists refer to the functional interdependence of social action, and structuralists like Lévi-Strauss propose to study society by way of studying the circu-lation and transformation of objects passed on between different contexts of social life. History itself appears as a succession of micro-situations chained together by a variety of interrelations. Pushed to its extreme, emphasis upon the interrelationship between micro-social episodes may lead to the position that there exists only one clear-cut all-inclusive system, Wallerstein's 'world-system' (1974). Characteristically, Wallerstein arrives at this position in the search for the context of analysis which encompasses *all* relevant inter-related historical events. To this, the above micro-sociological per-spectives supply the antithesis of a monadic conception of internally structured micro-episodes considered in relative isolation.

However, there need not be any contradiction between these extremes. The fact that social events are interrelated does not cata-pult them out of micro-situations. World-system transactions no less than confessions to oneself in the dead of the night arise in micro-situations and should be studied in these situations. Yet at the same time micro-transactions always in principle transcend the immediate situation. By this I mean that they make reference to, and indeed may only exist by virtue of, other micro-transactions. It is plain that the occurrences in a social situation always answer to, and have implica-tions for, other social situations. It is apparent, too, that the authors of the above hypotheses recognize the presence of situation-transcending references in micro-transactions. But not much is made of this particular aspect of episodes. This can be illustrated in regard to the Hypothesis of Unintended Consequences. I want to propose that there is nothing esoteric about unintended consequences of social action, at least as far as social consequences are concerned, if we give sufficient weight to the interrelationship of social situations.

Elsewhere I have used C.V. Wedgwood's history of the Thirty

Years War to illustrate what was apparently a whole explosion of unforeseen events (Knorr-Cetina, 1981a: 31ff). According to this fine historian, the Thirty Years War is an outstanding example of a meaningless conflict which nobody wanted, which proved economically destructive and socially degrading for most who engaged in it, and which solved no problems and left both the Catholics and Protestants involved unsatisfied:

> The overwhelming majority in Europe, the overwhelming majority in Germany, wanted no war; powerless and voiceless, there was no need even to persuade them that they did. The decision was made without thought of them. Yet of those who, one by one, let themselves be drawn into the conflict, few were irresponsible and nearly all were genuinely anxious for an ultimate and better peace. Almost all – one excepts the King of Sweden – were actuated rather by fear than by lust of conquest or passion of faith. They wanted peace, and they fought for thirty years to be sure of it. (Wedgwood, 1967: 526)

How was it that the ruling powers of Europe 'let themselves be drawn into the conflict, one by one'? The first thing to note is that not one of the leading politicians ever decided for the 'Thirty Years War'. They decided to seize upon an advantage or to curtail somebody's power, to help out with troops or money, to intervene or to sacrifice a participant. For at least seventeen months after the date of 1618, traditionally associated with the outbreak of the war, it was apparently not clear 'even to the leading men in the countries most deeply concerned', that the revolt of 1618 rather than any other incident in that stormy time had initiated a war (Wedgwood, 1967: 12). The original incident consisted in the overthrow of an unpopular Catholic (Habsburg) government by rising Protestants in Prague. Subsequent incidents connected to the revolt led to a continuation of the conflict.

To begin with, the Elector Palatine Frederick of the upper Rhenish Palatinate became convinced that the revolt in Prague was an occasion to break the Habsburg succession to the imperial throne by wresting the crown of Bohemia from the Habsburg family. His advisers may even have played a role in engineering the revolt. Frederick moved to Prague where he tried to join forces with the rising Protestants. His move was unsuccessful. The Protestant princes of Germany decided not to support him; they hoped to end the war by sacrificing Frederick. While Frederick still busied himself in Prague, the Spaniards moved into his Palatinate. This was felt to be crucial in bringing the manpower of the North Italian plains into action in Flanders, which they planned to attack after an earlier truce had expired. The German princes were moved to further action by the Spanish invasion of German territory. Equally, the Dutch moved against the Spanish plan by subsidizing Frederick, who had lost Bohemia, hoping that he would regain his Palatinate on the Rhine. In the meantime, a new Habsburg emperor had been elected. He renewed the Habsburg coalition with Catholic German princes and proceeded against Frederick. And so forth.

There is no need to continue the historian's story of moves and countermoves grossly summarized above for the first three (!) years of the War. The point I wish to make should be obvious. First, we are dealing with events *chained together* by participants' concrete projects, by their mutual expectations, imputations of interest, fears, grudges or misread communications. Second, there appears to be *nothing unintelligible* in principle about this chain of events and its 'unintended' outcomes if we take the trouble to look concretely at the relevant episodes and their, however complicated, interrelations. If participants' intentions were continually frustrated in this conflict, it is, according to the historian because they were built upon assumptions about other relevant agents which did not hold water, and it is because other participants moved against these perceived intentions. The 'Thirty Years War' is a construct proposed and investigated by local and professional historians. As such, not one of the participants could have known or intended it. But within the sequence of events to which we refer as the 'Thirty Years War' participants account for each episode in terms of other episodes which thereby become related to each other. The historian who assembles these accounts provides a step-by-step rationale for the cumulative effect of these interrelated episodes, and thus has no trouble in explaining an unanticipated and presumably undesired macro-event.

Unintended macro-level consequences of the sort of a war of thirty years lie within reach of micro-social methodology, provided it focuses on the interrelationship between participants' definition of the situation. Consider once more the idea of emergent properties; of unanticipated outcomes, that is, best explained by 'structure', which means by relationships which obtain between the constitutive parts of macro-social units. Think of these parts as transactions in micro-social situations rather than as individual persons. Then there can be no problem of the dubious ontological status of 'structures' (structured groups individuated as wholes) beyond a certain moderate level. We do not need to identify such groups in order to account for unanticipated macro-consequences. Instead, we can relate such outcomes to action–reaction sequences of the sort exemplified by the history of the Thirty Years War. In such sequences, participants define their situations by reference to other agents' projects and circumstances, thereby legitimating the historian who considers the series as a unified sequence of 'interrelated' events. From the micro-scale perspective upon events, the overall outcome of the series is perfectly intelligible.

However, this does not make them predictable for participants, or for on-the-spot analysts. It is in this sense of their likely unpredictability *out of a specific contributing situation* that macro outcomes retain an 'emergent' quality. But of course, there is no difference in this regard between macro-outcomes and micro-situations. Recall that micro-situations have been associated earlier in this chapter with a dynamic of their own whose outcome we cannot fully predict by knowing the attributes of individual participants or the structural properties of the situation. Participants themselves are often pre-occupied with making the outcome of crucial situations more predictable, with variable success. Thus, the immediate outcome of micro-transactions appears to be no less indeterminate than the global result of a sequence of interrelated transactions. In fact, if the outcome of micro-episodes is underdetermined by pre-existing structures, then the apparent unpredictability of the global outcome of many micro-episodes may simply be a consequence of the unpredictable dynamics of contributing episodes.[8]

Suffice it to say that 'emergent' properties of macro-units due to 'structure' (interrelationships between micro-episodes) are well within scope of a micro-approach. In fact, if the above example can be generalized, it might well be that such emergent properties can *only* be fully accounted for by micro-analysis of the respective events. Now focusing on these episodes, we can choose between two strategies. We can either adopt a bird's-eye perspective and attempt to reconstruct the network of 'relations' which emerges from various definitions of the situation. This is the perspective which underlies much macro-theoretical research. Or we can take a step back and start from the representations by which participants construe these interrelations. I shall pursue the consequences of such a step back in the rest of this chapter.

It is perhaps the major thrust of the work of Cicourel and some other micro-analysts to document the interactional and organization accounting procedures whereby situated events are routinely transformed into summary measures, bureaucratic records, aggregate distributions, and similar macro-information.[9] Stimulated by Schutz' analysis of common-sense typifications (1967, 1973), this line of thought suggests a view which differs from the above models of the macro as a straight aggregate of micro-episodes or as their unintended and unknowable outcome. Instead, it allows us to see the macro as a *summary representation actively constructed and pursued within micro-situations*. Phrased differently, the macro appears no longer as a particular layer of social reality on top of micro-episodes –

a layer composed of the interrelation (macro-sociologies), the sum total (Aggregation Hypothesis), or the unforeseen effects (Hypothesis of Unintended Consequences) of micro-situations. Rather, it is seen to be part of these micro-episodes where it results from the structuring practices of participants. The outcome of these practices is typifications of various degrees of abstraction which 'stand for' the events they typify. Participants work out and employ these typifications to represent and interpret their situation-transcending involvements and other aspects of the more global circumstances of their life. I shall call Representation Hypothesis the view that the macro-order is first and foremost an *order of representation*, that is, of summary references pursued within micro-situations.

The fallacy of unwarranted subsumption

Structural relationships have loomed large in macro-sociological approaches. I have argued that micro-approaches ought to confront the issue, and proposed that we view these relations and their consequences from a Representation perspective. But there is a deeper issue concerning the macro-social order. At least since the turn of the century (Marx, Durkheim), structure has been identified with social constraints. We are talking about power relations, or about regularities that acquire the status of normative obligations.

Take a combination. It is plain that there is no difference in scale between the transactions of those we have elected into power (and thereby bestowed with authority) and of those we think powerless. 'The State' as a term of reference is a highly simplified large-scale representation. But 'the State' as a level of political-administrative action involves nothing larger in scale or more complex in structure than the situated interactions of (in the USA) members of Congress and of those who frequent the White House or other government locations. But the issue is evidently not the scale of transactions. The issue is that some of these transactions are thought to be more consequential than others. Political societies have long been defined by an internal structure that allows some of its members, namely the government, 'to find habitual obedience for their acts of command' (Voegelin, 1952: 37). The 'European centres of power' to which Wedgwood referred by definition 'control' the affairs of the realms of which they are the 'centre'. Or consider someone who has 'learned to obey' the authorities, like Crainquebille in Anatole France's story of a small vegetable dealer in Paris who is brought before court because he allegedly insulted a police officer.[10] When Crainquebille took his seat in the magnificent, solemn court-room and saw the judges, clerks and lawyers in their robes, the court attendant carrying the chains, the Academy officer with his palms attached to his chest, the bare heads of silent spectators behind a bar, and the busts of Christ and the Republic towering the room as if all divine and human laws were hanging over his head, he was stunned and terrified by the spectacle of justice. Penetrated by respect, he was ready to give himself up to the representatives of authority, even though he knew – or had perhaps once known – that he was innocent.

The deeper issue, then, is a difference in control and authority between the 'lower' and the 'higher' order, between Crainquebille and the judge who represents the law and the State, between the small farmer and the power centre. It is precisely this perceived difference in control which persuades us to subordinate certain layers of social life to others, and to identify 'the macro' with the subordinating structure while defining the 'micro' by a lack of control. Now it is plain that if macro-structures effectively controlled micro-events, if they furnished the variables which define micro-situations, then there might indeed be no need to bother about micro-situations. It does not matter for this argument whether macro-structures are seen in terms of power relations, normative obligations, or culturally shared grammars of cognitive rules and orientations. To make the case for a conception of the macro based upon a micro-sociological foundation, it is not enough to appeal to an order of representations arising out of internally structured micro-episodes. One must also make it plausible that macro-structures cannot be taken to unproblematically subsume (control) micro-situations.

I want to propose that the macro-structuralist mistake amounts to a *fallacy of unwarranted subsumption* rather than, as is often claimed, to a failure to refer (to a problem of reification). It is a failure to see the parallel evolution of provinces of transaction (and representation) as realities in their own right, irrespective of mutual claims of subordination. (Power) structures appear to constrain social life all-the-way-through, to the point where nothing of sociological importance is left to say about the reality they 'cover'. This is not surprising, since the power of the macro-structural argument depends on the degree to which it can legitimately claim to represent the reality it subsumes. Yet it is practically incorrect for any type of macro-structure. Macro-structures do not subsume, they coexist. An example might help. I shall draw upon someone immensely interested in the history of modern capitalism, this society's alleged economic macro-structure (Braudel, 1979).

In an attempt to assemble the factors which produced modern capitalism, Braudel finds that he must recognize, in the relevant period of the fifteenth to eighteenth centuries, the parallel evolution of not just one but several economies. These 'face each other, draw upon each other's support, and also contradict each other' (1979, vol. 1: 8ff). The first, easy to grasp and even transparent, is the market economy which dominates our statistics. This is the economy of production and exchange linked to the activities of farmers, craftsmen, shopkeepers, travelling merchants and, later, stockbrokers and bankers. It is the economy of booming twice-a-week markets and small-town fairs, of the slow replacement of payment in kind by bullion and 'paper money'. This economic 'spectacle' is privileged by the fact that it is well documented. Almost every single one of the respective economic transactions leaves a trace: an entry into a balance sheet, a letter transmitting an order, a permit to display one's goods, a receipt. A sufficient number of these records survive and facilitate the task of the historian. By focusing their discourse on this 'easy' plane, economists have locked themselves from the beginning into a blatant but partial reality at the price of excluding others.

These others, it appears, were no less important. Below the public spectacle of the market economy, Braudel finds a self-sufficient subsistence economy of fantastic dimensions. This is the stagnating, repetitive, routine infra-economy of rural life by which the majority, 80–90 per cent, of the population of the world survives. It continues an ancient, material life which changes too, but very slowly, and which coexists with the market economy protected by distance and isolation. Importantly, it continues to persist today in the form of an 'underground' economy of directly rendered services, illicit work, housekeeping occupations and various forms of tinkering. And even today it appears to be sufficiently important to worry economists; they estimate that 30–40 per cent of the gross national product thereby escapes all statistics in industrialized countries (Braudel, 1979, vol. 1: 9f).

Finally, above the surface level of the market economy, Braudel identifies a supra-economy of special means which, intentionally or not, stirs up the established order and creates anomalies and economic crises. On this level, some merchants in Amsterdam in the eighteenth century or in Genoa in the sixteenth century had the power to influence, from a distance, whole sectors of the European (world) economy. It includes the exchange business with its links to distant markets and its complicated credit games, a sophisticated art accessible only to a privileged few. This level of economic activity is what Braudel calls the very domain of capitalism, but it is a capitalism of exception from the rules and methods of market exchange, a capitalism that is from the beginning transnational, like the networks of representatives entertained outside Europe by the Fuggers and Welsers and other merchant families and companies (Braudel, 1979, vol. 1: 7ff, vol. 2: 125ff).

There are, then, systematic differences between the 'capitalists'' supra-economy and the market economy, and between these and the infra-economies of rural life.[11] One might think about these econo- mies in terms of the parallel evolution of distinctive provinces of practice (transactions reproduced as 'essentially similar' according to participants' or analysts' representations). To be sure, they draw upon each other, and they may on occasion promote massive disturb- ances in their counterparts. But it would be a mistake to ignore their relative isolation. The ruptures between them are not accidental: behind the public exchange at fairs and markets and in shops there develops a private 'counter' market *designed* to circumvent official means of exchange. Think of the merchants who buy the crops wholesale before they get to the market, through special and profit- able deals with individual producers at the source of production. Or think of the creation of trade monopolies and, to take an example from organization theory, of the parallel existence of formal and informal organizational structures. It is plain that these counter- structures thrive upon low publicity. To keep them effective, partici- pants keep them to themselves. The office which organizes today's monthly meeting of the governors of European national banks ('BIZ') issues no press releases and publishes no reports. The 'black market' and the infra-economy of illicit work can only survive as long as they remain outside the grip of the internal revenue services and other government agencies.

There is also a more general point regarding the parallel evolution and apparent lack of integration of these structures. For a regularity to persist and orient expectations it needs to be reinstantiated as 'essentially the same'. Homogeneity arises from the reproduction of regularities in everyday transactions. Recall Wittgenstein's thesis that meaning arises from use, or Bloomfield's finding that 'the most important differences of speech within a community are due to differences in density of communication' (1933: 46), or anthropolo- gists' conclusion that the degree of cultural difference varies directly with the degree of isolation between participants and groups (Berre- man 1978: 57f; Gumpertz, 1958). Thus common characteristics de- pend upon the interaction of those who share them. Structures in the sense of regularities experienced by participants appear to extend no further than the practices of actually interacting groups.[12]

I am suggesting, then, that structural regularities are tied to partici- pants' actual practices instantiated in networks of mutually related (via representations) micro-transactions which coexist in parallel to each other. Hence, the existence of regularities which transcend micro-situations is not ruled out in the present perspective; but their grip is limited, so to speak, to the reasoning practice of interacting groups. 'Structural' properties, too, are locally accomplished; but 'local' is defined in terms of the accessibility of participants for each other, not in terms of space.[13] The relevant networks may extend over several countries, as illustrated by the transactions of European centres of power during the Thirty Years War, or continents, as exemplified by Braudel's (and today's) supra-economy. Mutually related transactions of this kind create provinces of relevances and routines within which the sociologists' 'structural' regularities have a certain reality of experience. These provinces may maintain their distinctiveness 'by design': there are, as we know, always barriers, and boundary conditions and issues of identity. But there is also the phenomenon that structures proliferate structures; participants may be prompted to invent and install regular ways of subverting identified practices by matching alternative practices. Moreover, some of these parallel provinces are routinely neglected by macro-statistics and other forms of written summary representations: either because they are considered irrelevant, as the 'overwhelming majority' of the people of whom, historians complain, they have no records left[14] or because participants do not desire coverage, and dupe the records.

Power reconsidered

My argument about the 'parallelization' of structures presumes a bird's-eye perspective. Its logic is roughly that those interested in reconstructing 'structural' patterns of regularities from interlocking micro-situations ought to consider, like Braudel, some notion of provinces of transaction evolving in parallel. From *within* a structuralist framework, I have argued against the implication of much macro-social theorizing that the micro can somehow be subsumed under the macro. To put it crudely, the macro appears no bigger than the micro not only in regard to the structure of underlying transactions, but also in regard to its control over ('micro') events. This raises the obvious question whether power can be dealt with at all in the present argument. Does the formula of the parallel evolution and relative isolation of provinces of social practice not suggest an imagery of peaceful coexistence that denies the very possibility of domination?

I think not. To establish the sense in which power is part of my concern I first want to extend the argument concerning the fallacy of unwarranted subsumption. Clearly this line of reasoning also applies to the idea of representation. One can define representations in terms of a seeming contradiction: they may be created and employed literally to represent an object, that is to stand for and replace the object in all relevant respects. Yet there is never an unproblematic

relationship of subsumption between the representing and the represented. Short of becoming the phenomenon, a representation cannot
capture all there is to the represented. Representations thrive upon
their right, however legitimated, to speak for the represented, yet we
must assume there is always more that could be said about the
represented.

It follows, I think, that the representing and the represented are
best considered to pertain to different, coexisting realities regardless
of the claim of one to speak and stand for the other. The case can be
made that claims to represent are at the same time political strategies,
potential topics and resources in the power struggles of everyday life.
Following Hobbes, Callon and Latour (1981) have argued that
micro-actors blow themselves up to macro-size by translating the will
of other participants, whose support they thereby enrol. Consider a
related example, described elsewhere as the 'Powell strategy'
(Knorr-Cetina, 1981a; Bailey, 1978: 206ff). Briefly, this consists of
promoting a definition of the situation that allegedly concerns a large
number of people, and to thereby push one's status along with one's
argument. Enoch Powell was a Conservative member of the British
Parliament who developed, with the help of this strategy, from an
eccentric but weak member of the party's élite to a national figure.
Through three formal speeches delivered in 1968, he transformed the
question of coloured immigrants in England from a matter of 'localized grumbling' in some poor industrialized areas to a matter of
national heritage and concern. By the time of his third speech he had
enormous mass following and considerably embarrassed his party,
which felt that Powell's ideas went far beyond Conservative politics
on race.

His critics countered with three kinds of answer: they denied the
'facts' which Powell presented; they criticized Powell for making a
mountain out of a molehill; and they accused him of racism. Interestingly, Powell was 'ditched' by the second type of response, promoted by one of his colleagues, Quintin Hogg. Hogg made many feeble
jokes about Powell's concerns, and reduced 'the race question' from
the level of the nation and its heritage to that of housing and job
opportunities in particular areas of particular towns. This level was
easy to deal with in local politics. By reducing the problem to one that
had nothing to do with race, or culture, or Britain, he also reduced
Powell as a spokesman of 'the people', and reaffirmed the party
establishment.

We can appreciate, then, how power effects arise from representations. One can see power strategies at work in the most esoteric and
sanitized of representations, that is, in the discourse of natural science, provided one takes the trouble of a micro-scale investigation

(see the analyses collected in O'Neill, 1983). Recent ethnographic studies of scientific work find such power strategies to be part and parcel of the production of scientific representations of reality (Knorr-Cetina, 1981b; Latour and Woolgar, 1979; Law and Williams, 1982; Zenzen and Restivo, 1982). The fruitfulness of analysing power-effects on a micro-scale has previously been exemplified by Foucault's work on the history of the prison and of sexuality (1975: 29–33, 1976: ch. 2) and by sociologically informed work on schizophrenia and the family (Laing, 1956; Laing and Esterton, 1964). These have shown a microcosm of infinitesimal violences no less complex than the power struggles traditionally attributed to the macro-scale. Thus, it is worth recalling that power as a micro-process of social life is a central topic of micro-scale investigation.

But, of course, this does not yet answer the question raised in the beginning. Can one reject the straightforward idea that micro-events are controlled by macro-level structures and yet retain, within the present perspective, a sense of domination? Consider once more the ruling powers of Europe in Wedgwood's account of the Thirty Years War. By definition, they 'rule' over their subjects. Yet Wedgwood also describes these subjects, the 'great majority' of the people of Europe that is, not only as ignorant of but also as indifferent to the dynastic ambitions which governed the relations between the centres of power. Of course, it was they who are said to have decided to fight for thirty years. Yet except for the actual districts of fighting, the civilian population 'remained undisturbed' by wars fought largely by professional armies, at least until the need for money caused an exceptional levy on their wealth (1967: 13). In a similar vein, Braudel had argued that the material life of the large majority of the rural population remained unperturbed by the emergence of market economies and multinational capitalist transactions.

One can go a step further. While those 'in power' make decisions which may affect the powerless, the latter also make decisions which may affect the former. For example, the rural population described by Wedgwood and Braudel makes hundreds of decisions which affect the agricultural production and thereby in the end the armies and the markets, the political and the economic power élites. Now consider a more extreme example. In his historical account of Napoleon's expedition into Russia Tolstoy argues that power cannot be regarded as the cause of historical events. The commands of individuals who 'rule the people' are mostly not executed, sometimes the very opposite of what they order occurs, and from all their orders only those which correspond to an actual (and independent) series of events are attributed to them – the others are forgotten (1966: 1313ff). Take a scene from the famous Battle of Borodino. From where Napoleon was standing the fighting was almost a mile away, so that he could not see more than an occasional glint of bayonets, especially since smoke mingled with mist covered the whole battlefield. But even in the midst of actual fighting it was impossible to make out what was taking place: Russians and Frenchmen, infantry and cavalry appeared, fired, fell, collided, screamed and ran back again. To be sure, Napoleon had sent out adjutants who kept galloping up to him with reports of the progress of the action,

> but all these reports were false, both because it was impossible in the heat of the action to say what was happening at any given moment, and because many of the adjutants did not go to the actual place of conflict but reported what they heard from others; and also because while an adjutant was riding more than a mile to Napoleon circumstances changed and the news he brought was already becoming false. Thus an adjutant galloped up from Murat with tidings that Borodino had been occupied and the bridge over the Olocha was in the hands of the French. The adjutant asked whether Napoleon wished the troops to cross it. Napoleon gave orders that the troops should form up on the farther side and wait. But before the order was given – almost as soon in fact as the adjutant had left Borodino – the bridge had been retaken by Russians and burned . . . on the basis of these necessarily untrustworthy reports, Napoleon gave his orders, which had either been executed before he gave them or could not be and were not executed. (1966: 892f)

Tolstoy goes on to argue that the marshals and generals, nearer to the battle but not taking part in the fighting, made their own arrangements without asking Napoleon. However, they fared no better since for the most part things happened contrary to their orders. Those who fought acted according to the mood of the moment, running back and forward depending on where safety seemed to lie, occasionally led by officers who were on the spot and who, in the heat of the battle, made their own *ad hoc* decisions spurred by bullets and screams and other occurrences of the situation. It is wrong, says Tolstoy, to think that the Battle of Borodino, Napoleon's invasion of Russia, or any other historical event results from the planned action of commanders or others 'in power' to whom they are traditionally attributed. He suggests that historians leave aside the kings and commanders – who may be causally coincidental to a sequence of events – and study the infinitesimally small transactions of the people who constitute these events. We are back with the idea of the reality in its own right of the occurrences of micro-social situations.

Yet it would be a mistake to conclude that this relative autonomy of micro-transactions – say of those who fight the battle in relative isolation from their generals – settles the issue. Asymmetries are the life-blood of ordinary social action. Surely the power of the prince somehow spills over and affects his subjects' daily transactions? The key to the solution, I think, lies in the word 'affect'. How do the decisions of sovereigns affect the people? I propose that we borrow a metaphor recently illuminated afresh by Michel Serres (1980) and conceive of these relations as *parasitical*. To conduct its own affairs, the 'centre of power' extracts a levy. It quite literally feeds upon tolls collected from its 'subjects'. Upon some, these affairs may break like a natural disaster, as upon those who happened to live in the actual districts of fighting in the Thirty Years War. But most, says the historian, remain unperturbed, and conduct their own business. Now Braudel's example. The local and transnational merchants depend to some degree upon the agricultural surplus, which they extract from the rural population. In their struggle for the surplus, they struggle against each other: the private counter-market circumvents official market prices and quantities, one parasite feeds upon another. The number of levels of parasites may well be indefinite. A final look at the Borodino case – at the inability of the commander, that is, seriously to command an army's action. The commander's contribution (and toll) appears to be intricately connected to his voice: he shouts at his subordinates and writes orders of the day. And from innumerable commands those that can be matched to the action adopted on the spur of the situation are recalled and preserved. They return to him, he extracts them from an actual series of events. The parasite plays the role of a catalyst. From the noise of the battle, there emerges a wilfully planned and orderly executed sequence of subordinate action. Kutuzov won a victory, Napoleon lost a battle.

But note: it is a condition for the survival of parasites that the 'host from whose table they feed' (Serres) remains intact, capable to act as a provider, that is, of goods that appease the parasite. Parasites work upon their hosts in a functionally isolated way. They must not disturb the functioning of the body they infest (although, occasionally, they do exactly that). Of course, what exactly it means to leave a province of social practice 'relatively unperturbed' may be a matter of continual controversy in everyday life. Yet the metaphor of parasitism provides for a sense in which we can think of the exertion of power upon, or rather the extraction of power-effects from, a field of practice that retains relative autonomy and isolation.

More needs to be considered to put flesh on this metaphorical sketch. Suffice it to emphasize, for the purpose at hand, that to conceive of power relations in terms of parasitical relations avoids the fallacy of unwarranted subsumption; that is, the argument that once power relations (or structural relations) have been identified, we have discovered the underlying mechanisms which effectively control micro-social transactions, and said all there is to be said about these transactions. I suspect it is this implication of the idea of power against which micro-sociologists rebel when they denounce, by neglect or contempt, macro-concepts of domination.

Notes

1. This conception of social situations derives from Schutz. He emphasized that non-social situations do not exist in everyday life; they can only be construed in theory, as a limiting case of participants' ordinary experience (Schutz and Luckmann, 1975: 253).

2. With respect to the neo-classical model, Friedman (1953) and Machlup (1967) among others have argued that the lack of realism in a theory's assumptions is unrelated to its validity. From an instrumentalist perspective, theories are useful fictions of science.

3. Quoted in Miller (1978: 403). Miller makes his argument in regard to methodological individualism.

4. See the summary in Denzin (1969). For those interested in these studies, Denzin provides further references.

5. As an example, consider Goffman's sketch of the features of social situations (1972).

6. This formulation of the problem follows Goffman (1972: 61f), though I am not sure that Goffman would agree with my further explication. Like other interactionists, Goffman appears to be interested in identifying rules that govern human conduct.

7. One difference between the Aggregation Hypothesis and the present conception is that the former considers such classifications as legitimate in as far as they capture what happens in repeated sequences of micro-social situations, while the latter concedes them only rhetorical status (Harré, 1981: 154ff). This has to do with the fact that the Aggregation Hypothesis as I have presented it starts from transactions in social situations, while Harré grounds his conception in 'individuals' and their relationships. Thus 'aggregationists' may regard the term 'working class' as a convenient shorthand for the sum total of individuals who engage in their working-life situations in specifiable confrontations with those who control the means of production; 'structuralists' of Harré's brand may insist that the members of the working class are not necessarily tied together by any relationships, and hence do not constitute any empirical grouping above and beyond the level of individuals. As we shall see, these viewpoints do not necessarily contradict each other.

8. For a somewhat more detailed discussion of the idea of underdetermination of social practice, see Knorr-Cetina (1981c).

9. See Cicourel (1964, 1968, 1970) as well as the summary in Denzin (1969). See also Mehan and Wood (1975) and Garfinkel (1967).

10. The story was published in 1901. I have been alerted to it by a comment of Schutz.

11. Lenin pointed out a similar difference between what he called imperialism (the new capitalism) and 'simple' capitalism, and Galbraith (1978) speaks about a juxtaposition of 'the market system' and 'the industrial system'. Braudel finds himself in accord with both – only these differences are not new but have existed in Europe at least since the Middle Ages, as has a grass-roots economy 'outside' market and capitalism (1979, vol. 2: 197).

12. This raises the question whether Braudel's rural infra-economy can plausibly be considered as encompassing an 'essentially similar' form of transactions across different countries and regions, that is, across different networks of concretely related

transactions. I think not. The issue of similarities across different networks of concretely related transactions needs further consideration.

13. See Giddens (1981) for a related interest in 'accessibility'. Compare also Giddens' definition of institutions as similar actions reproduced across time and space.

14. For example, Braudel makes reference to the problems created by missing or unreliable records throughout his writings (1979).

References

Alexander, Jeffery (1982) *Theoretical Logic in Sociology*, vol. 1: *Positivism, Presuppositions, and Current Controversies*. Berkeley: University of California Press.

Bailey, F.G. (1978) 'Tertius Gaudens aut Tertium Numen', in Fredrik Barth (ed.), *Scale and Social Organization*. Oslo: Universitetsforlaget.

Berger, Peter and Luckman, Thomas (1967) *The Social Construction of Reality*. London: Allen Lane.

Berreman, Gerald D. (1978) 'Scale and Social Relations: Thoughts and Three Examples', in Fredrik Barth (ed.), *Scale and Social Organization*. Oslo: Universitetsforlaget.

Bhaskar, Roy (1979) *The Possibility of Naturalism*. Brighton, Sussex: Harvester.

Birdwhistell, Ray L. (1971) *Kinesics and Context*. London: Allen Lane.

Bloomfield, Leonard (1933) *Language*. New York: Henri Holt.

Braudel, Ferdinand (1979) *Civilisation matérielle, économie et capitalisme, XVe–XVIIIe siècle*. 3 vols. Paris: Armand Colin.

Brittan, A. (1973) *Meanings and Situations*. London: Routledge & Kegan Paul.

Callon, Michel and Latour, Bruno (1981) 'Unscrewing the Big Leviathan: How Actors Macrostructure Reality and How Sociologists Help Them to Do So', in Karin Knorr-Cetina and Aaron Cicourel (eds), *Advances in Social Theory and Methodology: Toward an Integration of Micro- and Macro-sociologies*. London: Routledge & Kegan Paul.

Cicourel, Aaron (1964) *Method and Measurement in Sociology*. New York: Free Press.

Cicourel, Aaron (1968) *The Social Organization of Juvenile Justice*. New York: Wiley.

Cicourel, Aaron (1970) 'The Acquisition of Social Structure: Toward A Developmental Sociology of Language and Meaning', in Jack Douglas (ed.), *Understanding Everyday Life*. Chicago: Aldine.

Cicourel, Aaron (1981) 'Notes on the Integration of Micro- and Macro-levels of Analysis', in Karin Knorr-Cetina and Aaron Cicourel (eds), *Advances in Social Theory and Methodology: Toward an Integration of Micro- and Macro-sociologies*. London: Routledge & Kegan Paul.

Collins, Randall (1981a) 'The Microfoundations of Macrosociology', *American Journal of Sociology*, 86: 984–1014.

Collins, Randall (1981b) 'Micro-translation as a Theory-building Strategy', in Karin Knorr-Cetina and Aaron Cicourel (eds), *Advances in Social Theory and Methodology: Toward an Integration of Micro- and Macro-sociologies*. London: Routledge & Kegan Paul.

Denzin, Norman K. (1969) 'Symbolic Interactionism and Ethnomethodology: A Proposed Synthesis', *American Sociological Review*, 34: 922–34.

Dewey, J. (1910) *How We Think*. Boston: D.C. Heath.

Ditomaso, Nancy (1982) ' "Sociological Reductionism". From Parsons to Althusser:

Linking Action and Structure in Social Theory', *American Sociological Review*, 47: 14–28.

Douglas, Jack (1970) 'Understanding Everyday Life', in Jack Douglas (ed.), *Understanding Everyday Life*. Chicago: Aldine.

Etzioni, Amitai (1970) 'Toward a Macrosociology', in John C. McKinney and Edward Tiryakian (eds), *Theoretical Sociology: Perspectives and Development*. New York: Appleton-Century-Crofts.

Fleck, Ludwik (1979) *Genesis and Development of a Scientific Fact*. Chicago: University of Chicago Press.

Foucault, Michel (1975) *Surveiller et punir*. Paris: Gallimard.

Foucault, Michel (1976) *Histoire de la sexualité*, 1: *La Volonté de savoir*. Paris: Gallimard.

Frake, Charles O. (1964) 'How to Ask for a Drink in Subanun', *American Anthropologist*, 66(6/2): 127–32.

Friedman, Milton (1953) 'The Methodology of Positive Economics', in *Essays in Positive Economics*. Chicago: University of Chicago Press.

Galbraith, J.K. (1978) *The New Industrial State*, 3rd rev. edn. Boston: Houghton Mifflin.

Garfinkel, Harold (1967) *Studies in Ethnomethodology*. Englewood Cliffs, NJ: Prentice-Hall.

Garfinkel, Harold and Sacks, Harvey (1970) 'On Formal Structures of Practical Actions', in John C. McKinney and Edward Tiryakian (eds), *Theoretical Sociology: Perspectives and Developments*. New York: Appleton-Century-Crofts.

Giddens, Anthony (1979) *Central Problems in Social Theory*. Berkeley: University of California Press.

Giddens, Anthony (1981) 'Agency, Institution and Time-Space Analysis', in Karin Knorr-Cetina and Aaron Cicourel (eds), *Advances in Social Theory and Methodology: Toward an Integration of Micro- and Macro-sociologies*. London: Routledge & Kegan Paul.

Goffman, Erving (1963) *Behaviour in Public Places*. New York: Free Press.

Goffman, Erving (1972) 'The Neglected Situation', in Pierre Paolo Giglioli (ed.), *Language and Social Context*. Harmondsworth, Middx: Penguin.

Goffman, Erving (1974) *Frame Analysis: An Essay on the Organization of Experience*. New York: Harper & Row.

Gumpertz, John (1958) 'Dialectic Differences and Social Stratification in a North Indian Village', *American Anthropologist*, 60: 668–82.

Gumpertz, John and Hymes, Dell (eds) (1972) *Directions in Sociolinguistics*. New York: Holt, Rinehart & Winston.

Gurwitsch, A (1941) 'A Non-egological Conception of Consciousness,' *Philosophy and Phenomenological Research*, 1: 325–38.

Harré, Rom (1975) 'Images of the World and Societal Icons', in Karin Knorr-Cetina, Hermann Strasser and Hans-Georg Zilian (eds), *Determinants and Controls of Scientific Development*. Boston-Dordrecht: Reidel.

Harré, Rom (1980) *Social Being*. Totowa: Rowman-Littlefield-Adams.

Harré, Rom (1981) 'Philosophical Aspects of the Micro–macro Problem', in Karin Knorr-Cetina and Aaron Cicourel (eds), *Advances in Social Theory and Methodology: Toward an Integration of Micro- and Macro-sociologies*. London: Routledge & Kegan Paul.

Knorr-Cetina, Karin (1981a) 'The Micro-sociological Challenge of Macro-sociology: Towards a Reconstruction of Social Theory and Methodology', in Karin Knorr-Cetina and Aaron Cicourel (eds) *Advances in Social Theory and Methodology:*

52   Karin Knorr-Cetina

Toward an Integration of Micro- and Macro-sociologies. London: Routledge & Kegan Paul.

Knorr-Cetina, Karin (1981b) *The Manufacture of Knowledge. An Essay on the Constructivist and Contextual Nature of Science*. Oxford: Pergamon.

Knorr-Cetina, Karin (1981c) 'Time and Context in Practical Action. Underdetermination and Knowledge Use', *Knowledge: Creation, Diffusion, Utilization*, 3(2): 143–65.

Laing, R. (1956) *The Divided Self*. London: Tavistock.

Laing, R. and Esterton, A. (1964) *Sanity, Madness and the Family*. London: Tavistock.

Latour, Bruno and Woolgar, Steve (1979) *Laboratory Life. The Social Construction of Scientific Facts*. Beverly Hills: Sage.

Law, John and Williams, Rob (1982) 'Putting Facts Together: A Study of Scientific Persuasion', *Social Studies of Science*, 12, 535–50.

Lemert, Charles C. (1979) 'De-centered Analysis: Ethnomethodology and Structuralism', *Theory and Society*, 7: 289–306.

Machlup, Fritz (1967) 'Theories of the Firm: Marginalist, Behavioral, Managerial', *American Economic Review*, 57: 1–33.

McKinney, John C. (1970) 'Sociological Theory and the Process of Typification', in John C. McKinney and Edward Tiryakian (eds), *Theoretical Sociology: Perspectives and Developments*. New York: Appleton-Century-Crofts.

Marx, Karl (1939) *Grundrisse der Kritik der politischen Ökonomie*. Moskau: Verlag für fremdsprachige Literatur.

Mayhew, Bruce H. (1980) 'Structuralism versus Individualism: Part 1, Shadowboxing in the Dark', *Social Forces*, 59(2): 335–75.

Mayhew, Bruce H. (1981) 'Structuralism versus Individualism: Part 2, Ideology and Other Obfuscations', *Social Forces*, 59(3): 627–48.

Mead, George Herbert (1972) *The Philosophy of the Act*, ed. Charles W. Morris. Chicago: University of Chicago Press (first published 1938).

Mead, George Herbert (1974) *Mind, Self and Society*, ed. Charles H. Morris. Chicago: University of Chicago Press (first published 1934).

Mehan, H. and Wood, H. (1975) *The Reality of Ethnomethodology*. New York: Wiley.

Merton, Robert K. (1957) *Social Theory and Social Structure*. New York: Free Press.

Miller, Richard W. (1978) 'Methodological Individualism and Social Explanation', *Philosophy of Science*, 45: 387–414.

O'Neill, John (ed.) (1973) *Modes of Individualism and Collectivism*. London: Heinemann.

O'Neill, John (ed.) (1983) *Science Texts*. Chicago: Chicago University Press.

Quine, W.V.O. (1969) *Ontological Relativity and Other Essays*. New York: Columbia University Press.

Schegloff, E.A. (1968) 'Sequencing in Conversational Openings', *American Anthropologist*, 70(6): 1075–95.

Schutz, Alfred (1967) *The Phenomenology of the Social World*. Evanston, Ill.: Northwestern University Press.

Schutz, Alfred (1973) *Collected Papers*, vol. I: *The Problem of Social Reality*, ed. Maurice Natanson. The Hague: Martinus Nijhoff.

Schutz, Alfred and Luckmann, Thomas (1975) *Strukturen der Lebenswelt*. Neuwied und Darmstadt: Luchterhand.

Serres, Michel (1980) *Le Parasite*. Paris: Minuit.

Simmel, Georg (1971) *On Individuality and Social Forms: Selected Writings*. Chicago: University of Chicago Press.

Tolstoy, Leo (1966) *War and Peace*. New York: Norton.

Voegelin, Eric (1952) *The New Science of Politics*. Chicago: University of Chicago Press.

Wallerstein, Immanuel (1974) *The Modern World-system*, I: *Capitalist Agriculture and the Origins of the European World-economy in the Sixteenth Century*. New York: Academic Press.

Warriner, Charles, K. (1956) 'Groups are Real: A Reaffirmation', *American Sociological Review*, 21: 549–54.

Watkins, J.W.N. (1955) 'Methodological Individualism: A Reply', *Philosophy of Science*, 22: 58–62.

Watkins, J.W.N. (1957) 'Historical Explanations in the Social Sciences', *British Journal for the Philosophy of Science*, 8: 104–17.

Wedgwood, C.V. (1967) *The Thirty Years War*. London: Cape.

Wieder, D.L. (1970) 'On Meaning by Rule', in Jack Douglas (ed.), *Understanding Everyday Life*. Chicago: Aldine.

Wieder, D.L. (1973) *Language and Social Reality*. The Hague: Mouton.

Wirth, Louis (1939) 'Social Interaction: The Problem of the Individual and the Group', *American Journal of Sociology*, 44.

Wittgenstein, Ludwig (1968) *Philosophical Investigations*. Oxford: Basil Blackwell.

Zenzen, Michael and Restivo, Sal (1982) 'The Mysterious Morphology of Immiscible Liquids: A Study of Scientific Practice', *Social Science Information*, 21(3): 447–73.

Zimmerman, Don H. (1970) 'The Practicalities of Rule Use', in Jack Douglas (ed.), *Understanding Everyday Life*. Chicago: Aldine.

2
AUTONOMY AMONG SOCIAL THEORIES

One of the critical matters to be raised about Knorr-Cetina's argument is whether there is any difference in the analytic approach she commends according to the nature of the research problem. For example, would a concern with the analysis of power in organization enjoin any particular procedures or variations? Arguments which are apparently about the 'facts' of some social phenomenon may actually be arguments about how the inquiry was set up in the first place. The extent to which the formulation of one's problematic is decisive for the kinds of solutions one can canvass is something which is perhaps acknowledged in sociology but its importance, Sharrock and Watson argue, is much underestimated there, with the result that partisan conceptions of the key problems are treated as though they were neutral between the different viewpoints in sociology. Nowhere has this been more so than in the argument over micro-sociological viewpoints in sociology, which have characteristically been criticized on the assumption that the opposition/complementarity of 'macro' and 'micro' structures defines the problem area within which solutions must be sought. This can be seen as to the detriment of symbolic interactionism and ethnomethodology, which find that the debate has been pre-empted and they are called on to satisfy criticisms made in the very terms they would prefer to dispute. In Sharrock and Watson's view, to conceive their efforts as designed to solve problems posed in terms of a macro–micro opposition is to divest many of their basic strategies of purpose, significance, and effect.

In this chapter, Sharrock and Watson pursue this contention by using the example of ethnomethodology to argue (a) that it is necessary initially to appreciate the degree to which ethnomethodology is motivated by the objective of comprehensively rethinking the problematic of sociology; (b) that this requires dispensing with many of the dualisms and oppositions which have defined sociology's established framework, including the macro–micro distinction; (c) that the macro–micro distinction involves a separation of action and setting in a way which ethnomethodology cannot accept, for it necessarily sees social action as situated in a setting and settings as manifest in the actions of participants; (d) with the result that the commonplace complaint that ethnomethodology evades the problems posed by environing social structures is false. It tackles those issues which sociologists characteristically located under the rubric of macro–micro relationships but it does so in ways which are not easily recognizable to those thinking in terms of the macro–micro connection.

To appreciate the depth of this critique it helps to highlight the controversial issue of the status of members' accounts collected as data. For example, if a notable feature of an interview with a client is an emphasis on the constraints on service presented by the organization's mode of service delivery, how necessary is it in determining if that is really a constraint that the researchers seek to establish it for themselves? Sharrock and Watson's case is that it is not the 'validity' of the complaint which counts but the way this presumed problem constrains the actions and options available to clients as spoken of in the transcript. Others argue that if interactions of a type which occur outside organizational settings are studied, researchers would be drawn more strongly to the 'duality of structure' argument because it would there be possible to show constraint that is internal or endogenous to the interaction. Sharrock and Watson would resist generalizing about constraints in this way; each case needed to be dealt with in its own terms rather than by linking, say, individually distinctive accounts to interactions outside organizational contexts. They argue that the 'duality of structure' approach simply incorporates all different approaches (as present in some fluid balance) in an indiscriminate fashion, reducing the prospect of the researcher deciding that, in some cases, one approach out of the alternatives actually did not apply.

Autonomy among social theories
The incarnation of social structures

Wes Sharrock and Rod Watson

Many sociologists are quite satisfied that they understand ethnomethodology at least well enough to know what it is about, whether they could hope to learn anything further from it, and what is wrong with it. We take the view, in the light of the characterizations and criticisms which emanate from these sociologists, that they do not understand ethnomethodology anywhere near as well as they suppose; but it is futile simply to reiterate this claim since those who are confident that they *do* understand will be unmoved by the insistence that they do not. To make and document the case that ethnomethodology is persistently and systematically misrepresented in much of the sociological literature would be an extensive exercise in its own right and not one that we want to undertake here, being more concerned to single out and tackle one particular problem in understanding which we say is quite common. The kind of misunderstanding which we refer to is the one which involves the persistent attempt to place ethnomethodology within the structure of dualisms which form the main focuses of contemporary sociological theorizing, despite the fact that ethnomethodology declines to formulate its project or its problems in terms of those dualisms. The attempt to treat ethnomethodology as a species of 'interactionism' crucially lacking a theory of large-scale social structure, as an approach that places emphasis on 'agency' at the expense of 'structure' or that prefers a 'voluntaristic' over a 'determinist' approach are all efforts in that same direction and ones which we shall suggest presuppose an apparatus of theorizing that is obviated by ethnomethodology's assumptions and strategy.

A procedural turn

We will try to do a little demythologizing of ethnomethodology, hoping that this will not only promote the interests of that pursuit but may also contribute something to the clarification of issues which are of interest across a wider area of sociological debate. We do not intend to promote ethnomethodology at the expense of other, 'rival' sociological strategies, setting out to elevate it and criticize them.

Indeed, part of our point is that there is a great deal of unnecessary rivalry, too common a tendency to set up the issues in such a way that one position can be taken only at the expense of some other.

Though we hope to point out that some disagreements are superfluous, this does not mean that we think there is abundant opportunity for reconciliation, that the apparently divergent sociological strategies are really fundamentally complementary, basically engaged in the same overall task and each making a specialist contribution to it. The attempts at comprehensive sociological schemes in which each strategy is given its particular place do not seem any more helpful than does the competitive approach. If the latter exacerbates difficulties, then the former simply avoids them, playing up broad and superficial similarities at the expense of deep and serious divergences.

We argue for a much greater appreciation of the autonomy of sociological strategies and for their (current) irreducible diversity. The topic of 'structure versus agency' provides us with an opportunity to argue this quite relevantly, since the 'opposition' between structure and agency is regarded as one of the polarizing dimensions of sociological thought, and since some of the more notable attempts at 'reconciliation' (such as that of Anthony Giddens) are designed to resolve that opposition. We can opportunely try to eliminate some mythology about ethnomethodology because that approach is routinely treated as one which places an exclusive and excessive emphasis on agency at the expense of structure. It does not, we will try to show, fall within the agency/structure dichotomy, but takes a way around that. In this way we might help clarify some issues in sociology by showing that the agency/structure polarity is the product of a set of assumptions about the aims and character of theorizing, rather than the necessary pre-condition of sociological inquiry. If successful, we might obviate one of the standard arguments against ethnomethodology, that it places wrong and undue emphasis on agency and requires (at least) correction by a suitably strong emphasis on the importance of structure. If that criticism is disposed of, then clearly the conception which most sociologists have of ethnomethodology's wider implications will need to be revised and, with it, their suppositions about what ethnomethodology might mean for their own enterprise. Though sociological strategies are (we think) rather more autonomous than they are taken to be, and do not therefore stand in relations of direct rivalry, they do none the less have *indirect* consequences for one another. However, it is no part of our purpose here to explore these, being engaged as we will be in the making of heightened contrasts of ways in which structure-and-agency is seen to present a problem.

Sociology thrives and stumbles on dualisms. Dualisms provide it with its problems, but at the same time they prove stubborn, resistant to quick disposal, focuses of polarized controversy, sources of persistent puzzlement. One can, of course, take one's stand within the space defined by such dualisms, one can opt for one side or the other, or one can attempt to overcome the duality. In doing this, though, one is asking what to do about the problem of this or that duality, rather than how one comes to be in possession of such a dualism to begin with. What is the relationship between 'structure' and 'agency'? The two seem inimical: 'structure' apparently means givenness, constraint, stability, whilst 'agency' seemingly implies creativity, autonomy, fluidity. How, then, do structure and agency relate in society: is it primarily one or the other? Does emphasis on structure marginalize or eliminate agency, does emphasis on agency dispose of structure? Which should we favour? Or should we seek an appropriate balance between them, saying that society is both structure and agency, that agency requires structure (or is only possible within structure) whilst structure is engendered by but emergent from agency? Asking about 'structure and agency' in this way, though, is to disregard the first way in which these two are related: they are presented as a dualism, given as terms in which to define our problematic. It is, though, possible to ask whether it is not the relationship of agency-to-structure within our theories which gives the problematic, but the character of our theories which sticks us with the dualism of agency-and-structure, and thus our attitude to theorizing which is problematic. Ethnomethodology approaches these matters in this way. It does not stand within the same conception of theorizing, does not affiliate itself to the received tradition of theorizing, but steps outside of that and thus outside of the collection of dualisms (including structure-and-agency) which comprise sociology's institutionalized dilemmas.

The opposition of agency to structure is not, itself, primary but derivative. It is also pretty directly derivative from yet another, more primeval, duality, between society-seen-from-within and society-seen-from-without. Structure-and-agency originates in a contrast of points of view, that between society as it appears to us within the sphere of our daily lives where we appear to be free agents, capable of deciding and choosing, and society as it appears from the larger, longer view, in which our actions appear as dictated not by our individual subjectivities, but by the objective requirements of historically assembled, large-scale organized structures. It is at just this point, though, that ethnomethodology rejects the dichotomization which will result if we treat society-seen-from-within and society-seen-from-without as distinct and finished alternatives. If we treat them thus, then we appear to have two independent alternatives, and a problem as to how to relate them: here are two views of (in some sense) the same thing, but in these two views the same thing appears very different. Which of these views are we to take, if either? Ethnomethodology (for reasons which we do not go into) looks into the origins of these views and finds that we do not have two *entirely distinct and contrasting views* but that one is a *modification* of the other. Society-as-seen-from-without is produced by idealization from society-as-seen-from-within. That society-as-seen-from-without is an idealization is no objection to it, for idealization has utility within the traditional framework of theorizing; however, this kind of idealization does not have utility for ethnomethodology, since it does not undertake those tasks in terms of which a conception of society-as-seen-from-without can find a place and a use. Ethnomethodology does not set out to provide a specific mode of comprehending society, a theoretical framework *within* which a substantive conception of society is to be construed, but determines (instead) to inquire into the *comprehensibility of society*, into the ways in which social life can be understood and described when seen from within by members, or when seen under the auspices of the idealizations of social science. It does not, in other words, concern itself with theorizing as an episte-mological and cognitive matter, but with theorizing as a social and organized affair: it does not, that is, pursue arguments about the correct form of theorizing but seeks to identify and describe those activities which are constituent of the work of theorizing. Those working within the tradition of social science theorizing can – indeed must – disregard the extent to which their activities are rooted in and organized through an understanding of society-seen-from-within, since these matters are (from the point of view of theorizing) entirely irrelevant. However, ethnomethodology cannot so disregard them, for it is concerned with precisely the ways in which these *theoretically* irrelevant matters are *practically* essential and consequential.

We bring out these basic points because they show how far back the divergences between ethnomethodology and other sociologies go, and how considerable are the differences between them. It is wholly misleading to treat ethnomethodology as though it were a different view of the same things that other sociologies are interested in, when it is, in truth, interested in very different things than they are, so much so that there is a sharp discontinuity between them, with ethnomethodology directing its attention to the very things which (under the rules of their tradition of theorizing) other sociologies must *systematically* disregard. Ethnomethodology must with equal systematicity give sustained attention to them.

This should indicate why we are deeply sceptical of the suggestion that ethnomethodology's point of view could, with relative ease, be reconciled with that of other sociologies or accommodated within some overall scheme which incorporates it and those other sociologies. The relationship between ethnomethodology's point of view and that of any other sociology is not like that between two perspectives on the same thing, such that these can be conjoined to produce a more 'rounded' picture of the object of attention. The relationship between these points of view is, rather, much more like that between the elements in a *gestalt* switch such that there is – again – a discontinuity: one can look at things one way or the other, but they are discrete and alternate, not additive, ways of seeing things, such that what is seen from one point of view 'disappears' when seen from the other. Those things which are the very stuff of ethnomethodology's inquiries are the same ones as must, perforce, be counted out of attention if other exercises in sociological theorizing are to proceed coherently and the attempt to take notice of them (without otherwise and massively readjusting themselves) will simply *distract* them from their intended business. It would make absolutely no sense for ethnomethodology to urge other sociologies to improve themselves by taking on board its concerns, for it is clear that those are directed to matters which are not casually overlooked by those sociologies, but which are necessarily and persistently excluded from their consideration (though they are, of course, ones to which a close and detailed practical attention must be pervasively sustained).

The problem that other sociologists have in reconciling structure with agency is, for them, a matter of settling causal/explanatory questions (though, we should stress, these are actually questions about the form of explanation, rather than about how actually to explain anything). This appears to ethnomethodology as yet another manifestation of a more general problem that such sociologies have, that of abstraction-and-restoration, that is, the puzzling difficulty of reconnecting within the theory things which have been analytically isolated and counterposed to constitute that very theoretical framework. Thus, the contrast between 'society-as-seen-from-within' and 'society-as-seen-from-without' is the very basis for the construction of (standard) sociological theories, the very licence for such theories to idealize and abstract from the appearances of daily life, but then the discontinuities thereby engendered between 'how things are in the natural attitude' and 'how things are viewed under the auspices of sociological theorizing' as a consequence of the deliberate transformation of the former into the latter, reappears as an analytical problem within the theory (this seeming, from our point of view, rather as if one were puzzled by the fact that a blueprint and a photograph of the same house did not look alike).

Thus, many topics which have been extensively discussed as substantive problems in sociological theory (like the structure-versus-agency dilemma) are, for ethnomethodology, ones which are better considered as products of methodological decisions which antedate the formation of the theories themselves and which require, therefore, re-examination at the most primitive pre-theoretical level, rather than within the given framework of dualisms, dichotomies, and dilemmas which, in view of the received traditions of sociological theorizing, we apparently face as immutable, granted suppositions of our sociological reasoning. Ethnomethodology offers the possibility that they are not the unavoidable dualisms which must frame our thinking about how to examine the organization of social life, but are dilemmas which we impose upon ourselves by the adoption of a particular (albeit widespread, and widely approved of) way of thinking. Thus, what many see as the thoroughly empiricist character of ethnomethodology might be better understood as an attempt to retrace the steps involved in some of sociology's most elementary methodological decisions.

To invite ethnomethodology to conceive itself through the opposition of 'structure' or 'agency' or to contribute to the mediation-and-resolution of this opposition is to ask it to situate itself in the terms of a dualism whose very constitution it finds problematic. Worse, to understand ethnomethodology as though it acquired its sense and role within a discussion conducted on the unquestioned basis of that decision (as if, for example, it were an instance of 'radical subjectivism') is to misread its entire character. Does it not, though, offer itself as just such a subjectivism, for does it not invite us to consider social phenomena as 'achieved' phenomena, as locally and interactionally accomplished outcomes of practical sociological reasoning, proposing to portray the ways in which such phenomena are made to happen? Is not this the same as saying that society is created by individuals, necessarily – and even fatally – overlooking the fact that individuals are created by society? Worse, is it not exactly the same as proposing that society is made up afresh, *de novo*, by individuals, as if they were free to make it happen however they wished? And does this not clearly – even fatally – underplay the fact that the members of society are not free to make it happen as they like, that there are tremendous constraints given by society itself on how they can produce social reality? They do not, indeed, produce society, they reproduce it.

There are numerous misconceptions compounded into such characterizations. One is, of course, that it supposes that ethnomethodology strives to produce the same kind of theoretical output as standard sociologies do, namely a synoptic characterization of society, or of 'social reality'. What is taken for an oversight with respect to the given and constraining effect of society-in-the-large is in fact a consequence of the refusal to begin from the dichotomization of society seen from without and within. A methodological decision, to study society purely as encountered from within the world of daily life, is treated as though it were an ontological or causal claim. The second significant mistake is that of taking ethnomethodology's aim as being that of the synoptic overview yielding a *causal portrayal* of individual action and/or the constitution of social structures. However, it is also to overlook the most rudimentary point of all, which is that ethnomethodology does not take as its puzzle the fact that people act in stable, regular ways (such that we have the problem of what keeps them behaving like that) but the quite different one of how it is that the stability and regularity of conduct is recognizable and discoverable, and recognizable and discoverable from within its own midst (which gives us the problem of how we go about the business of identifying people's actions and finding explanations for them). The third crucial mistake (and the last one we will discuss here) is to take the suggestion that social phenomena be viewed as 'achievements' as an argument about the causal production of social structure (as these are understood within the conventions of more standard sociological frameworks). We are, again, dealing with a methodological step, and one which encourages us to examine social phenomena as procedural affairs, replacing the questions 'why do people do X in the first place?' and 'what keeps people doing X?' with 'what do people have to do to be (routinely, unremarkably, but recognizably and readily so) doing X?' This formulation serves one purpose quite satisfactorily. It shows just how different the central question which ethnomethodology puts is from those to which sociological theory conventionally gives priority. We make no comment on whether this question of ethnomethodology's should take priority over or even entirely displace those others, or whether starting from ethnomethodology's question we would eventually be in a better position to answer the other ones. In another respect, our formulation may not be so satisfactory. It can be misinterpreted as focusing upon individual action, opening the way to a repetition of the claim: it ignores 'social structures'. There are ways in which one can formulate ethnomethodology in such a way that 'the individual' drops out entirely and one can say, quite firmly, that ethnomethodology is interested in actions, activities and courses of action, and not in individuals at all (thus, one can talk about 'the member' not as a 'person' at all, but as a 'mastery of natural language' (see Garfinkel and Sachs, 1970: esp. 342–5)), but we avoid these since they make argument cumbersome and elaborate, and perhaps even harder to understand. The way to avoid this kind of misapprehension on this occasion is (perhaps) to say something about the way in which we ask 'what is involved in doing X?' which is not to be understood as 'what is involved in an individual doing action X?' since this gratuitously formulates the question in a way which isolates individual and action, when the question will, for ethnomethodology, be more characteristically (say) 'what actions are involved in carrying on the orderly business of a history lesson in junior school?' or 'what actions are involved in making up a crowd following a football match?' or, again, 'what actions are involved in executing the day-to-day tasks of a medium-sized business?' These are all queries about how actions make up orderly patterns, how actions comprise the day-to-day business.

Furthermore, we may suggest that the procedural emphasis together with the construal of the queries in this way combine to highlight the collective/collaborative character of the matters being investigated, allowing (indeed!) an emphasis on this to a degree that cannot be matched (and certainly cannot be exceeded) by sociologies which are (supposedly) vastly less individualistic than ethnomethodology. It is not, after all, that ethnomethodology conceived social phenomena individualistically, for it conceives them as essentially collaborative phenomena. Thus, for example, ethnomethodology should ask not 'how does a teacher maintain the order of a classroom?' but 'how do teacher, pupils and others not necessarily present there collectively engender a-classroom-routinely-and-recognizably-going-about-its-business?' This last question is not at all the same order of question as the first.

For many sociologists, the notion of showing that something is 'social' involves, essentially, establishing that it takes place within society, and that it bears the marks of the society within which it takes place. Ethnomethodology has a different notion: showing that something is social involves showing how it is done together. The conception of society from a collectivist or individualist point of view involves an emphasis on the relation and connection of positions and persons respectively but for ethnomethodology it involves the connection of activities with, as far as we know, a unique concentration on the way in which actions are co-ordinated and concerted. Just to avoid any impression that there is some underlying – and erroneous – assumption about the amount of consensus in real life, let us say that the expressions 'collaborative' and 'co-ordinated' are not to be understood as meaning (for example) 'done in a spirit of collaboration' or 'done with the aim of helping each other out'. From this point of view, a radical disagreement would be a collaborative production, would be 'made to happen' by the various parties to it.

To reinforce this, let us point to that basic, but frequently ignored, notion of the 'documentary method' to which ethnomethodology gives such play. Part of the purpose of articulating that notion is to make the case that there is an inherent tension between the methodological canons which many social-science researchers adopt and the actual requirements of factual investigation in social life, such that anyone wanting to say what definitely happened on any occasion must employ reasoning which cannot conform to the demands made by ideals of analytical reasoning which, it is widely supposed, sociology must comply with. That is a point with far-reaching consequences which, if taken seriously, would require the extensive revision of sociology's self-understanding with respect to its methodological ideals and practices, and their relationship. However, we mention the 'documentary' method here just to note how the idea of an opposition of 'individual action' and 'social structure' is entirely incongruous with ethnomethodology's root conceptions. The whole point of it is to show that we cannot conceive of an individual action except as an-action-in-a-social-structure, any more than we can conceive of a single word as other than a-word-in-a-language. What the word is depends upon which language it is part of, and what someone's action is depends upon which social setting it is part of. The relationship between 'action' and 'social structure' is not to be conceived at this level as one between cause and consequence (whichever way the causal connection is supposed to run, from action to structure or vice versa or dialectically between them). It is, instead, to be conceived as that of pattern and particular, where the articulation of the two provides for their mutual visibility: the particular is recognizable for what it is as part of the pattern but the pattern itself is made out of and manifested in the particulars (as the elements of a mosaic and the mosaic-as-a-whole comprise one another). The pattern and particular are mutually constitutive and that is why ethnomethodology cannot make the analytic separation of action and social structure, nor face the problems which arise from it: an action 'isolated' from its social structure can only be discovered in and through the actions which make it up. The 'documentary' method is a set of members' common-sense methods for imputing sense, visibility and recognizability to conduct-in-a-social-structure.

One last point in this section. The arguments given have been designed to show just how distinctive ethnomethodology's problems are from those which motivate other forms of sociological inquiry (without any inclination on our part to argue that ethnomethodology's are preferable ones), and to show that, far from locating ethnomethodology at the extreme 'agency' end of the agency/structure polarity, it obviates that polarity completely. It places such weight at such a fundamental level on the fact that actions cannot even be identified except as actions-in-a-social-structure that the issue cannot be problematic in the way that it is for other sociologies. Having said all this, however, there is perhaps a need for one further argument, which has to do with 'comprehensiveness'. It may be thought that ethnomethodology is not so 'comprehensive' as other sociologies, and that, though distinct from them, it may none the less need complementing by them. It is itself capable of dealing only with face-to-face situations and cannot deal with the large-scale social phenomena that provide other sociologies with their stock-in-trade: life goes on outside the immediate situation. Indeed it does, but this fact is not particularly relevant to ethnomethodology's project nor to any arguments about whether it needs to be (let alone could be) complemented by any of the other available sociologies.

The problem here is what is understood by comprehensiveness. We have said that ethnomethodology and other sociologies look at quite different things, but that makes it sound (perhaps) as though, in concentrating on the things it looks at, ethnomethodology thereby notices some aspects of things, whilst other sociologies notice different aspects. Surely they need to be added or taken together to give us a more rounded, a more complete picture? It is not, though, in the *phenomena* that the divergence between ethnomethodology and other sociologies originates, such that there is a specialization between them, with one dealing with certain substantive aspects of the phenomena and the rest noticing various other ones. The difference originates in the point of view such that ethnomethodology and other sociologies may often look at what is, in one sense, 'the same thing', but because they regard it from such different standpoints that they see quite different things. Ethnomethodology need not regard itself as any less comprehensive than any other sociology, since for it comprehensiveness comes not from looking at some object of interest from numerous different (and probably incommensurate) angles, but from looking at any and every topic from one and the same point of view. There is, thus, no reason for it to suppose that it is precluded from inspecting phenomena that other sociologies freely tackle, because they fall outside its purview. It cannot examine the phenomena that other sociologies tackle because, in the very act of inspecting them, they become *different kinds of phenomena* than they are for those other sociologies.

Two illustrations

One of sociology's real problems may be that it reasons discursively. We do not intend this as one of those facile criticisms which says that sociology is inadequate because it reasons discursively and that it had better, therefore, hasten to abandon this way of carrying on and adopt formal ways of thinking. It seems to us that we are (at least for the foreseeable future) stuck with reasoning discursively, and it may be that it is only through discursive reasoning that many things we want to do can be done. Discursive reasoning is a problem in the sense that it is hard to do, and that in it we run the continuing risk of losing track of the steps we have already taken, losing sight of the origins and character of the things we are doing, and of failing to perceive the connections between facets of our argument. The issues which sociology currently faces are large, complex and interdigitated, with the result that the necessary brevity imposed here ensures that distinct and elaborate issues are compacted together.

We have tried to indicate that some of the apparent problems and misunderstandings which are involved in the structure-and-agency problem are a result of discursiveness. We have focused on the place of a 'synoptic view' within sociological analysis, since many problems, though not the same as it, are closely bound up with it, and have insinuated that there is precisely a tendency, because of the discursive character of sociological reasoning, to lose sight of the fact that 'a synoptic view' is a methodological device and that its utility and indispensability are not to be presumed without regard for the nature of the problems at hand, and the terms in which they are proposed. Society, synoptically viewed, tends to be treated as if it was the point of origin for and environment of sociological analysis, but 'society, synoptically conceived' is a result of sociological reasoning, and is built upon particular sets of assumptions which just happen, we have indicated, to be those which ethnomethodology cannot honour. Losing sight of the fact that 'society, synoptically conceived', is a methodological device, there is a tendency to treat those who find no room within their approach for such a device as if they were engaging in substantive controversies about ontology and causality, as if they were arguing that certain phenomena had no existence or as if certain facts were illusory. It is for this reason that ethnomethodology is so commonly accused of offering an implausible account of the nature and causes of social action, and of overlooking, if not actively denying, the character of real-world social structures.

These issues, as we say, interdigitate. Disclaiming a use for the synoptic view we also reject the need for something else which is thought to be provided through the synoptic view, namely, a portrayal of social reality from a point of view independent of that taken by the members of society – the issue modulates into that of the objective-and-subjective character of social phenomena. We cannot (obviously) go any distance into that one, save to say that one of the reasons why there is no need for the construction of a synoptic view is just because there is no role in the inquiry for 'social structures, independently described'. A social structure, independently described, is an alternative nomenclature for 'a social structure, theoretically conceived' and that, if introduced into ethnomethodology, would resolve into 'a social structure, ethnomethodologically conceived' but this latter notion is an incoherence. Ethnomethodology does not incorporate the attempt to describe social structures in any sense comparable to that in which it is usually undertaken: it does not aim to describe the stable features or operating principles of social settings, portraying these abstractly. It has absolutely no need to say on its own behalf how a social setting is organized, for its concern is not with 'social settings in themselves' (so to speak) but with 'social setting as practically encountered', its objective not being to describe the features of such settings, but to identify the eponymous methods, the ordinary procedures, whereby such settings are discovered, identified, described, and so on, by members ('society as a procedural phenomenon' has replaced 'society as a standing arrangement' throughout). The contrast between 'things as they really are in themselves' and 'things as they appear to members of society' is not abolished by this step, but it is relocated. It is no longer treated as being realized in the contrast between the theorist's synoptic view of society as seen from without and the member's (supposedly) perspectival view of society seen from within, in the counterposition of the sociologist's 'objective' view, and the social actor's 'subjective' one. It becomes, instead, a distinction which is made by the members of the society and which is methodically employed within the course of their everyday affairs as a routine feature of their fact-finding and decision-making.

The advisability of reshaping the quite fundamental presuppositions of (much) sociological theorizing in this way is, of course, open to argument. We could not rule out the possibility that we are making wrong moves, but we will not be persuaded of this on the strength of criticisms which treat our point of view as a manifestation of *naïveté* about elementary and obvious facts of social life, especially when those critics seem themselves quite naïve about (or at least inattentive to) the methodological background of their own favoured standpoints, let alone ours. The argument thus far has been unrelievedly abstract, and has perhaps given the impression that the determination to reshape presuppositions arises from a desire to make the methodological points for their own sake, but this is not so. The methodological argument is consequential because it bears upon access to phenomena. The claim, on our part, is that the standard assumptions of sociological analysis deny us access to the very topics that we want to discuss. These assumptions were not, of course, designed with our topics in mind, nor is there any reason why they should have been, but if – as we allege – they not only do not but cannot accommodate our interests, then they cannot serve as the basis for our inquiries.

The kinds of difficulties we are pointing to can be expressed in terms of the issue of the synoptic view. The synoptic view provides a picture of society, theoretically conceived, and the preparation of such a view requires the disentangling of society's organization from its local and practical environment, a portrayal of society's structure as it appears independently of any particular inhabitant's point of view. This may be just what is required for the perspicuity of some modes of analysis, but it is not what we want. Given that our concern is with society as mundanely encountered, it is precisely the elements with which we are concerned, namely the local and practical organization, which are 'lost' in the process of constructing a synoptic point of view. By moving 'up' to a level of abstraction which surveys society 'as a whole' we do not gain any clearer view of the matters we wish to attend to, but obscure them from our view.

In the light of the importance we give to access to phenomena, the abstractness of the discussion should be relieved by some examination (albeit brief) of two illustrative instances, which will serve to show the application in analytical practice of some of the points we have made above.

Allegedly, ethnomethodology's policies restrict it from being able to appreciate the extent to which social actors are placed within a particular kind of system, prevent it from recognizing, for example, the extent to which their situation and activities are dictated by being located within a market. Such criticisms really, though, only amount to the objection that ethnomethodology does not take note of, for example, market organization in the way that other sociologies do, but that is, it ought now to be clear, only to be expected. Consider, for example, the situation of a 'purchasing officer'[1] in an organization which uses petroleum products, who is firmly located within an international market for petroleum products, and whose day-to-day work is oriented to the state of that market as one of its leading circumstances. The conditions of the purchasing officer's relation to that market are, then, occupational, and as such they are dominated by the need to ensure that flows of appropriate, storable, usable quantities of suitable products are available as and when they are required in terms of the officer's own organization's production flows, and at prices which have regard to organizationally supplied budgets and acceptable standards of costing. The purchasing officer is required to track and anticipate the state of the market, timing purchases in such ways as to ensure the appropriate flow of incoming supplies whilst postponing decisions long enough to take advantage of expected price falls or bringing them forward to escape the consequences of predictable rises. The petroleum market is, from the purchasing officer's point of view, a given structure, with properties which are more or less definitely known and with proclivities of movement which are beyond the purchaser's own control, but part of the work is to determine the properties of that market and to work out the ways in which features of it interact to bring about price movements or complications of supply. It is also the case that the officer's investigations into these matters are under organizationally supplied conditions, that they are to be done in and as part of the daily round of work.

Thus, our concern is not with the market as it might appear from no particular point of view, from a theoretician's standpoint, but with the market as it can be found in invoices, telex print-outs, telephone calls, personal contacts, newspaper stories, office lore; how its workings are discoverable in what are, for the purchasing officer, familiar, routinized, atypical, wholly exceptional, puzzling or downright equivocal circumstances; and what kind of techniques of ordering, scheduling, bargaining, calculating, and analysing provide the working practices for making such discoveries.

The problem of how far and in what ways the market 'constrains' the purchasing officer's activities is not, itself, either an abstract or an external question: it is one for the actual purchasing officer. It is one of the officer's troubles that the market is dominated by a single supplier, and it is an issue of some uncertainty as to how much control can be exerted relative to that supplier. Thus, it is one of the purchasing officer's routine practices to distribute orders around smaller suppliers (and to let the dominant supplier know that he or she is doing this), although it is the case that these orders are placed at prices less advantageous than would be obtained from the dominant supplier, since this is, from the purchasing officer's point of view, a way of acquiring somewhat more bargaining power with the dominant supplier than he or she might otherwise have. It is at this point, though, that someone might see the need for a synoptic point of view, against which we could check whether this technique has the efficacy its user envisages for it. But what kind of efficacy does the user envisage? It is not the kind of efficacy that is sought and achieved under ideal or theoretically desirable conditions, but an efficacy which is sought all things considered, which is aimed for in the light of what are, for the persons contriving and employing it, the unavoidably relevant conditions of their local placement, the deficiencies in their information-collecting and analysis, the multiple and (perhaps) irreconcilable requirements that their organizational positions place upon them, the paucity of resources provided relative to the tasks they are supposed to accomplish, and so on. It is enough for them, for example, that a technique works as best as they can tell, where they have – so far as they can see – little room for manoeuvre, and where they cannot envisage any more assuredly effective and practically implementable practices for achieving the same end.

For a second, somewhat (although minimally) less sketchy example let us look at these fragments of data (derived from Watson, 1978):

D.236   *Client* [*sob*]: No fire, no light, no nothing, it's terribly lonely [*sob*] . . .
D.237   I wish I were dead (as was god my judge) [*sobs*] I do I wish I were
D.238   dead (. . . you're no good dead). Oh dear god (I hope to) . . . [*sobs*
D.239   *five seconds*] I am not asking for nothing, no charities, I don't
D.240   want nothing.
D.241   *Counsellor*: But y – you know there are times when you've got to ask for things, Mrs L.,
D.242   you know, as I said, I will see if I can get somebody.
D.243   *Client*: I have not asked anything, it was a bit of company I wanted
D.244   (and) I can't even have that in this country, there's black people come in this
D.245   country and get more than what (I), than what white people get (no good).
D.246   I am not against blacks everybody has got to live but I've never in my
D.247   life known how hard it was till I (tried it) it's disgusting (how the
D.248   country is run) disgusting. I am only one in a million, I am going to
D.249   tell you this, I am only one in a million but I'll spread it about,
D.250   what the church can do for you it can do nothing, the Catholics do more
D.251   *every day* in every week than what the Protestants do I think it's disgusting
D.252   I do really and truly . . .
D.253   *Counsellor*: Do you – have you spoken to your vicar or to anyone at church? Do – do they know that you're infirm?
D.255   *Client*: (I am not needy) I am not one of them type(s) that come screaming//
D.256   *Counsellor*: Well no: I:/we) you don't have to go screaming if – if they just know
D.257   (I) I mean people do care but they've got to know before they can care,
D.258   haven't they?
D.259   *Client*: I don't know who knows, (I'd never feel like) ringing the bell to tell
D.260   because I am not one of – I am not that type to do so. I am not
D.261   that type to do so.

E.411   *Client*: (You tell me) what good you meant on the way in, I've got
E.412   nobody to please, nobody, no I couldn't, no I couldn't, I could not
E.413   do that, never will do, knock on anybody's door.

E.414 *Counsellor*: Uhum.
E.415 *Client*: No, beggars do that, I haven't become one of them yet, (I'll never live
E.416   to see a beggar's day, your) prayer, I'd sooner put my head in that
E.417   gas – gas oven, I would [*sobs*].
E.418 *Counsellor*: Um.
E.419 *Client*: The Jewish people, the Catholic people are all better looked after than
E.420   (me), there's only one that isn't, that's Protestants, I can tell you
E.421   that on the phone, I do know that (... it is) my husband's death,
E.422   god forbid that I should say such a thing but the (...), no, charity
E.423   begins in the church (doesn't it), (that) my church, what they've done
E.424   for me I'm very thankful for, nothing at all.
E.425 *Counsellor*: No I know its/very har//
E.426 *Client*: (I think) it's disgusting, really disgusting, I'm really disgusted
E.427   with what I've had help from them is nobody's business (and I) don't need
E.428   no help...

It is attention to materials like these which probably does more than anything to confirm the impression that ethnomethodology is an 'interactionist' approach which analyses only relations between individuals and which may indeed be so incapable of generalization that it is confined entirely to the appreciation of the particularities of unique situations. We would certainly want to insist not only upon the value, but also upon the indispensability of examining materials like these, and would regard it as legitimate to treat them as instantiating properties of social interaction *per se*, but it seems important to get these things in the right perspective. On the one hand, there is the danger of thinking that treating such materials as instantiating social interactions is the 'rock bottom' mode of analysis, that it is instances of 'social interaction' which such transactions basically consist in. On the other hand, there is the tendency to dismiss the investigation of such materials as capable of 'nothing more' than the analysis of social interaction. As far as we can see, the treatment of such materials as instantiating social interaction involves not the identification of the organizational substructure of these activities, but a particular form of abstraction from them. One can indeed analyse such materials in complete disregard of the fact that the activities making them up also comprise particular events in social settings, organizations, and so on, and one can achieve a great deal of analytical penetration thereby, but this does require a systematic exclusion of certain orders of visible fact about the transaction so analysed. This particular telephone call can, for certain purposes, be analysed as an exchange of talk which might be between any two persons whatsoever; it might be inspected to see what features it exhibits by virtue of being an exchange of talk. It can, that is, be analysed as talk-as-such. It would, though, be quite mistaken to think that recognizing the legitimacy of analysing materials in this way commits us to something like the strategy of 'methodological individualists' who want to 'build up' from characterizations of individuals' actions to institutional facts, treating the individual actions as concrete and the institutional order as abstract. As we have noted, it is the treatment of the transaction as an interaction between individuals which is abstract, for the transaction with which we are concretely, really, dealing here is between a caller and an organization. To treat this call as though it were entirely between two individuals would be to misrepresent the character that it has for the participants themselves (which is what we are interested in, after all): the caller is not calling nor dealing with this particular person who happens to be taking the call, but is calling and dealing with the organization Helpline. This call is, first of all, irreducibly an event in the operations of an organization, such that we cannot abstract out its organizational relevances and retain its real-worldly character. It is, we have suggested, by misreading the commitments involved in the treatment of talk-as-social-interaction that one draws the conclusion that one deals with all social phenomena as 'primarily' or even entirely as relations between individuals.

The further supposition is that one is driven to insist upon the uniqueness of situations, to deny any possibility of generalization (though such a supposition implies that one is still attached to the conception of generalization which comes with the tradition from which there has been a withdrawal). The concern with the uniqueness or generality of situations comes usually, in sociology, from a standpoint outside the situations. The question as to whether this situation is unique or standard is to be decided by the comparison of this situation with others. Thus, the interest is in regularity-as-counted, in the fact that some number of situations exhibit recurrent features, that things occur in this situation as in that one, and so on. However, what we have been pointing to throughout is the centrality of the situation seen from within. It would be entirely false to the character of social situations, as they are encountered, to present them as if they were undergone by those involved in them as entirely unique, for it is part of the character of social situations as they are experienced that they are undergone as if they were (amongst other possibilities): absolutely standard, entirely typical and predictable, for the umpteenth time, with a sense of *déjà vu*, something that does not happen every day, a once-in-a-lifetime opportunity, an almost unprecedented occurrence. Whether and how this situation is uniform with others are not questions extraneous to the transaction, but are constituent parts of them.

For those who call organizations like Helpline it can be an issue for them as to whether they have called this organization before, whether in making this call they are doing something unusual, even abnormal, whether they are like the other people who make such calls. Such issues are intrinsic to the management of the call, for how a recipient responds to such a call depends upon the extent to which the caller can be presumed to be familiar with the working practices of the organization, the conditions of its services, and such like. For the caller, such issues are consequential to how they appear, whether they (for example) appear as though they are always asking for help, whether they are by asking for help from this source categorizing themselves with people they would rather be dissociated from and so on. The caller, in this case, is much occupied with the fact that what she is currently doing is what many others also do, and that she may therefore be categorized with those other people as a 'complainer'; so she tries to present herself as someone who is not really complaining, and in so far as she is doing this is not doing so because she is a regular complainer. The business of being a complainer, and someone who asks for things, is intertwined with the character of her problem and the particular difficulty which she has, which is that of getting something she is entitled to without having to ask for it.

Thus, her complaint is against her church which has failed to deliver the attention and care to which she is entitled from her co-religionists – just like anyone else, including those who belong to religions which her own church would regard as its moral inferiors. She is unable to ask for the help she requires from the church, since this would compromise her entitlement, and make it seem that she was seeking charity rather than that which is her entitlement. The problem that she has is not, however, peculiarly her own; it is a much more general one. It has to do with the way the whole society is going, and with the way people in her position (established and taken-for-granted members) are neglected in favour of newcomers, and this, of course, makes her situation a hopeless one. Getting that situation altered is not just a matter of making some simple moves, but of going against the whole tide of social change. Hence, she is pushed into calling Helpline because she does not like to ask for help, but needs it and can find no other way of asking for it without appearing to want charity.

The caller is offering something like 'this must sound like the kind of call you get all the time, but it isn't one of those', and the differentiation of the respects in which her problem is and is not like that which other people have is integral to the specification of what her problem is, it being an equally integral feature of people's problems that they are, for them (amongst a range of possibilities), 'much the same as everyone's', 'the sort that only happen to me', 'a result of things affecting everyone', 'the product of my own peculiarities', and the extent to which they are one or the other of these are matters which are (for participants) posed and resolved in the situation itself. Once again, the point at issue proves (if we are right) not to be about whether one can recognize and accommodate certain (rather obvious) facts – such as that situations have standard typical reproducible features – but how is one going to respond to those facts, what kind of treatment is one going to give them? It is, and must be by virtue of the very materials we deal with, as plain to us as to anyone that situations are encountered which are routine, familiar, standard, and so on, but our problem is not 'what, from outside those situations, ensures their routine, familiar, standard character?' but 'how are recognizable routineness, typicality and standardization built into the situation?'

One last point will enable us to round off the discussion. We were going to say that we have allowed that these activities are situated in an organizational setting, but this sounds as though we have made a concession, admitted a point that we would rather deny. We prefer, then, to say that we have *insisted* that these events are located within an organizational setting. Having done so, do we not need to acknowledge that the activities taking place within the organization's setting are constrained by its structure? Do we yet fail to see that what is going on between caller and counsellor is limited and directed by structural facts which are outside their control and even outside their ken? The steps these people take are not (surely) determined purely by their own free choice, but are limited by all kinds of structurally accumulated factors. If they have the delusion that they can do what they like, there is no need for us to share it (though we are, presumably, tempted to do this through our persistence in looking at society only from within).

Again, though, this interpretation of the options before us is only possible if one picks out some of the things we have said, somewhat distorts those, and overlooks the whole pattern of argument in which they are placed. It overlooks, for important example, the fact that we are concerned with 'the practical actor' and that that very title indicates anything *but* a person under the delusion that they are free to do whatever they like. The contrast has again been drawn in the wrong place, as though it were between the sociological theorist, aware of the presence of constraint, and the practical actor, unaware of any constraint. We have, though, dissociated ourselves from just this contrast, arguing that the contrast is properly between the sociological theorist conceiving 'constraints' abstractly, and the practical actor encountering them as real-worldly circumstances. The caller and the counsellor on the Helpline do not imagine themselves free to do whatever they like, for they are only too plainly aware of the fact that they are inhabitants of an organizational environment, and that decisions as to what they can do must be made with respect to how those organizations work, what they will allow, prohibit, countenance, facilitate, and with regard to what it takes to get in touch with them, to mobilize their attention, direct their effort and so on and on (for an apposite formulation of formal-organizational constraints, see Bittner, 1974). Far from treating the transaction as one which is isolated from social structures, we have proposed that it be treated as an event which is firmly located within a social structure and which is being carried on as an inquiry into social structure. It is, though, an inquiry which is conducted in terms of the relevances of (from the counsellor's end of things) dealing with a potential suicide, of needing to decide what to do quite quickly, of having to find out what needs to be known in the course of the particular phone call, from a person who is distressed and perhaps disoriented, of having to find them out whilst talking in ways which will avoid exacerbating the distress or making the problem worse and so on. The counsellor, then, is (presumably) only too well aware of being very highly constrained in terms of what he can say, of what he can ask or suggest (for example, see line D.242). These are not necessarily constraints of the order that some sociologists have in mind, for the ones we have been pointing to are ones which originate in the particular situation, in the problems of dealing with a 'hysterical', suicidal, caller, but there are constraints of a different order, constraints which come from the organization's overall structure, from the fact that it has (amongst other things) a division of labour, a bureaucratic hierarchy of power, and so on. So far we show no sign of 'taking account' of these things. Does that show that we cannot deal with them?

Many of the previous arguments reapply. We have pointed out that this transaction is with an organization, and can now add that, of course, from the point of view of someone contacting a service organization, the fact that it has a bureaucratic structure and a division of labour is something to be dealt with as part of making the contact and acquiring the service. To say that an organization has a division of labour or a hierarchical arrangement of power/authority is not to say just *what* division of labour and hierarchical structure this organization has, nor is this something that a person making a first contact with such an organization knows either. They perhaps know perfectly well that there will be some specialization in work, that there will be issues of autonomy and authority which will regulate rights to make decisions, respond to requests, dispatch services, and so on. This knowledge presents them with problems of finding their way around an organization whilst finding out (something) about the way it is organized, focused upon the problem of 'finding the right person to talk to/take your particular problem to'. These are, for someone contacting an organization over the phone, problems of how to organize your talk, how to identify yourself, whether to try to identify the person you are trying to contact or whether to present the reason for your call and hope that the person you are talking to will be able to determine, from that, who you need to talk to, and may generate the troubles of being given the wrong person to talk to, finding that the person you are talking to cannot do anything 'off his own bat', being 'given the run-around' between people all of whom disclaim responsibility and so forth.

Surely, the rules of an organization, its division of labour, its chains of command, and so on, are encountered by those who seek assistance as quite palpable features of the talk that they have with those who speak for the organization.[2] For those in this latter position, those same matters – the apparatus of rules, the separation of competences, the hierarchy of authority – are present as things to be attended to in deciding what to freely say, the helpfulness that can be volunteered, the kinds of commitments that can be made, the persistence with which claims are resisted or the ease with which they are acceded to, the kind of disagreements that can be undertaken, and the like. Far from wishing to deny the relevance of those things sociologists would wish to list under the heading of 'structural constraints', we too would maintain their essential importance, but would not see this as requiring any shift from the general policy of treating social settings as 'known from within' by members.

Conclusion

We have said nothing new. The points we have made have been made before, but the passage of time since they were first made has only shown that they were not noticed or, if noticed, were not appreciated. We do not imagine that we will have succeeded in clearing up confusion over the few points we have managed to cover in this chapter. We will be satisfied if we have managed to insinuate a few doubts as to the extent to which the formulation of sociology's issues in terms of a dilemma between structure and agency properly represents the choices which are now before us.

Notes

1. We are indebted to Richard R. Harper (Sociology Department, Manchester University), whose research provided the basis of this example.

2. See Bittner's (1974) comments on persons deemed competent and entitled to act in some organizational capacity.

References

Bittner, E. (1974) 'The Concept of Organization', pp. 69–82 in Roy Turner (ed.) *Ethnomethodology*. Harmondsworth: Penguin Books.

Garfinkel, H. and Sacks, H. (1970) 'On Formal Structures of Practical Actions', pp. 338–66 in John C. McKinney and E.A. Tiryakian (eds) *Theoretical Sociology: Perspectives and Developments*. New York: Appleton-Century-Crofts.

Watson, D.R. (1978) 'Categorization, Authorization and Blame-Negotiation in Conversation', *Sociology*, 12(1): 105–14.

3

SEMIOTICS AND SOCIAL THEORY

In any theoretically informed research, a critical point is how much 'pre-casting' of the analytic approach there should be. Sharrock and Watson's stance is to examine the data initially to see what is apparent on the data's 'own' terms and to help analysts recognize what they felt comfortable doing. But this may present the theoretician with problems. Theoreticians may want to pursue a more 'interventionist' approach by pre-defining the research problem and seeking particular data. In practical terms, both versions are 'interventionist' in that both culminate in the analyst more than likely pursuing what is conducive in the data, but Sharrock and Watson's approach at least compensates for that somewhat by seriously addressing the concerns of research subjects as a tenet of inquiry.

Effort to apprehend the subjects' world from their perspective obliges the researcher to come to terms with the contradictions subjects routinely tolerate while not resolving them. From such a perspective, constraint and power may indeed be regarded, and analysed, as the same concept. Peter Manning's notion of 'loose-belief analysis' reveals such reasoning on the part of the élite band of scientists charged with regulating safety in nuclear installations. At the very least he shows that beliefs (in this case, about safety) are much more than the manifestation of structure. To cement his case, Manning introduces the essentials of semiotics in order to describe how they may be applied to identify the semantic role of organizational discourse, and so indicate the relationship between beliefs, discourse, and power. That is, the core elements of semiotics, an established analytic system in its own right, can be drawn on to clarify the relation of beliefs about safety and the public and private organizational discourse out of which the organization member's sense of its structure is maintained.

To many, the great virtue of a structural analysis of society (increasingly its chief positive feature) is its notion of resources. One can get a considerable insight into what goes on in interaction in terms of the constraints operating over it. Some are plainly external, whatever their 'local' manifestation. 'Resources' could prove a more useful term for this perspective than 'constraints'. Those who see this only as a possible analytic strategy among others, with no special primacy, do so because they resist a generalized, decontextualized forecast of what people are like or how they will behave. A rejoinder is that one must have some orientation to external constraints on interaction in organizational contexts because members use such knowledge to get resources, gain control, and exercise power. An organization's 'reality' is formed out of both the real external constraints and members' beliefs about them. Peter Manning pursues the problem of the disputed status of 'structure' vis-à-vis 'beliefs' in the context of beliefs about safety and risk in the nuclear-power industry. Beliefs about uncertainty and trust are 'mapped' so as to support a first version of the organization's view of its 'internal stucture' and external environment.

Semiotics and social theory
The analysis of organizational beliefs

Peter K. Manning

It has long been assumed that beliefs are either the bases of social structure, for example in the case of myths, rituals, or ceremonies (Geertz, 1971), or on the other hand, that structure is the source of beliefs (Durkheim, 1965). Others do not detail the causal flow, insisting that it works both ways, or either way, or analyse belief as a kind of independent category as in the sociology of religion (Bellah, 1975). As Needham (1973) has shown in his exquisitely detailed analysis of belief, it is not a clearly explicated concept. Belief is a notion that is only partially captured in language. Even when a linguistic term is used to signal intent or seek acceptance of a meaning (a difficult matter at best to discriminate), distinct ideas may not be conveyed (1973: 242ff).

An examination of language use in organizational context may lead us to further question the notion of a single coherent category of belief. Ideas that are taken to be beliefs are diverse and bounded by organizational discourse which is itself arbitrary and limited by a set of presuppostions about the organization and its articulation with the environment. Organizational discourse is one feature of the socio-logy of symbolic systems. If one considers the categories found in a domain of meaning, some principles which organize them, and the boundaries to which such terms can be stretched or applied, that is, system limits, then one has something of a map of the semantic space which organizations occupy. Organizational discourse is *about* the internal structure and process of the organization (see Manning, 1970), as well as indexically referencing the speaker's relationship *to* the organization.

Further connections can be drawn between organizational dis-course and ideology on the one hand, and power on the other. Organizational discourse defines the semantic space occupied by terms having organizational referents, omitting from thought other types of discourse, and building upon pre-defined sets of conceptions of action and typifications of motives, intent, mandate, and relevance (see Schutz, 1964). It is thus an ideological form, or *pre-definition* of the nature of events which interchangeably mixes fact and belief (Geiger, 1969). The potential contradictions between various facets of a symbolic system (its levels of analysis, changes through time, and multivalent terms with shifting referents) are made unitary by beliefs or ideology. Power, or the ability to persuade (if necessary) others to act in spite of their resistance, in turn is dependent upon belief. The temporal development of elements of belief and power yields a form of *structuration* (Giddens, 1976: 118–26). By ordering the semantic space occupied by organizational discourse, with special emphasis on the role of beliefs in a particular domain, it is possible to connect discourse, power, and organizational beliefs. Beliefs are the basis for an organizational mandate (authority), a selective focus on aspects of the external environment, and the basis for enacting the mandate.

The analysis of this chapter is a preliminary exposition of the internal structure of several semantic domains relative to safety, risk, and trust in one organization, the British Nuclear Installations In-spectorate (NII). This chapter uses semiotics formally to map organizationally grounded beliefs about the nature of the organizational environment, and to show how these beliefs are related to structure, resources, and trust.

Organizational discourse

Organizational beliefs constitute one form of organizational discourse, or organizational language. They include a view of the organization's goals and objectives, its structure and boundaries, characteristics of roles and statuses within the organization, and explanations of the cause of problems, their ideal solutions and posited consequences of such interventions. Organizational beliefs are thus a part of organizational culture on the one hand, and an explanation for that culture on the other. The degree of organization of segments of this discourse is a *variable*. There are odd parables, stories, anecdotes, and tales; common rules of thumb, shorthand recipe-knowledge, principles, and working rules (Manning, 1982). Organizational analysis may also yield more formalized and myth-like explanations.

The model which guides this investigation assumes that language as a system of signs interpreted within codes provides a model for analysis of other systems of signs. This idea has been explored in organizational research which suggests that a linguistic model can be extended to describe facets of communication within organizational structures (Bittner, 1965; Fine, 1984; Lemert, 1979; Manning, forth-coming). Elsewhere, it is argued that organizations are formally and authoritatively structured message systems based on technologies, social roles and organized codes or principles for assembling, validating, and reproducing diverse communications (Manning, forthcoming). Communications are 'heard' within a structure of belief which is not independent of what is heard; it is a mode of encodation of meaning within a bounded ecological system. Organizations produce a form of culturally and socially meaningful differentiation and constraint and map on to the world their implicit vertical and horizontal rankings, and their understandings of social and juridically bounded relations. Organizationally marked differentiation is given to political, legal, moral, and social values. Such differentiation becomes part of other systems of classification such as the law.

The primary products of police organizations, for example, are symbolic messages conveyed to social groups about their moral well-being, their social positions (horizontal and vertical rankings), identities and statuses, and the degree of their acceptance within a legal-power order (see Douglas and Isherwood, 1979). Organizations as symbolic interpretative modes reproduce a larger cultural system of rules, beliefs, power and authority, practices and actions (see Giddens, 1976, 1981). Organizations act as a kind of screen, transducer, or feedback-interface between an external environment of potential messages and an internal processing system. A scheme within which organizational discourse can be viewed is semiotics.

Semiotics

Semiotics is the science of signs, and seeks to derive the principles of signification; to explain how the meaning of objects, behaviours, or talk is produced, transformed, and reproduced (Culler, 1975). A sign, based on the ideas of Saussure (1966) and Peirce, is 'anything that determines something else (its interpretant) to refer to an object to which it itself refers (its object) in the same way, the interpretant becoming in turn a sign and so on ad infinitum' (Peirce, quoted by Eco, 1979a: 69). The interpretant connects an *expression* or signifier (a word, a picture, a sound) with a *content* or signified (another word, image or depiction). The process of connecting expression and content is dependent on an interpretant within a system of relations, and patterns of opposition, analogy, similarity, or contiguity. Thus, within a system of colour coding, white/black are each a word and image (the word 'white' and an image of a colour are heard/seen as one) and take on meaning as oppositional colours (or non-colours). A sign (such as 'white') on its own is always 'incomplete' in so far as its meaning arises from its relations to other signs.

The links made between expression and content as well as those between signs are variously conventionalized. These links may be analogous or homologous and the connections *syntactical*, or based upon understood relations between and among signs, or *semantic*, meanings which arise from the connections of expression and content. Signs are also seen as *units*, or *syntagms*, within a system such as a list of colours (beige, brown, fuchsia, and mauve). The units can be arranged in a syntagmatic chain so that they stand in part–whole relation: such as in *metonymy* (each colour is like the others, but also distinctive), or they can be connected by logical associations or *metaphoric* clusters that create cognitively assembled groups (mauve/ fuchsia, beige/brown). These groups or clusters are created or seen within *paradigmatic* or associative contexts and subcontexts. The principles of a *code* which permit associating signs (encoding and decoding them) in *context* may be formal and written, or informal and almost tacit. This understanding is assumed to be a basic competence of speaker–hearers of a language. *Context* is a fundamental sociological concept in semiotic analysis because it refers to aspects of knowledge assumed by speakers but not necessarily expressed in an utterance. These include such matters as expectations for action, past experiences, respect for the speaker, and other background understandings (Garfinkel, 1967; Levinson, 1983; Schutz, 1960). A *context* and a code are meta-messages, messages about how a message is to be heard (Bateson, 1972; Goffman, 1974).

The concepts of code and context mean that any delineation of the paradigms, or associative contexts, found within an organization will at least in part be physically and temporally situated. Since there are many codes and paradigms, not all of which are officially sanctioned, they cannot be easily read off from organizational rules, procedures, or even practices. Observation, interviewing, and document analysis may be required to establish the links between organizational discourse, paradigms within such discourse, and the external environment. Giddens' concept of 'knowledgeability', or the tacit sense actors have of what is correct, adequate, and workable, links formal semiotics schemata with practical actions (1981). However, this link is vague, sporadic and not well understood. Terms are loosely coupled to structures and actions. The organized perceptions which tie beliefs about trust, risk, and safety to segments of the organization as well as their mutual associations, cannot be understood entirely by discerning the linguistic mapping of organizational discourse. This suggests an approach which will be termed loose-belief analysis.

The methodology of loose-belief analysis

Semiotics provides a number of tools for formal analysis of beliefs in the form of myths (Barthes, 1972; Douglas, 1973; Lévi-Strauss, 1963). Cognitive anthropology has similarly advanced tools for formal lexical analysis using eliciting (Tyler, 1969). What is more diffi-

cult is the identification and systematization of loosely held or articulated beliefs which do not form a *closed system* of meanings that fully
exhausts the contours of held beliefs.

It is assumed that there is a loose connection between given terms
associated with beliefs (Needham, 1973), between the terms and
contexts in which they are used (Weick, 1979) and between the rules
that govern meaning (codes and meta-codes) and terms (Eco,
1979a,b, 1983). Nevertheless, a map is the first approximation of
cognitive domains of interest. In using a linguistically derived model
of analysis and trying to make formal the identified relationships (see
Kurzweil, 1980; Robey, 1973), one need not accept the conventions
of semiotic structuralism (Lemert, 1979). However, once one
assumes an open rather than closed system of meaning, and sees the
unfolding nature of discourse and its uses, then the relationship
between the actor's model of reality, the rules that frame their
experiences (Goffman, 1974) and the codes and formal terms employed become subject to analysis. Thus, in presenting a model of
terms and their relationships, no assumption is made about the
similarity of the perspectives of the actors. The model is an outline of
minimum necessary meaning.

A related point is the nature of the relationships between ethnographic material and semiotic analyses of belief. The formal aspects of
this approach have been criticized (Berreman, 1966; Faris, 1968;
Manning and Fabrega, 1976; Psathas, 1968). Two sets of issues arise.
The first is the question concerning how one identifies the head
terms, such as in this case, 'safety', and how taxonomies (such as
those found below in Figures 3.1, 3.2, and 3.3) are created. The
second issue is how one links ethnographic materials to the analysis of
semiotic data. Each requires some discussion.

Head terms arise in the course of open-ended interviewing, and are
usually thematic in answers to several related questions. Some connection is normally drawn between the goals or strategies or tactics of
an organization and these key terms. Safety, for example, is a primary responsibility of the NII, but the realization of this as either a
static system state or process is left undefined in the relevant acts of
the British Parliament and working documents. Thus, it is discussed
in different contexts such as the technical assessment of the reactor,
systems of management and safety, plans for evacuation in case of an
accident, inspection and supervision and evaluation of inspectors by
principal inspectors. It is also a concern of the public at large. It
contrasts implicitly with non-safety. The revealed meanings are
based upon interview comments made by inspectors when asked
about the idea of safety. They are not quantitatively selected by
frequency of mention, but by virtue of their clustering as having

similar denotative meaning. Each of the contexts is a referent or *content* referred to by the expression 'safety'. Each of the subcontexts is clustered within an associative context and they in turn are reclustered under other analytic focuses. The analytic focuses are chosen by the investigator to bring out aspects of the organization, or the cultural bias or preference for kinds of information and ideas demonstrated by such contexts and subcontexts. The process of deconstructing a term into its sub-expressions begins with the discovery of contexts. Transformation of meaning from denotative to connotative meaning and back to denotative (one such transformation) is based upon ethnographic knowledge about the organization, its practices and ideologies. These, in turn, may be characteristic of one of the five branches of the organization. Thus, one can work from the formal taxonomic arrangement to change in meaning and associate this with ethnographic data which describe the social base for this knowledge and perspective. Figure 3.1 (see below) represents a preliminary outline of these social linkages and usage. It indicates key terms central to the mandate of the organization.[1]

Loose-belief analysis includes organizational discourse, and articulates levels of abstraction.

1 Organizational discourse includes in its focal concerns a view of a resource base, the location (mapping) of problematics and trust in the environment, as well as a set of techniques, modes of assessing this environment, and hypothecated aims. It thus creates a loose encodation of the social and physical world signified by its key terms and paradigms.

2 Organizational discourse frames reality for units with the force to enact a role (Greimas, 1966) and produces the means by which 'new data' are selectively perceived, retained, and believed (Weick, 1979: 135).

3 Organizational discourse maps ideas, symbols, chunks of meaning upon nature, creating ideas about nature or a 'cultural bias' (Thompson and Wildavsky, 1985). Cultural bias is a kind of authority which defines the relevant facts or information and is the basis for the assumptions underpinning those facts. It both constitutes and sets out the nature of problems. Within organizations, however, differences in 'bias' exist.

4 Institutions, or broad groupings of interests, stratify preferences as well as deny others (Thompson and Wildavsky, 1985), enhancing some modes of uncertainty (information absence) and rewarding 'plural rationalities' for coping with this uncertainty.

A linguistic model focuses on the arbitrary distinctions made within discourse based on contrasts implicit in language, captured in paradigms and in 'systems of differences from which utterances are selected' (Lemert, 1979). The reasoning employed is that encoded signs of practical behaviours (tokens) are located in designated semantic fields. Explanation involves 'a semantics of sociological signs' producing statements that meaningfully organize previously encoded values (sign systems, discourse units) (Lemert, 1979: 943–4). As the MacCannells (1982) have argued, sociological analysis is the study of signs about signs, or social differentiation.

What is required preliminarily is a search for *key concepts*, particularly those that anthropologists consider 'head terms', or labels for important cognitive domains. These can be related to the perceived aims and goals of the organization, as well as its rationale or mandate (see Agar, 1986; Faris, 1968; Manning and Fabrega, 1976). An understanding of the constitutive cognitive *elements* within that domain can be elicited. These are the *denotative meanings* for which head term(s) represent a connotative gloss. This process can be continued to find further levels of denotation metonymically ordered within metaphoric or associational context(s). These denotative elements can be reorganized into additional metaphorical groupings or associative contexts or subcontexts. This involves reorganization of the interpretants. The contexts in which these meanings are assembled can be linked to organizational segments and roles. It should be further noted that broad questions of the organizational 'mandate' are encompassed by the integration of various 'lower level' contradictions and paradoxes at 'higher' levels of organizational discourse.

The setting and techniques

This study draws on data from interviews gathered with members of the Nuclear Installations Inspectorate in Britain in order to carry out a loose-belief analysis (see Notes at the end of the chapter). The aim is to explore how some apparent organizational paradoxes, especially those surrounding the uncertainty of safety and its meanings, are resolved at other levels. Furthermore, the organizational segments within which the beliefs are situated make apparent the need for 'resolution'. Uncertainty produces paradoxes at one level which are resolved at other levels.

The NII was established in April 1960 following the introduction of the Nuclear Installations (Licensing and Insurance) Act of 1959. It was established in part as a response to a serious fire at the Windscale Fuel Reprocessing plant in 1957 (Patterson, 1983) and the Fleck Commission Report published in December 1957. The Health and Safety at Work Act of 1974 shifted NII from the Department of Energy to the Health and Safety Executive, under the Minister of

Employment, in a consolidation of health and safety inspectoral functions. The NII presently employs about one hundred inspectors, specialists and policy analysts in five branches (current installations, reactors in progress, fuel reprocessing, future reactors, and policy), who are located in Bootle, Lancashire, and in London. They are trained in a variety of disciplines, and virtually all until recent years have had prior experience in the nuclear-power or electrical industry. Each branch save the policy branch employs both specialists and inspectors, but the line is not sharply drawn since to a large extent the people are interchangeable.

Although inspections are made at the discretion of the inspectorate, the initiation of requests is made by the industry in the form of applications for the design, construction, staffing, and operating of a nuclear-power plant. These applications are often quite lengthy and involve making a case for the safety of a given aspect of the site (for example, the evacuation of the plant, management and staffing, the maintenance plan, the pressure circuit). There are three licensees, the Central Electricity Generating Board (CEGB), the South of Scotland Electricity Generating Board (SSEGB) and British Nuclear Fuels (BNFL), who are engaged exclusively in fuel reprocessing. The responsibility for the safety of the installations lies with the licensee, the NII acts to judge the adequacy of the safety cases submitted to them. Their work is in large part reactive and seeks to maintain compliance by bargaining, consultation, negotiation, and frequent meetings. The NII prefers to act informally and use persuasion rather than its rather considerable non-appealable powers to revoke licences, to fine, and to close sites. They assume that they can apply the 'reasonably practicable means test' (a rough rule of thumb) to decide whether the licensee has achieved safety and/or failed to do so. Through a variety of techniques, they monitor safety, observe plant operations, review proposals for changes and alterations in plant structure, and work within the current government's policies to balance safety and productivity.

The history of the development of nuclear technology in Britain is characterized by an initial and continuing concern for safety (Hall, 1986; Patterson, 1983). The development of particular reactor designs over the period from 1948 to present, including the current question of building the pressurized-water reactor (PWR), is dominated by safety concerns. The initial choice of the Magnox reactor over other designs such as the CANDU and the PWR was based on the lower volatility of the gas-cooled reactor and the reduced likelihood of radioactive release (Williams, 1980). In addition to a concurrent safety focus in the development of the industry and the designs chosen, the NII has developed increasingly orderly, rationalized, and clear procedures for licensing and principles around which this activity is to be organized (see, for example NII, 1982). Three licensees, in turn, are responsible both in moral and legal terms for the safety of the plant. The seriousness of this commitment is evidenced, it is argued, by the long record of safety in Britain and the absence of a serious nuclear accident (events at Windscale in 1957, 1979, 1984, and the 1983 releases into the sea are not viewed as major events). The CEGB, BNFL, and SSEGB have enormous resources, time, and staff which enable them to ensure safety, it is believed, even if it entails great cost. Given this historic pattern of development, the NII is seen as something of a 'watchdog' or 'conscience' for the industry, and the neutral, professional, and objective detachment of NII provides a 'counterbalance' to the Generating Boards' eagerness 'to get on with the job of providing cheap electricity to the consumer', as Sir Walter Marshall, head of CEGB, once said. These five elements of safety can be glossed as technology, design, procedures, licensee responsibility, and the NII as a conscience.

The stages of the investigation are as follows. The concept SAFETY[2] is seen as a key concept among several others which form the mandate of the organization and its legal and moral legitimation.

SAFETY can be deconstructed into five contexts, each containing a set of contrasting elements (NII views, techniques for assessment, the bases of knowledge of safety, the bases for authoritative knowledge and public perceptions of the safety of nuclear power). These are seen as types of *goods* in economic terms. They are the basis for reordering of items in the context into types of *cultural bias* (modes of rejecting and accepting information), which are designated as either *hierarchical* (stabilized and institutionalized basis of valuation), *entrepreneurial* (market-based competitive basis for valuation) or *sectarian* (equalitarianism as a basis for valuation). Nuclear safety is seen as a kind of valuation contest between hierarchical and entrepreneurial cultural biases.

Semiotic analysis of safety

Interviews with members of the NII at several levels from chief inspector to inspector reveal that the concept SAFETY is a key term, both with respect to the centrality of the idea in the history of the inspectorate and its present mandate. The head term, 'safety', from the NII's point of view, is associated with a number of contexts. Five of these are shown in column B of Figure 3.1. Context is a paradigmatic association or grouping of ideas, each of which is denotative in nature. The items in the subcontexts labelled (a), (b), (c), etc. (column C) represent the denotative meanings associated with each

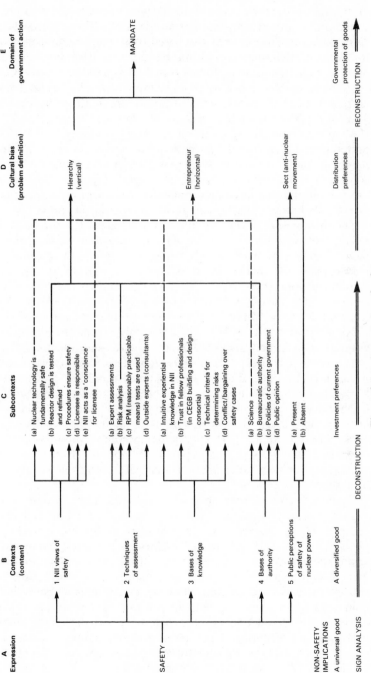

Figure 3.1 *A semiotics of safety*

of the contexts or the content(s) linked with the expression 'safety'. Column D regroups or reassembles the various context terms into clusters based on new connotative bases for problem definition. Note for example, that sect as a cultural bias is based upon public views that reactors are unsafe (columns B and C) and public opinion as a basis for authority. Sect in column D contrasts with hierarchical and entrepreneurial bases of problem definition, both of which are foundation points for NII's mandate (column E).

GOOD in column A is seen as investment preference, distribution preferences and governmental protection claims. These are groupings of meanings of SAFETY in economic perspective. While SAFETY in column A is a sign, it is deconstructed (placed in new contexts of association) in columns B and C but reconstructed or regrouped into broader and more inclusive categories in columns D and E.

The first context shown in column B of Figure 3.1 is *NII views of safety*; the second context is *techniques of assessment*. Four techniques are used to assess *safety*: expert assessments, risk analysis, reasonably practicable means (RPM) test, and hired outside experts. Within the context *technique*, the four subcontexts are denotative meanings. The third context in Figure 3.1 is *bases of knowledge* used to establish safety. There are four of these (column C): intuitive or judgement bases, trust in fellow professionals, technical-engineering criteria, and conflict/bargaining over standards and principles. The fourth context is *bases of authority*. Given the *concept* SAFETY, a question arises concerning the authoritative bases upon which it is to be established and maintained. These can be scientific, bureaucratic (in the sense of organizational policies), political (policies established by the government in power), and public opinion. These are listed as sub-contexts (column C). The fifth and final context within which the expression 'safety' is viewed is public perceptions of the safety of nuclear power. These are stark and binary: it is seen as either present or absent.

Figure 3.1 also shows that as one moves from left to right, one expands meaning from deconstruction to reconstruction and sees goods as being changed from general matters to more specialized phenomena which are differentially allocated and supported by governmental action (next to bottom line of Figure 3.1). Hierarchical and entrepreneurial bias or authority dominates problem definition and interacts to produce conceptions of governmental action (column D). Thus, meaning expands and contracts, and powerful official forces move to redefine range and infinity into fixed and finite problems and actions (column E). Plural rationalities, of course, remain as long as SAFETY has such diverse meanings and the contexts within which it is located are so numerous.

Several brief observations about this tree or semiotic diagram (Figure 3.1) can be made. The head term or sign-vehicle 'safety' (column A) can be seen as having meaning within at least five distinctive contexts (or contents) listed from top to bottom of column B. Each of these contexts or paradigms is related metonymically and stands in part–whole–part relation to each of the others. The subcontexts are a further specification of denotative meanings and represent content for the expressions listed as context 1, 2, etc. For example, *bases of knowledge* is a content for the expression 'safety' but in turn is an expression linked to the content, *intuitive experiential knowledge* (column C, 3a). In column D, this is one semantic element of the entrepreneurial bias in organizing goods for development. Thus, as one moves from left to right across the figure, one is seeing meaning unfold from denotative to connotative, what Eco (1979a) calls, 'unlimited semiosis'.

There is also a metaphoric or paradigmatic relationship to be found among the items listed in column B. The items within each of the subcontexts have an associational basis (1–5 in column B). However, note that there is a potential for conflict in meaning or contradiction and opposition as one moves from the head term. Is it precise to gloss a sign like SAFETY with a single subcontextual item like risk analysis when it is integrally linked semantically to alternative meanings? Furthermore, there is an organizational basis for this potential semantic conflict. Some NII branches (namely 2 and 4) rely more on risk analysis than others. Most likely to use it are members of the future developments branch, which is assessing the safety case being made by the CEGB for the proposed Sizewell 'B' pressurized water reactor (PWR). Thus, loosely coupled meanings are organizationally segmented. What may appear to be contradictions are not so when examined semantically. Different meanings of the term 'safety' are employed in different branches of the organization. Finally, note that internal and external standards need not be consistent. NII's views of the public views of SAFETY, either present or absent, stand in stark contrast to the more elaborated semantic space allocated to the idea by members of NII. It is unlikely that discussions of nuclear safety involve people talking about the same thing or shared referential conventions.

Figures 3.2 and 3.3 show, respectively, a mapping of the *internal* environment of the NII in respect of the location and techniques used in safety and modes and aims of safety work, and a mapping of the *external* environment in regard to risk, modes of assessment, resources, and degree of trust in the efficacy of these assessment modes. Note in Figure 3.2 that technology and design (column A), experts (column B) and science as a closed system (column C) are

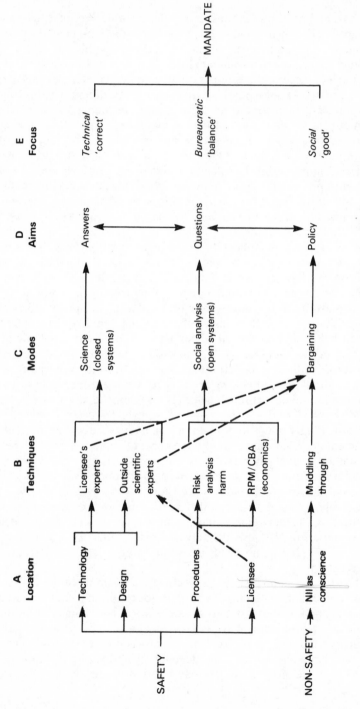

Figure 3.2 *A mapping of safety: modes and aims in the NII, 1985–6*

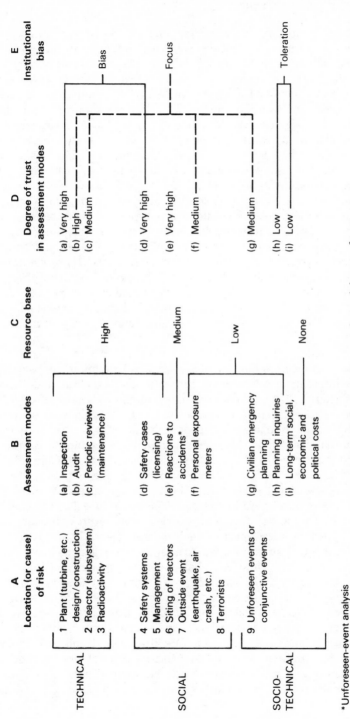

Figure 3.3 *Risk: assessment modes and degree of trust*

*Unforeseen-event analysis

seen as producing 'answers' (column D), and these connections contrast with a 'procedures approach' linking risk analysis and reasonably practicable means (RPM) tests with social analysis regarding costs and values (or costs and benefits, CBA) and producing 'questions' (column D). The notion that NII functions as a conscience is consistent with an independent line of thought: 'muddling through', using experts and risk analysis producing a bargaining or compliance approach to policy. These three strands of meaning, which may be termed 'technical', 'bureaucratic' and 'social' are potentially in some conflict or are oppositional, as shown by the arrows (column D) in Figure 3.2. While the focus of technical operations is to reify a correct, scientifically reproducible answer(s), a bureaucratic focus centres upon producing and reproducing a balanced set of answers which reflect an open and developing questioning approach. A social focus seeks the good in political and economic terms, derived from bargaining and assessments. The organization holds disparate beliefs about itself. The overall mandate of NII is indicated by the bracket to the right of column E in Figure 3.2.

Figure 3.3 shows RISK in three semantic domains: technical (1–3), social (4–8), and socio-technical (9) in column A. They see modes of assessment (column B) as independent of types of risks since one or more modes can be used to assess any risk. However, the amount of resources given to these modes varies, and attention and resources are differentially allocated to technical, socio-technical, and socially defined risks. The NII resource base (column C) is most reflective of a concern with technical risks, secondarily with social risks, and is in danger of overlooking socio-technical risks (what Perrow, 1984, calls 'normal accidents'). This means that inferences about the degree of trust in the efficacy of the different modes vary, as shown in column D. The themes of degree of trust can be combined into *meta-themes* of 'organizational bias' (as used above) and the social construction of the nature of relevant knowledge. This might be called the *cultural authority* of the NII: their ability to define the nature of the facts and their meanings in respect of nuclear safety (Starr, 1982). A second meta-theme is attention given to auditing and reactions to accidents (column B (e)). Note also that planning inquiries and long-term political, social, and economic costs (column B (i)) are recognized or 'tolerated' within the inspectorate, but NII possesses little or no capacity to gather, analyse, or document these matters. The overall concern of the NII with technical and selected features of social risk means that high-risk, rare events are little studied, and the combination of unforeseen events and human error (9 in column A), although recognized, is given no systematic attention. There is perhaps a necessary tension between these organizational biases, focuses, and blind spots; any organization will combine such tensions and potential contradictions.

'Trust' is an unexamined willingness to give control over some aspect of one's own life to others, and is seen in Figure 3.3 as belief of members of NII in the efficacy of the risk-assessment modes used (column D). One consequence of this resource/trust combination is that high-risk matters, for example, the reactor, safety systems, and radioactivity, are given relative emphasis in resource terms. Some areas seen as high risk in socio-technical terms are given rather low resource allocation (column C). High risks that are known, but not foreseen, those believed possible but rare, are little guarded against. Thus, rare-event analysis, the unanticipated conjunction in more than one system of an error or accident, is a logical partner to current assessment modalities. (Ostberg, 1986: Ostberg, Rydnert and Ofverbeck, 1987).

By drawing out themes in the degree of trust in the efficacy of certain approaches (column D), and recombining those that are very highly trusted – (a), (d), and (e) – those that are trusted – (b), (c), (f), and (g) – and those that are tolerated – (h) and (i) – a grouping indicative of the organizational bias, focus, and toleration of these approaches can be derived (column E). The progression from types of risks to assessment modalities, hence to resource allocation, trust, and finally to the character of the organizational bias, suggests how the NII views the world of nuclear safety, what it is prepared to 'see', and what it imagines it does, can, and will do about this contingent world.

Conclusion

Beliefs can be mapped, and the outlines of such maps are a first approximation of the organization's view of its internal structure as well as its external environment. Some organizational theories (Scott, 1981: ch. 10) assert the importance of a conjunction of perceived uncertainty, resources, and dependence. Perhaps these theories do not sufficiently attend to the relevant counter to such uncertainties, trust (Short, 1984). A theory of encoding and structuration of relations should include risk and trust as posited features of the external environment. The codes by which individuals order such experience will also be required. Loose-belief analysis, like psychoanalysis, suggests that blind spots in organizational cognition are related to differential allocation of resources and actions. Thought and action are linked through such encoded beliefs, but within systems which are neither logically nor semantically closed.

Notes

This study is funded in part by a grant from the Health and Safety Executive to the Centre for Socio-Legal Studies, Wolfson College, Oxford, which provided support from April 1983 to April 1987. The research incorporates economic, legal, historical, sociological, and social-psychological perspectives and data, and includes, at various levels of time obligation, some eight to ten persons. The author's work includes a joint project with Keith Hawkins on decision-making generally, as well as the study of the NII. To date, the work consists of field-work in four of the branches of the inspectorate, including meetings, site visits and correspondence, interviews with some twenty-one staff from the chief inspector to inspector, and field-notes. It also includes analysis of official documents, transcripts of the Sizewell Inquiry (1983–85), histories of the origins and development of nuclear power in Britain, France, and the United States, and newspaper clippings from 1982 to present on nuclear energy in Britain and related problems such as waste disposal, the economics of electrical energy, pollution, and international developments in nuclear power.

   1. A less formal mode of analysis was used in a previous paper on the metaphorical context of selected key terms used by narcotics police (Manning, 1980). It was argued that meanings such as *source* (of drugs), *major violator*, *informant*, *success*, and *case* vary by organization, by speaker–hearer dyads (e.g. their past knowledge of each other), and by the horizon of expectations embedding the current investigation. These provided the *action consequences* of a particular meaning (Manning, 1980: ch. 6), thus linking semantics and organizational praxis. *Narcs' Game* represented an initial and rather general exercise in describing *semantic variation* using a few social variables, and was based on *pragmatics*, or the study of meaning attached to utterances, sentences, or larger bits of discourse, rather than meaning derived from syntactic or semantic structures. The analysis failed to show how such broad notions, often contradictory in their implication, were connected, either metaphorically or metonymically. Furthermore, it did not formalize the structure of meaning through semiotic analysis.

   2. It is contrasted with another key term: Non-Safety. Conventions: quotes around a word ('safety') indicate the expression, or signifier, and italicizing a word (*technique*) indicates the content or signified. Capitals (SAFETY) indicate a sign in the sense of the combination of '*content*' and *expression*. Connotation and denotation result from seeing a set of meanings as being represented by a single term.

References

Agar, M. (1986) *Speaking of Ethnography*. Newbury Park, Calif.: Sage.

Barthes, R. (1972) *Mythologies*, sel. and tr. Annette Lavers. New York: Hill and Wang.

Bateson, G. (1972) *Steps to an Ecology of Mind*. San Francisco: Ballantine.

Bellah, R. (1975) *The Broken Covenant: American Civil Religion in Time of Trial*. New York: Seabury Press.

Berreman, G. (1966) '"Anemic" and "etic" Analyses in Social Anthropology', *American Anthropologist*, 68: 346–54.

Bittner, E. (1965) 'The Concept of Organization', *Social Research*, 31, 240–55.

Culler, J. (1975) *Structuralist Poetics*. Ithaca: Cornell University Press.

Douglas, M. (1973) *Natural Symbols*. New York: Pantheon.

Douglas, M. and Isherwood, B. (1979) *The World of Goods*. New York: Basic Books.

Durkheim, E. (1965) *The Elementary Forms of Religious Life*. Glencoe, Ill.: Collier.

Eco, U. (1979a) *The Role of the Reader*. Bloomington: Indiana University Press.

Eco, U. (1979b) *Theory of Semiotics*. Bloomington: Indiana University Press.

Eco, U. (1983) *Semiotics and the Philosophy of Language*. London: Macmillan.

Faris, J.C. (1968) 'Validation in Ethnographical Description', *Man*, n.s., 3(1), 112–24.

Fine, Gary A. (1984) 'Negotiated Orders and Organizational Cultures', pp. 239–62 in R. Turner and J. Short (eds), *Annual Review of Sociology*, 10. Palo Alto, Calif.: Annual Review Press.

Garfinkel, H. (1967) *Studies in Ethnomethodology*. Englewood Cliffs, NJ: Prentice-Hall.

Geertz, C. (1971) *The Interpretation of Cultures*. New York: Basic Books.

Geiger, T. (1969) *On Social Order and Mass Society*, edited with an introduction by R. Mayntz. Chicago: University of Chicago Press.

Giddens, A. (1976) *New Rules of Sociological Method*. London: Hutchinson.

Giddens, A. (1981) 'Agency, Institution and Time–space Analysis', pp. 161–74 in K. Knorr-Cetina and A.V. Cicourel (eds), *Advances in Social Theory and Methodology*. London: Routledge & Kegan Paul.

Goffman, E. (1974) *Frame Analysis*. Cambridge, Mass.: Harvard University Press.

Gowing, M. (1964) *Britain and Atomic Energy*, vol. I: *1939–45*. London: Macmillan.

Gowing, M. (1974) *Independence and Deterrence* (2 vols), vol. II: *1945–52*. London: Macmillan.

Greimas, A.J. (1966) *Sémantique structurale*. Paris: Larousse.

Hall, A. (1986) *Nuclear Politics*. Harmondsworth, Middx: Penguin.

Kurzweil, E. (1980) *The Age of Structuralism*. New York: Columbia University Press.

Lemert, C. (1979) 'Language, Structure and Measurement', *American Journal of Sociology*, 84: 929–57.

Levinson, S. (1983) *Pragmatics*. Cambridge: Cambridge University Press.

Lévi-Strauss, C. (1963) *Structural Anthropology*. New York: Basic Books.

MacCannell, D. and MacCannell, J. Flower (1982) *The Time of the Sign*. Bloomington: Indiana University Press.

Manning, P.K. (1970) 'Talking and Becoming', pp. 239–56 in J.D. Douglas (ed.), *Understanding Everyday Life*. Chicago: Aldine.

Manning, P.K. (1980) *Narcs' Game*. Cambridge, Mass.: MIT Press.

Manning, P.K. (1982) 'Organizational Work: The Enstructuration of the Environment', *British Journal of Sociology*, 3: 118–39.

Manning, P.K. (1986) 'Signwork', *Human Relations*, 39(4): 283–308.

Manning, P.K. (forthcoming) *Signifying Calls*. Cambridge, Mass.: MIT Press.

Manning, P.K. and Fabrega, H. (1976) 'Fieldwork and the "New Ethnography"', *Man*, n.s., 11: 39–52.

Needham, R. (1973) *Belief, Language and Experience*. Oxford: Basil Blackwell.

NII (Nuclear Installations Inspectorate) (1982) *The Work of H.M. Nuclear Inspectorate*. London: HMSO.

Ostberg, G. (1986) 'Learning Lessons of Bhopal'. Unpublished paper, University of Lund, Sweden.

Ostberg, G., Rydnert B. and Ofverbeck, P. (1987) 'How Decision-makers Deal with Low Probabilities'. Executive summary, University of Lund, Department of Engineering Materials.

Patterson, W. (1983) *Nuclear Power*, 2nd edn. Harmondsworth, Middx: Penguin.

Perrow, C. (1984) *Normal Accidents*. New York: Basic Books.

Psathas, G. (1968) 'Ethnomethods and Ethno-science', *Social Research*, 35: 500–20.

Robey, D. (ed.) (1973) *Structuralism*. Oxford: Oxford University Press.

Saussure, F. de (1966) *General Course in Linguistics*, translated and edited by C. Bally *et al.* New York: McGraw-Hill.

Schutz, A. (1960) *Collected Papers*, vol. I, ed. M. Natanson. The Hague: Martinus Nijhoff.

Schutz, A. (1964) *Collected Papers*, vol. II: *Studies in Social Theory*, ed. Arvid Brodersen. The Hague: Martinus Nijhoff.

Scott, W.R. (1981) *Organizations*. Englewood Cliffs, NJ: Prentice-Hall.

Short, J.F., Jr (1984) 'The Social Fabric at Risk: Toward the Social Transformation of Risk Analysis', *American Sociological Review*, 49: 711–25.

Starr, Paul (1982) *The Social Transformation of American Medicine*. New York: Basic Books.

Thompson, M. and Wildavsky, A. (1985) 'A Cultural Theory of Information Bias in Organizations'. Unpublished paper, October 1985.

Tyler, S. (ed.) (1969) *Cognitive Anthropology*. New York: Holt, Rinehart & Winston.

Weick, K. (1979) *The Social Psychology of Organizing*, 2nd edn. Reading, Mass.: Addison Wesley.

Williams, R. (1980) *The Nuclear Power Decisions*. London: Croom Helm.

4

MICRO-SOCIOLOGY AND POWER

At root, one gains from Manning a view of organization member as both creator and creature of organizational structure. But the case of nuclear-safety inspectors shows how much more subtle the situation is than that. It indicates the need to differentiate one's analysis in order to look at the components of the symbol-sets which may be assembled under the heading 'beliefs about safety and risk'. Such headings are as misleading as they are broad; not all the symbols work in the same direction. The disjunction of formal from informal organization implies the working of something more capricious and unstable than one assumes when regarding an organization and its products from the outside. With this in mind, one may move from analysis of the beliefs of strategically located organization members to their actions. Where Manning schematizes belief, revealing contradiction as well as the drift in a general direction, Rock describes the meandering and fitful interplay between the formulations of officers and the reaction of audiences significant to them.

The stance taken towards the theory of micro- and macro-social reality reveals divergent perspectives but a coherent view that treatment of micro and macro as formal opposites is indefensible. Data cannot be assigned to one or another level; the 'levels' are indistinct, and meld into each other. It requires a new and refined sense of the workings of familiar concepts. Paul Rock's sensitive treatment of the emergence of a policy initiative in a government agency brings such insight to bear on concepts of power and bureaucracy. His starting-point is the methods he employed in the early phases of research in the Canadian Ministry of the Solicitor-General as he attempted the reconstruction of the bureaucratic life-worlds or symbolic habitats inhabited by officials and composed of organizationally prominent and familiar figures, processes, strategies, and eventualities. It is within such habitats that civil servants formulate, manage, and inspect their plans of action, and it is upon them that those plans may return to work changes. Policy-making is perceived here as an evolving exchange between frameworks and purposes, and organizations themselves are described as little more than loose clusters of many interchanges.

Micro-sociology and power
A natural history of research on policy-making

Paul Rock

For quite some time it has been a routine criticism that arguments allied to symbolic interactionism and phenomenology have failed to address analytic problems of power. Gouldner (1971: 382), for instance, wrote of their neglect of 'overpowering social structures'. There is nothing in principle that would bar the use of qualitative sociology in the description of powerful organizations. It is certainly to be expected that ensuing analysis would not embody the concerns and imagery of the critics, but there are no good epistemological or methodological reasons why it should do so. Interactionism will beget interactionism, not Marxism or structuralism. Interactionism will set its own agenda, treating a bureaucratic setting as if it were only a special case of a small social world. To be sure, the features of that special case may be very distinctive indeed, but they can be inspected with customary ethnological techniques. The results may not please structuralists, but that was not the intention. It has also been alleged that the accessibility of the powerless to ethnography is not mirrored by the accessibility of the powerful. That contention has not often been illustrated or tested, but it remains. The idea of an ethnography of powerful government ministries then became somewhat tantalizing.

What follows is a description of the relatively simple methods I employed in the early phases of two linked pieces of naturalistic research on policy-making in bureaucratic settings. It would be too grand to call them a methodology. Rather, they exemplified Ken Plummer's AHFA principle, the use of Ad Hoc Fumbling Around as a tentative, pragmatic, and exploratory technique of working in an unfamiliar research environment.

During the last few years, criminal justice ministries in Canada and the United Kingdom have become involved in an emerging politics of victims, and I have spent some time studying the history of their involvement. In one case, that of the Ministry of the Solicitor-General of Canada, I was invited to Ottawa as a Visiting Scholar in 1981 and was encouraged to explore the Justice for Victims of Crime Initiative that was then under development. I was given free access to documents, meetings conducted within the ministry, to officials and to politicians. In the other case, I gained a fairly intimate background knowledge of the files and routine practices of the Home Office when I was attached to that Department as a research consultant in 1984 and 1985. Home Office officials and politicians have subsequently given me aid and advice in my reconstruction of that organization's work with criminal injuries compensation, victims-support schemes, and reparation and mediation projects. Throughout, I have sought to understand what happens when officials work together on policy-making, how policies evolve and attain social and organizational character, and how they come to form a presence in government and in the landscape around it. In particular, I have tried to reconstruct a few of the more important symbolic environments within and around bureaucracy, environments that are constituted by locally significant groupings of figures, processes, strategies, and eventualities. It is within such environments that civil servants formulate, manage, and inspect their plans of action, and it is upon them that those actions may return to work changes. Understanding their composition is vital to an interpretation of policy-making itself.

Analysis has been relatively grounded and inductive, emerging step by step out of the process of inquiry rather than being imposed from the outset. If it were to be categorized, it could loosely be identified as symbolic interactionist, although it has also been influenced by the work of such qualitative sociologists as Weick, Bittner, Van Maanen, Punch, and Manning. I shall allude to the two Departments throughout the whole of this chapter although almost all my argument should actually be taken to refer to my research on the Ministry of the Solicitor-General of Canada: that work is now complete, it was the more substantial project, and my comprehension of it is consequently firmer.

It was inevitable that I had to come to the two settings with an anthropologically naïve attitude. After all, both the Ministry of the Solicitor-General and the Home Office had had only a shadowy presence in my life until I chose to embark on research. I had known little of the Home Office and almost nothing of the ministry. Both bodies had seemed interesting, as many institutions are, but they had never obtruded so urgently that I had to put other things aside and examine them closely. I had worked in the Home Office a long time ago and have had intermittent dealings with its officials as friends, acquaintances, and colleagues since. Yet I had never stopped and thought about the Home Office as a topic which demanded searching scrutiny. I had talked with people about the two ministries, but my talk had never been an interrogation. I understood the ministry and the Home Office in much the same casual way as I understand other background features of the environment, my knowledge being based on occasional visits, professional gossip, cursory surmise, limited reading, and a rather haphazard grasp of the two ministries' effects on the world of criminal justice. None of this had been orderly, purposive, reflective or meticulous. I was aware I could not give solid historical, structural, or political context or feature to what was really a miscellany of unscholarly impressions. In short, I had knowledge *about* the ministry and the Home Office, knowledge that was practicable enough for ordinary use in everyday life but not for prolonged or detailed dealings with those organizations themselves. I was fully conscious that I had no knowledge *of* the Departments.

Eventually, to be sure, knowledge about a phenomenon will prove a valuable topic and resource in sociology. It is an amalgam of working assumptions, gossip and fragmentary understanding that constitutes a social organization. Bureaucracies themselves are gossipy, fragmented, and loosely coupled assemblies of people. They are based on rumour and idle conversation, and rumour and conversation can come to play a part in their explanation. Nevertheless, in the beginning, they may do little more than cloud understanding. It is difficult to know how to give them weight, background, or meaning. Indeed, an appreciation of their local usage is one of the principal goals of research. I was in no position at the start to determine how instructive were the ideas with which I approached the two institutions. Being so placed would have required the sort of detailed map and guide to an organization that sociologists seek at the end of a lengthy process of exploration. At first, mere knowledge about an organization seemed to be very little better than none at all.

In the very beginning, then, conscious of my ignorance, I placed myself in an office and started reading a file called, in the one instance, 'Victims – General', and, in the other, 'Victims – Social Aspects of Crime'. My reading a file quietly and unobtrusively served a number of ends. In organizations given to the copious production of written reports, where decisions are recorded as a matter of routine, where relationships flow along paper, where policy papers may well be the culmination of activity, files have a centrality as ends and means. As Erikson and Gilbertson (1969: 389) observed of another kind of organization, a hospital, 'if a stranger were to notice how many . . . resources were devoted to the task of recording information . . . he might very well conclude that the main objective of the institution was to generate information and keep systematic files . . .' The files of government officials have an even greater prominence: after all, policy-making is almost entirely given over to the drafting of arguments. Ottawa itself has been described as a 'paper world' and I had an obligation to capture its special character. Moreover, reading files gave me something to *do* in the early irresolute period of research. Surrounded by obviously busy people, imagining that there was a presumption that a competent sociologist should know how to do research without excessive fuss, not knowing what local identity I might have acquired, and recognizing little of the position, character, or stance of the civil servants around me, I refrained from asking too many questions. I could not construct telling questions and I suspected that I might not be able to make sense of some of the replies that I would receive. I had not by then acquired sufficient confidence or standing to subject strangers to what might be silly inquiries. When I finally ventured out into the organization, I wanted to be prepared. Obscurity seemed to be sensible in that opening phase. Indeed, I had little choice: I was unable to navigate the bureaucracy with assurance, purpose, or a grasp of geography.

Obscurity and isolation did reinforce my awareness of the uncertain and contingent character of meaning. I read file after file but they were not wholly intelligible and I was never sure of what I had discovered. The rationale for opening, employing, maintaining, or retrieving a particular file was not always apparent, especially in Canada where much was done in thinly recorded meetings and chance encounters in corridors and rooms. Some of the Canadian files were little more than piecemeal and unsystematic accumulations of paper. They were not always used, as they were in Britain, as a starting-point, reference, and periodic end of action. But it was to be a while before I could ascertain what kinds of social objects they were. Canadian files, too, lacked the marginal commentary that knits documents together and imparts the relatively anonymous sense that a proficient insider is expected to follow. They were not compiled for strangers. In the Home Office, as I was to discover, much communication, thought, and activity are conveyed in circulating memoranda. Being 'good on paper' is praise in a setting where people do not meet formally and frequently. It is a central skill in a large organization with a long past and a preoccupation with precedent. In Canada, there is no such commendation and documents are obstinately indexical. There especially, at first, not only could I make little of the names, organizations, and events that peppered papers, I was reluctant to seek immediate clarification through questioning. I felt privileged being able to conduct research in a setting that sociological folklore portrays as closed and mystified. There was pressure flowing out of timetables. The outcome was that, suspending the natural attitude, urgently poring over everything that came before me for what it might portend, searching for pattern, I found myself creating or enhancing the delphic features of my environment, impregnating them with meaning. I was anxious that I should miss nothing of possible interest. The casually discarded or scribbled note could become the key to an enigma. The formal organization of a typical file might disclose the deep structures of bureaucracy. I suspected that the positioning, combination, and juxtaposition of papers engendered significance, papers being their own context. A document could acquire meaning from its mere presence in a particular file. Indeed, the 'same' document in two different files might not be the same at all. The filing of a copy of a newspaper cutting, speech, or letter could be a purposive act that was intended to direct the reader towards very particular conclusions. It might not. Yet there was no bold logic of the files that could enlighten someone like myself who had never been schooled in the interpretative practices of the organizations: I felt sure that I was not ascertaining the 'real' import of what I was examining. And it was a valid enough doubt: my activity at that stage was confined to extracting sense from a product without knowing anything of the aims, methods, and concerns of its producers and audience. All I could turn to was my competence as a reader of documents in general and almost assuredly fallible typifications of bureaucratic conduct. When examining Canadian files, for example, I had necessarily drawn on my loose stock of knowledge about the British civil service. I had no other, and it proved subsequently to be unreliable: Canadian officials were indignant when, in an early draft, I endowed them with the typical motives and customs of their British counterparts. Later, in London, I was to search fruitlessly for the organizational conventions of Canadian bureaucracy. In both instances, clarification stemmed ultimately from what proved to be the use of perspective through incongruity. At the start, however, I had no appreciation of incongruity and I was more than a little adrift. I tended to record everything that came before me in the hope and expectation that it would yield meaning at a later point. I was not in a strong position to determine what could be excluded. My response was quite typical of the first phase of field-work. Barley (1986: 55) observes, 'The prevalence of factual data in anthropological monographs stems, I am sure ... from an attitude of "when in doubt, collect facts". This is, in a sense, an understandable approach. The fieldworker cannot know in advance what is going to prove important and what is not.'

The earliest files did not furnish anything that resembled an adequate model of official conduct. Rather, they were lists of individuals, organizations, and happenings that were embedded in as yet rather precarious environments of meaning. Each new file tended to be an addition to my stock of information; it changed my sense of the structure of policy-making and it underscored the provisional and plastic quality of my conjectures. Yet, little by little, a kind of tacit sociology of government did begin to appear. It is somewhat difficult now to reconstruct the process by which that immature theory first came. It seemed to have been an emergent property of disciplined anxiety, a sociological aesthetics that produces or heightens recognition of patterning in the world, an unusual attention to social life, a catalytic environment and a kind of pre-reflexive brooding on details and anomalies that the sentient mind could not even describe. In practice, all those states and qualities were experienced as one and they cannot be reproduced neatly or methodically. William Foote Whyte observed of the same condition, 'Probably most of our learning in [the] field is not on a conscious level. We often have flashes of insight that come to us when we are not thinking about a research problem at all' (1951: 510). In retrospect, it was all quite easy. *In situ*, the chief sensations were a compound of muddle and an alarm that, whatever may have happened in the past, it could well be that no plausible sociology would unfold *this* time. Indeed, I do not think I was even aware that a theory was attaining shape.

A rough model of bureaucratic organization grew out of a slow process that identified a few 'manifest' attributes of the files, began to treat those attributes as analytically teasing, and then proceeded to employ a tentative homology to transform them into the properties of their parent social institution. What was done in and to reports became a working facsimile of things reported and the context in which reporting took place. To be sure, I was mindful even at that early phase that the files were not autonomous and entire descriptions of events and actions: after all, they did not embody what people could not, would not or did not record; they reflected unstated purposes; they were themselves objects set in fields of uninscribed meaning; and they did not contain rules for their own successful translation. Yet it was reasonable to suppose that there would be a necessary working affinity between the logic-in-use of the file and the logic-in-use of the civil servant, between the terrain described by the file and the practical social landscape of bureaucracy, and it was that logic and that terrain that I wanted to capture. In the beginning, too, I had no other clues but documentary phenomena, structures and connections. It may have been a vulnerable method of reasoning but it was the only route that could take me beyond the bald contents of reports and letters.

Let me list some of those manifest attributes. I could learn about the names and locations of those who peopled the bureaucratic world. Even if I could not thus far decipher the organizational or policy reasons for mentioning a particular person or group, their very inclusion gave detail to a map, forming a cast of those employed in the policy-making process. The files were directories of bureaucracy's significant others, those who constituted a world and affected action. Further, I could learn something of the manner in which those others were classified and arranged in space and time: they began to take on recognizable patterns. They were not mentioned in isolation, but as members of committees, working parties, Departments and sequences of command and decision-making. The landscape they inhabited became increasingly lumpy and uneven, composed, as it were, of different masses and elevations. I could infer a little from the apparent chronology of events: items following one another in time and gathered together in a file have all the appearance of a causal chain. It could be presumed that the guided steps of an initiative or decision followed a kind of teleology that merited description. What was important, too, I was presented with a paper facsimile of bureaucratic interaction: reports about files and letters travelling from one person to another, names and organizations being invoked, permission being sought and consultation undertaken, meetings and conferences being arranged, amounted to a plan of social relations. The files also conveyed something of the way in which the world of appearances is ordered for bureaucratic purposes. There is a distinct rhetoric in official documents that may be read as a local grammar of motives and action. Things reported to oneself, to colleagues, to superiors, and to the outside world are reported for reasons, and those reasons revolve around things that are considered to be especially important. Finally, each file could itself be treated as a more or less coherent image of the world, a way of seeing; each represented a more or less distinct cluster of events, an episode; and each was an inflection that illuminated particular phenomena and obscured others, an organization of emphases. Each file was thus a discrete glimpse of an official environment. Together, the files were a linked array of perspectives that gave depth and breadth to processes changing over time. It was as if phenomena were rotated to reveal the different faces that interested bureaucracy, and the outcome was local history seen through a complex eye. Eventually, that combination of a topography, causality, population and imagery gave me a somewhat ramshackle representation of bureaucracy. I have remarked that that representation was largely tacit at that stage, too formless to be more than an intuition of how things might fit together, a proto-theory. It certainly could not be defended. But it did furnish a catalogue of people to question and a shaky conception of their relations with one another, the departments and their emerging attitudes towards the victims of crime. Producing it had taken time, and, during that time, I had begun to form a few rudimentary connections with people that were uncontaminated by inept questions. I had not yet tried to interview or observe too minutely. I had merely gossiped over coffees and photocopiers. Now, equipped with that catalogue, I could advance a little further into the organization.

I did by that second stage have enough to give a sharper focus to research. A critical benchmark in any project will have been passed when one begins to recognize what questions should be asked, and I was at that point where I could identify a preliminary tier of gaps, puzzles and anomalies requiring elucidation. My ultimate objective, only dimly conceived at that time, was to employ interviewing and observation to reunite papers and statements with those who had drafted them and those who were supposed to be their audiences. The result would be a history re-joining its own heroes, heroines, narrative, utterances and authors. Thus, in one concrete case, I was to reproduce and interweave the accounts of those who had commissioned a policy paper, the paper itself, and the minister who had presented it to Cabinet, conveying the interplay between evolving ideas and their objectification, reception, and implementation in a series of linked scenes. Such a chronicle would set document against draftsman and reader against document, each contrast building a layer of analysis in a kind of counterpoint. It would be phenomenologically adequate, enabling history to be draped around its subjects' own stories.

That final objective could be attained only by a progression of sweeps into the terrain about me, and a sympathetic government bureaucracy given to social investigation is an ideal setting for such work. On both occasions, I was established in the research wing of the ministry and my preoccupations and procedures were not regarded as strange. On both occasions, I was given an office to which I could retire. All meetings were attended by people taking notes and my own note-taking was not untoward. The outcome was a staggered series of forays into the organization and its environment for interviews, documents or meetings. Each foray was designed to illuminate a particular line of development that had its origins in the coagulating proto-theory: thus, in one instance, it pursued the part played by Canadian women's organizations in promoting a politics of raped and battered women; in another, it was pointed at the influence of Ontario politics on federal policy-making; and, in a third, it examined the effects on the Canadian Government of the 1980 UN Congress on Crime Prevention. Each foray would be a piece of snowball sampling in which little clusters of people and reports would be revealed and explored. And each foray would be succeeded by a short period of retreat in which every new batch of information was reviewed and old ideas were recast in preparation for the next expedition. Interviews and papers led to one another in succession: each new stage seeming to invite reflection on the materials of previous stages, raise new problems and new questions, and prompt a reappraisal of what was to come. For a long while, no part appeared to remain stable. The constituent elements of my somewhat unsettled conception would change in sympathy with every fresh answer. From the very first in this process, ways of seeing and ways of questioning were facets of the same vision. In fact, an evolving proto-theory is little more than a state of focused and purposeful puzzlement. It fuses the observer, observation, and the observed world in one rather restless movement, and it is there that sociological knowledge and sensibilities can play their part as a seemingly natural phase of the research experience. The proto-theory did modify its course as new ideas or facts were encountered but, because of that indissoluble relation, the broad drift of interpretation did tend to appear inexorable. Uninterrupted, it would have pursued its own momentum and direction. It was only when it received a rude check that a correction was made to its progress.

Apprehensiveness and prudence ensured that the earliest sweep was directed at those officials I knew and trusted the most, and it was to those officials I returned repeatedly as other sweeps took place. I found myself often consulting them about strategies, structures, and problems. It was in this manner that an inevitable nervousness about approaching those who were more remote or powerful led to a method of sampling that created, refracted and reinforced my own relationships with the social structure of the bureaucracy. In the Ministry of the Solicitor-General, I was a close friend of one senior official and had been placed under the tutelage of two, later three, rather more junior civil servants who were my 'project officers'. It was against their judgement and organizational common-sense that I pitted my own ideas. The result was that my earliest perspectives embodied the preoccupations and situated assumptions of limited segments of the bureaucracy, and those assumptions were not necessarily 'typical'. One of my supervising officials, for example, was structurally peripheral to the Justice for Victims of Crime Initiative, and her observations would echo her marginality: she gave a detached, witty, and laconic commentary and was reflective enough to acknowledge the linkages between her social, functional and interpretative distance from events (as one who had studied phenomenological sociology at university, her reflexivity was massive and labyrinthine). It was inevitable, too, that I should not have known enough in those dawning sweeps to give proper balance and context to the ideas I received. My vantage points at that time were anchored in only a few sites. I was however mindful of the soft and undeveloped character of my thoughts, knowing that I did not know enough to be firm. Later, I was to restore proportion as I observed and spoke with other people in other parts of the ministry.

I was to discover that wandering around an organization brings with it numerous opportunities to speculate. Indeed, everything that moved became a datum. As sweep followed sweep, I became increasingly visible and visibility itself gave rise to an inadvertent mapping of my environment. As I moved around, especially in Canada, I was introduced to people, became obliged to give an account of myself, saw who was frequently to be seen in the company of whom and on what occasions, and met with suspicion, interest, and helpfulness. My journeyings thus provided the materials of a survey. It became possible to form conjectures about bureaucratic styles, personalities, and relations as I marked reactions to me, my project, and those whom I met. To be sure, much of this was provisional and weakly founded, but there was something of a congruence between official responses to myself, my work, and other facets of bureaucratic life. For example, the idea of territoriality was later to loom large in my analysis, and it was prompted in part by the impression I received from time to time that I had crossed an invisible border into some official's private preserve. Similarly, the very process of arranging interviews with the most august members of the ministry, the Solicitor-General and Deputy Solicitor-General, revealed the problems and etiquette of communicating across large areas of organizational space. Both men were to prove affable when I met them, but access to them was not secured in a casual fashion.

Again, travelling around the departments with the purpose of interviewing gave me evidence of how officials had domesticated their offices, building themselves a symbolic surround; showed me how officials comported themselves; and gave me a sense of the ecology of government. I observed the bureaucratic world at work. In Canada, for instance, it was instructive that groups of offices were intentionally clumped together to promote intense interaction between their occupants (people were forever 'popping in'). The offices of all but the most senior civil servants were walled by so much glass that there was little to prevent outsiders monitoring what took place within them. Officials would move along the paths between work stations and offices to meeting-places near lifts, photocopiers and coffee machines, and there, too, could be found intense local interaction. And the whole was set in the context of a more or less 'open planned' space that reduced privacy, enhanced the accessibility of equals, and promoted mutual surveillance. Many officials knew the doings, conversations, and associations of their colleagues. They were quite substantial figures to one another. There were many chance meetings and little conversations. When discussion was contemplated, it would just as readily be conducted face to face. Theirs was a public life and a kind of communality of effort and knowledge emerged. Writing took place. Indeed, there was a more prolific writing because of the greater abundance of formal meetings in Canada. But much of it was indexical, lodged in a framework of 'what everyone knows'. The Home Office, by contrast, is a mass of long corridors with numerous closed doors and a quiet, thin trickle of traffic between them. Projects are initiated by 'putting papers up', not by informal conversations. There are portions and divisions of the Home Office that seem never to meet at all.

Obtaining documents and attending meetings led me to give explanations, display self and talk with those I met, but they were passive enough enterprises. Interviews, however, were staged encounters which demanded a performance. One unexpected consequence of my forays was that I found myself repeatedly having to articulate ideas that might otherwise have remained silent and unorganized. Not only did I offer an account of what I was doing, but I phrased current preoccupations into arranged sequences of questions. Increasingly, interviews and discussion gave shape and objectivity to thought. I discovered myself describing the Justice for Victims of Crime Initiative as if I had some firm conception of its genesis and evolution. Even more, each succeeding interview audibly elaborated that conception: I heard myself theorizing. The situational exigencies of interviewing created order. More, the interviewees' answers and demeanour were a running commentary on the perceived adequacy of what was unfolding before them. Even before I was ready, each meeting tended to negotiate the structure and development of argument.

I have described each sweep as a probe that disclosed the relations, composition, and boundaries of different clusters of activity. In a policy-making organization, such probes can be quite ambiguous in their effects. First, policy-making is centrally directed at the manufacture of political reasoning, symbolic unities, and plausible relations. In its early stages, it is almost entirely constituted by spoken and written words. It is rhetorical, and rhetoric can absorb new materials very readily. Astute bureaucrats spend much of their time pondering the possibilities of argument. They can do a considerable amount of creative work with questions that are put to them, wondering aloud about connections and influence. From time to time, I believed myself to be witnessing the birth of new structures of causality. Interestingly, too, those musings were not necessarily misleading: they displayed the bureaucratic method at work in thought-experiments. They could do little about the grosser, more anonymous and general facts of the Initiative's history, but it is perfectly conceivable that they added detail and complexity to its vaguer and more recondite features.

Secondly, as a peripatetic interrogator, wandering about Canada at different periods over four years, I was to be found continually asking questions of people engaged in the various stages and tasks of policy-formation. There were but a few people occupied with the Justice for Victims of Crime Initiative. Almost inevitably, my questions objectified and emphasized what they did, making their projects concrete and suggesting paths of development and association. Addressing them as officials whose significance resided in their work on victims, inviting them to reflect on their own role in the process, alluding to a history that was being written, I may well have conspired in giving flesh to what was often little more than a marginal, uncertain, and speculative enterprise. I was certainly accused by a criminologist working at the Ministry of Justice of having affected the course of the Initiative.

Thirdly, I was mindful that the structure and frontiers of different clusters were a mirror not only of the world but also of my method of interrogation. Exploration was driven by the analytic imperatives of my project, not by the endogenous character of the clusters themselves. Thus, inquiring into the politics of federalism or feminism, I was concerned almost exclusively with their bearing on the course of policies for victims. Federal and feminist politics were only very marginally engineered around victims, and a concentration on victims deformed them. Exploration followed routes prepared by materials and people: I could not go where there were silences and absences. Further, exploration would invariably cease with the 'solving' of particular puzzles, although problems and answers invariably revealed themselves as emergent features of inquiry that changed from moment to moment. No puzzle was ever solved once and for all: its apparent solution was little more than a temporary subduing of its more vexatious characteristics, a lessening of my sense of curiosity. Answers were not final although they were reported as if they were so. Finally, exploration was bound by time and setting. I unearthed segments of processes as they were available to me at that moment and as they seemed to touch on the problems that then loomed large. I could not forever return to documents. Still less could I repeatedly petition people for interviews. There were some whom I questioned and observed over a length of years, but there were others whose examination was confined to one or more intervals along that length. I could learn only what had taken place until that interval. I could ask only those questions that had occurred by that phase. The result was an accumulation of snapshots capturing a long train of responses to an evolving political process, my changing judgement of what was happening, and my shifting relations with its events and participants. At the beginning, my comprehension and identity were weak. At the end, I was consulted to establish 'what had really happened' and officials would turn and repeat themselves to ensure that I had managed to record even quite sensitive conversations. Different samples of clusters reflected the uneven, staged, and developing quality of the process and subject of investigation.

None the less, those clusters did take on a shape and independence. They represented reasonably distinct universes of action. Thus people would talk and move confidently enough within their own spheres but did not know, and knew that they did not know, much about the incidents and logic of adjoining phases or areas of policy-making. What was to become in July 1981 a modest initiative on victims was actually the confluence of a number of disparate strands with very different origins, casts, objectives, and patterns of movement. It assimilated attempts to resolve the effects of decarceration in Ontario; the problems of assaults on women; promises made to curtail violence that had been made when capital punishment was finally abolished in 1976; the stirrings of the American victims' movement; and much else. Each of those constituent histories described zones of action and knowledge, and there was no necessary overlap between them. One who had busied herself with battered women need never have encountered the victim–offender reconciliation programmes that were being inaugurated in the 1970s. A person manning a crime survey might have had little to do with briefing a new minister on departmental policies. It became apparent that victims had very different meanings and destinations in these settings: they could be indicators, violated women, instruments of crime-prevention programmes, alienated witnesses or problems in 'de-institutionalization'. It became apparent, too, that officials dealt with those settings in various ways and for differing lengths of time. Promotions, demotions, childbirth and retirement fed staff in and out of the flow of process, often in a most intricate fashion (a success in managing a policy could lead to advancement and other issues, for example). Some bureaucrats would be brought in to command a specific phase of an initiative and then retreat to have no more business with it. Others would be so intimately identified with a policy that actions towards a proposal could be construed as a gesture towards a person. Understanding, motives, and commitment would move in sympathy. Thus it was that the extent, linkages, and organization of officials' knowledge of victims became a critical topic and resource: once they were described it was but a very short step to final analysis.

It was about that point that I embarked on writing the first draft of what was to become *A View from the Shadows* (Rock, 1987). On one level, writing can never be a simple, unmediated report or synthesis of what has gone before. It is *sui generis*, capable of yielding its own problems, involvements, and meanings. Very often, ideas and problems will be experienced anew in writing, as if they had never been encountered before. There will be a difficult confrontation with all the elisions and evasions that had been made during field-work: what was neglected in observation can embarrass later analysis. Writing is a solitary effort to establish what it was that one was accomplishing all along, a process of discovery in its own right. It has its disciplines. Above all, there is the discipline imposed by an uninterrupted inspection of all the little pieces and notions that had been gathered in haste, at different times and with different purposes. What had once been casually assumed to form a unity may well look less than coherent. Numerous misconceived or unasked questions, anomalies and gaps will begin to thwart understanding. Long periods may then have to be given to the gentle and barely controlled musing that can sometimes produce intellectual leaps and impart or restore structure to a disorderly pile of observations. Such a leap is difficult to manage and sometimes impossible to reverse. When a problem has been so reconstituted, it will never again be seen as once it was. Indeed, it cannot be the same. What bedevils this process is that a solitary examination of a problem, lacking immediate checks from without, can sometimes take a most eccentric path. Apart from the field, and secluded with little but his or her thoughts for long intervals, the lone writer is akin to the solipsist whose world appears ever less recalcitrant to the will. What was formerly solid and independent can take its shape from the organizing intelligence of the sociologist. Further, the world will lose more of its obduracy and objectivity with every new thought. Analysis induces a methodical forgetfulness, replacing an empirical muddle with a kind of conceptual cuckoo that is neat, clean, and much too simple. Very often, too, the multi-vocal character of the world permits more than one representation (how else could there be Marxists, phenomenologists, functionalists, structuralists, and all the others?) Alone in this setting, a sociologist is prone to confuse sheer plausibility and elegance with truth. As layer upon layer of formal argument is interposed between the subject and object, the object gets shrouded and obscured. Unless the object can 'answer back' it will have been lost altogether.

Thus it was that I returned to Canada with a plausible enough first draft to learn that parts of my characterization were misconceived. For instance, there was a scattered and uneven reaction to my description of Canadian officials as the disinterested, dispassionate servants of the State that I had known in Britain. Some found my portrait acceptable enough. Others evinced considerable resistance (one official claimed that I had portrayed them as 'scarecrows twisting in the wind'). As I considered how it was that such varied objections could be levelled at my argument, I began to apprehend the importance of the diversity of positions that structured the bureaucracy. It became clear that motives and passions are embedded and changing features of a policy-making organization that touches its participants in very different ways. Those who are at its heart and stay with it the longest may acquire symbolic property in an initiative. Those who are at the margins will be only marginally attached. And marginality and centrality will shift from stage to stage, transforming commitments as they move. Structures of activity were then revealed as structures of engrossment.

I was to discover that there were other mediations of place and role. Indeed, staff did not seem to work in the same organization at all. Some informed me quite forcibly that I had not grasped how undifferentiated their work was over time: whatever appearances and titles might suggest, there was an inner unity of effort. Other staff gave me to believe that theirs was a life of little dislocated episodes. It became evident that in that discrepancy was yet another interesting property of bureaucratic structure and, in its explanation, another analytic tier.

I came to recognize that those disparate perspectives were a mirror of the division of bureaucratic labour. In the Ministry of the Solicitor-General, research and policy staff have been apportioned between separate sectors of activity. Their experience of work and time was correspondingly distinct. Very often the bureaucratic sensibility defined research as relatively slow, continuous, and incremental. It translated its work materials into a gradually expanding and diffusely interconnected programme of action. Segments of that activity might be displayed under different names as public representations of policies and their budgets changed, but research staff regarded it as but one coherent and largely uninterrupted enterprise. Since the ministry was founded in 1966, it had concentrated on crime prevention, diversion, police–community relations, assistance to victims, and a host of other measures. It was really all one to the research staff.

By extension, proprietorship was itself diffuse and incremental. There were seen to be no abrupt fissures or faults that announced the abandoning or supersession of the research staff's concerns. Projects and programmes did not seem to end suddenly. Instead, they blurred into one another. They also tended to be paced slowly by the local standards of bureaucratic time, consisting of activities that might last three years in isolation but would stretch over much longer periods when yoked together. The life of a single piece of research could be quite lengthy, undertaken by officials or contracted to outsiders, planned, discussed, organized, piloted, executed, assessed, and reported. It might take years before an answer of any moment appeared.

By contrast, policy work is characteristically designed to grasp the propitious moment. It is dominated by a sense of the timeliness of things, an apprehension that the advantageous moment can appear and disappear, sometimes with disconcerting rapidity. Some policy officials would then construe their work as a series of responses to opportunity. There is a presumption that an occasion lost can condemn a policy, and it may lead policy officials to seize their chances even when research staff would protest that they are not ready. There is rarely a perfect coincidence of research and political timetables because the opportune moment is often independent of official planning. A project can become timely when a government or a minister or an economy changes, and policy officials will then fashion together what they can in response. To be sure, policy staff can modulate their environment and create openings for themselves. They can also reconstruct events and projects so that they complement one another in argument. But there is always the problem of the adventitious happening, the colliding timetable, or the sudden accessibility of funds. When the moment occurs, other timetables must be aborted or distorted. Although research work may not be in a state of readiness, what has been done will have to be used. Typically, all that can be said is that there is evidence of activity and commitment. A flag will have been planted and a history started. At such a juncture, it cannot often be claimed that there is incontrovertible proof of the wisdom of a course of action. It is in this manner that research can fall prey to a kind of temporal untidiness, ideas being exploited as best they can. In such an environment, there are the seeds of a disparity between the half-lives of different ventures, and it was a disparity that proved illuminating.

I have offered those perspectives on organizational work as an illustration of the kind of material that can be forced to appear when an initial draft is exposed to the critical view of its subjects, is offered objections or comments, and the resulting contradictions are resolved. With hindsight, it is not at all apparent a number of 'obvious' arguments should have escaped me. One may presume that many arguments will evade detection (there is always something more to be said), and that it is only a jolt from outside that forces their recognition. The pursuit of a few principal themes can blur one's focus and capture one's attention, blotting out much else. It may only be by engineering encounters between an author and his or her subjects that there can be a major opportunity to reconstruct and amend what has been said. It is imperative to allow the world to 'answer back' in some noisy fashion. To be sure, I was particularly fortunate with my subjects: having as a research population a group of sociologists, psychologists, and political scientists centred on reflective policy-making in the criminal-justice system. During a process of redrafting that continued for three years, description became part of a dialectic that progressively incorporated my subjects' world-views and reduced the solipsistic character of my own account. It must be noted that there was an inevitable unevenness of response to *A View from the Shadows*. In the end, too, mine was a sociological argument that housed assumptions that some found a little alien. But most seemed content and, in their approval, there was a validation of my argument.

References

Barley, N. (1986) *The Innocent Anthropologist*. Harmondsworth, Middx: Penguin.

Erikson, K. and Gilbertson, D. (1969) 'Case Records in the Mental Hospital', in S. Wheeler (ed.) *On Record*. New York: Russell Sage.

Foote Whyte, W. (1951) 'Observational Field-work Methods', in M. Jahoda *et al.* (eds), *Research Methods in Social Relations*, vol. 2. New York: Dryden.

Gouldner, Alvin (1971) *The Coming Crisis of Western Sociology*. London: Heinemann.

Rock, P. (1987) *A View from the Shadows: The Ministry of the Solicitor-General of Canada and the Justice for Victims of Crime Initiative*. Oxford: Oxford University Press.

Note

I should like to thank David Downes and Mary Tuck for their comments.

5
MICRO-SOCIOLOGY AND MICRO-ECONOMICS

Rock's bureaucracy is one in which informal organization subverts any useful sense in which formal, regulated hierarchical power can be regarded. As elsewhere, the formal map, or organizational chart, is not the territory; adherence to the theory of organization-as-bureaucracy leads one astray. Economics is one of the relatively few areas of social science where there are finely applied theories which purport to explain social behaviour in a causal sense. In their research Clark and Pinch used the tools of micro-sociology to study an area of economic activity: buying and selling in the market-place. One of their concerns was to investigate how far economic concepts, especially those of micro-economics, can be used to account for the practices they documented.

The corpus of data consisted of some sixty hours of audio-video recordings of market traders, in particular 'pitchers' selling goods on a variety of markets in the UK with a sales 'spiel', which was transcribed using the conventions of conversation analysis. Clark and Pinch show how economic conceptions, especially 'bargains', can be treated as locally managed productions and achievements. They document a variety of interactional strategies by which pitchers attempt to sell their goods, and deduce members' economic reasoning from a detailed investigation of the interaction between sellers and buyers. The data suggest that buying and selling can be better understood as an interactional, social accomplishment rather than an economic one. It is on this that they base their argument that rules of micro-economic behaviour concerning buying, selling and exchange can only be understood in terms of the exploitation of culturally held social conventions. The formulation of rules and systematic practices outside localized contexts of interaction should only occur as a second-order analysis derived from members' own practices. The case again reinforces the need to evaluate taken-for-granted assumptions of macro-level theory in light of behaviour strongly at variance with them.

The critical points such strong claims must meet include the matter of whether the setting studied so intensively may in some way have been a unique kind of market, where economic conventions may not be expected to apply. It often enjoins further study in different settings, in this case, for example, stock-market transactions. In pursuing the matter of power, it could be argued that the obligation to buy acts as a constraint, existing in the conversation and interactional tactics used by vendors in the setting. In demonstrating both the enabling and constraining character of pitching, it could be argued that this study exemplifies Giddens' development of structure, with constraint the objectification of human agency. The presence or otherwise of power in the situation is critical in evaluating such a theoretical claim.

Micro-sociology and micro-economics

Selling by social control

Colin Clark and Trevor Pinch

Most of the time we sell things that people don't want, they can't afford and they have no earthly use for. If they don't want it then we just tell them that they want it, make them want it.

The Brewster (a pitcher)

This chapter will explore one method by which market salespeople regularly manage sales transactions. We aim to demonstrate that sales, at least in this particular selling context, are essentially a locally managed interactional achievement. That is to say the success or failure of the sales transaction crucially rests upon the seller utilizing special interactional practices ('sales techniques') to 'control' people to make purchasing decisions. Our analysis largely stems from an examination of a corpus of audio-video recordings of the sales activities of market 'pitchers' – those salespeople who attempt to sell their goods by an extended verbal sales rhetoric as well as by other interactional methods.[1] Unlike most market traders, pitchers actively tout or 'graft' for the public's custom. Through the use of highly formalized sales routines they attempt to attract the attention of passers-by so that they will stop, listen, and buy the goods on offer.[2]

For the purposes of this chapter we will investigate a selling technique which is a central feature of many pitchers' sales routines. Specifically we shall examine a variety of procedures utilized by the pitcher, which serve to place members of their audience in a position which makes it difficult for them to walk away from the sales site (the 'pitching stall' or 'gaff') without having made a purchase. We shall see that this usually takes place by the pitcher soliciting some form of response from audience members. This response is then constituted as a purchasing-implicative commitment which is routinely treated by those audience members as rendering them under an obligation to buy the pitcher's goods.

Our examination of the interactional organization of this sales strategy shows that pitchers are able to appeal to and to capitalize upon the normative features which commonly underpin and regulate sales transactions. We show how pitchers structure and organize sales transactions such that exchange-implicative actions are made by both parties (that is, the buyer and the seller) *prior* to the actual moment of exchange. Furthermore, we show how the exchange-implicative actions of each party may be sequentially reordered and expressed in a non-equivalent fashion. By such means pitchers are able not only to obtain purchasing-implicative commitments from audience members that 'oblige' them subsequently to buy the goods, but also on occasions to sell those goods at a price which is higher than the punters can have anticipated. Finally, we show that in spite of the unorthodox nature of the sales transaction, pitchers appear to accomplish these types of sales with little difficulty, and with few complaints from 'punters'.

One general topic which we shall also address concerns the status – relative to macro-sociology – of research in what has been called the 'micro' domain. We reject many of the pejorative associations of the term 'micro' which imply that it deals with limited, trivial, and inconsequential aspects of social life. We shall argue that such traditional macro concerns as inequity, power, and control are pertinent to our analysis and furthermore that it is only when such concepts are approached through the micro domain that their analytical import can be fully understood.

We shall address the macro–micro debate in the following two ways.

Normative features of the constitution and reproduction of social organization   We shall argue that the normative practices which manifest themselves in these types of sales transactions, in having both 'constraining' and 'enabling' qualities,[3] provide a felicitous means by which an empirical examination of actual interactional practices can show members themselves attending to and working with both 'micro' and 'macro' concerns within their daily interactional transactions.

Social control and power   One criticism frequently levelled at micro-sociological analysis is that it is unable to address concerns relating to power relationships. Although power may have been neglected in micro-studies we would claim that there is no reason why micro-analysis *per se* cannot address this topic. Indeed, we hope in this paper to demonstrate one way in which social control is effected and a 'power relationship' constituted; however, in doing so we are critical of the notion, prevalent in much macro-sociology, that relations of power pre-exist and in some way determine the course of interactional outcomes.

Constituting obligation

'Back nailing'

The following sale occurs between a market pitcher (P) and two members of his audience (A1 and A2).[4] Immediately before this sequence the pitcher has sold a number of china vases for £2 each. Now, no other audience members apparently want to purchase the vases. However, the pitcher still attempts to obtain more sales of the same types of vases from that same audience:[5]

Extract 1

P: (. . .) an' 'oo's gonna buy the other one an' ah'll make the buggers cheaper than two quid? Come on? (1.5)
P: *Come on?* (1.7)
P: *'oo's gonna buy the other set?* (1.2) [*A1 raises hand.*]
P: Lady here. (1.7) An' 'oo 's 'avin' the *very* very – [*A2 raises hand*] gen'elman there. (0.5) Knock 'em all the profit off, (0.3) [*BANG*] one ninety-nine an' a 'alf. (.) Now then 'ere y'are.
[*Throws goods down to pitch crew – they are then exchanged for money from A1 and A2.*]
As: [*Laugh.*]
P: Theh wasn't a lot of –, (0.9), there wasn't a lot of profit on them ah'll tell yuh now.
As: [*Laugh.*]

In the above sequence the pitcher, as a means of attempting to sell more vases, offers them for less than their original selling price of £2. Upon hearing this, two members of the audience raise their hands. The pitcher then announces the new, lower selling price of the goods (£1.99½p).[6] Finally, the goods are exchanged for money from the two hand-raising audience members.

Before we analyse this extract we shall first summarize some of the features evident in 'everyday' acts of buying and selling (such as shopping). Usually in everyday economic exchange it is buyers who initiate transactions and they do so by expressing an intent to purchase (for example, by taking goods to a supermarket check-out). Furthermore, in most such sales transactions buyers know the selling price of the goods or request the price *before* initiating the sales transaction. Another feature of everyday buying and selling is that the commitments and obligations of both parties are incurred concurrently with or very close to the actual moment of exchange. In the simplest case sellers are under an obligation to sell goods at their designated price, and to hand over the goods if they receive the requisite money from buyers.[7] Similarly buyers have an obligation to pay for and accept the goods that they have expressed an intent to purchase. These obligations are incurred by both parties once the transaction has been initiated by the buyer. In such cases the act of economic exchange occurs at the same time or follows on shortly after the buyer's intent has been expressed. Finally, it is a feature of everyday economic exchange that each party enters into the sales transaction with full knowledge of the other party's obligations (for example, that sellers will sell the goods at the stipulated price, and that buyers, once they have expressed an intention to purchase particular goods, will buy them at that stipulated price). As part of this unambiguous feature of ordinary sales transactions the commitments made by sellers and buyers are marked or displayed for the benefit of both parties in an unequivocal way. Goods for sale are clearly distinguished from the shopkeeper's own private goods, and prices if not clearly marked on goods can be obtained unproblematically. Similarly, the shopper's expression of an intention to purchase particular goods (for example, the handing over of money) unequivocally commits that shopper to purchase those goods.

The sale in Extract 1 differs from these everyday sales transactions in several ways.

Inversion of instigation of transaction   The instigation of the transaction has been inverted – now the seller, rather than the buyer, initiates the sale. The transaction is instigated by the pitcher's announcement of an offer to sell: ' 'oo's gonna buy the other one an' ah'll make the buggers cheaper than two quid?' The offer to sell is formulated as a question – an action which is built to, and which does, eventually elicit a response (raised hands) from two audience members. The pitcher in this case only obtains a response after he has reiterated the offer and pursued the audience responsiveness, 'Come on? 'oo's gonna buy the other set?' Also, in this instance, the two responses are obtained separately; having obtained a response to his first offer to sell the pitcher asks 'An' 'oo's 'aving' the very very . . .' This produces a second response.

Inversion of knowledge of final selling price vis-à-vis an intent to purchase   Unlike the case in everyday exchange where buyers commit themselves to a purchase only *after* knowing the selling price, in this case an expressed intent to purchase and thus a commitment to buy is made *before* knowing the final selling price. The pitcher does not reveal the exact selling price of the vases but merely stipulates that their price will be 'cheaper than two quid'. It is upon the basis of this information that the two audience members raise their hands.

Displacement of exchange-implicative actions   In the sequence above – as in everyday acts of buying and selling – the exchange of goods for money occurs after the buyer knows the selling price (that is, after the pitcher has announced the selling price of 'one ninety-nine an' a 'alf'). However, unlike the case in everyday exchange the two audience members' indication that they wish to purchase the goods is made prior to and separate from this point. The buyer's intent to purchase has become displaced from the moment of economic exchange (that is, the handing over of goods in exchange for money). In other words, the moment of economic exchange does not coincide with, but occurs after, the offer to sell *and* the intention to buy have both been made.

Non-equivalence of the buyer's and seller's exchange-implicative actions Whilst in everyday acts of buying and selling each party enters into a sales transaction with full knowledge of the other party's obligations (that the seller will sell the goods at the stipulated price and that the buyer having demonstrated an intention to buy those goods will buy them at that price), in Extract 1 this is not the case. On the one hand, the hand-raising actions by the buyers clearly and unequivocally display their acceptance of the pitcher's offer and their intention to make a purchase relative to those other members of the audience who do not raise their hands or respond to the pitcher's offer to sell. On the other hand, the pitcher's offer to sell and in particular its price component is equivocal relative both to an explicit announcement of a selling price as well as to the two buyers' demonstration of an intention to make a purchase. The pitcher does not say what the exact selling price will be, only that it will be 'cheaper than two quid'. Moreover it is this price component of the offer to sell which forms the basis on which the offer is accepted. After all neither of these two punters had bought or demonstrated an intention to purchase these vases at the earlier price of £2.

Discussion
We take the sequential inversion and displacement of these exchange-implicative actions, and the manner in which each party's intentions are formulated and expressed, to be strategic on the part of the pitcher. Specifically, as illustrated in Extract 1, the pitcher, by instigating the sale, and displacing exchange-implicative components from the moment of exchange, has been able to obtain purchasing commitments from audience members prior to the actual point of sale. Indeed, by virtue of the pitcher formulating the price component of his offer to sell in an equivocal fashion and soliciting acceptances of his offer on that basis he has been able not only to sell two additional vases that otherwise would not have been sold, but also to sell them at effectively the same price as he had originally charged.[8]

Why do audience members express an intention to purchase before knowing the exact selling price and before the actual exchange of money for goods occurs? Although in his offer to sell the pitcher does not say exactly how much cheaper than £2 he will sell the goods for, we take it that those two audience members who express an intention to make a purchase do so in the expectation of a greater reduction in price than that which ensues. Audience members such as these under these circumstances share the cultural assumption that in this context cheaper means a significant and substantial reduction in price. In Extract 1 this is evidenced by the audience at large (and the two punters themselves) greeting the announcement of the ½p reduction with laughter. Here the pitcher can be seen to be exploiting the indexical features of the term 'cheaper'. Indeed, the pitcher also provides additional information to the audience which reaffirms the prospect of the selling price being a more substantial reduction from £2 than that which follows. Just before the announcement of the selling price he states that he will 'knock 'em all the profit off'. Thus 'cheaper' is built to be heard to mean 'a lot cheaper' and, likewise, 'profit' to mean 'a sizeable profit' (certainly one which is greater than ½p).[9]

Given that the selling price of the goods is likely to have been higher than the audience members can have anticipated, it is perhaps surprising that on these types of occasion few punters 'jebb out' from the sale (that is, refuse to purchase the goods) and/or attempt to take the pitcher to task for having deceived them. It seems that a key element in the pitcher's success here is his skilful use of humour. On many occasions humour works by creating a puzzle which is then solved in a candid and unexpected way. The pitcher's offer to sell the goods cheaper than he has previously done so can be said to create such a puzzle for the audience. Those that have previously paid £2 will feel cheated if he goes lower. But, on the other hand, he has just offered to go cheaper and knock 'all the profit off'.

The announcement of the 'reduced' selling price is greeted with laughter. Both the joke and the sales transaction has been at the expense of the two hand-raising members of the audience rather than at the expense of those who have bought earlier at a higher price or at the expense of the pitcher. Not only does the laughter make it difficult for the two punters to claim that they have been deceived, it also characterizes their actions as being based on greed and thus deserving of having to pay for goods at the minimal price reduction which has ensued.

The interesting and perhaps significant aspect of the pitcher's use of humour is that the *humour is used to do serious work* (Jefferson, 1984; Mulkay, 1986). In many cases of humour it is made clear that a joke is being told – jokes are often prefaced with special work by the teller which serves to indicate that a joke is to follow or that actions are displayed to be clearly taken as humorous (Sacks, 1974). In the case examined above it is not made clear that humour is involved until after the pitcher has announced the final price. In other words, there appears to be an issue as to whether the activity being conducted is serious or humorous (Drew, 1986). By retrospectively constituting what initially had the character of being a serious activity into one which transpires to have had also a 'humorous' element, the pitcher has exploited humour in order to manage his 'serious' interactional project of selling goods in an orderly, non-hostile fashion (Mulkay, 1986).

Nailing the punters as a resource to accomplish mass sales

The sequence which we have examined above, whilst it forms a common aspect of pitching routines, is somewhat exceptional in that it is a remedial sales strategy designed to sell one or two more of the same items after reaching the Sales Relevance Place (SRP) – the first point in a pitching routine where the selling price is announced and goods are exchanged for money.[10] Pitchers, however, build their routines to achieve mass sales. Indeed, the solicitation of purchasing-implicative responsiveness from audience members which then evidently commits and constrains them to buy the goods is a central feature of many pitcher's standard sales routines. By regularly being able to solicit such commitments from large numbers of audience members *before* the announcement of the selling price at the SRP the pitcher is able prospectively to manage mass sales success.

In what follows we shall be examining a variety of such strategies. In the manner we shall present them, the different practices we encounter become progressively more complex. As the price of the goods being sold increases the pitchers' routines tend to utilize a particular type of 'nailing' technique. In general as the price of the goods offered for sale goes up the pitcher's offer to sell is presented more and more equivocally, the audience's initial responsiveness becomes similarly more equivocal, and the exchange-implicative actions are displaced back further and further from the SRP (that is, they occur much earlier in the selling routine). This displacement enables the pitcher incrementally to manage the responsiveness solicited from audience members into having been purchase-implicative commitments which act as obligations upon those audience members to buy the goods. In each case that we shall be examining the audience members' commitments are rendered in such a fashion as to make them enter into more and more ineluctable obligations to buy.

We shall continue to analyse the various strategies in terms of the central properties of this type of economic exchange as outlined in the above section.

'Getting the Forks Up'

This technique is the most rudimentary method by which a pitcher attempts to solicit purchasing-implicative expressions from audience members – it occurs in the vast majority of pitching routines. In Extract 2 the pitcher is attempting to sell a number of sets of pens:

Extract 2

P: (. . .) ah *won't* charge yuh *five* ninety-five, (0.8) ah WON'T charge yuh *three* ninety-five or *one* ninety-five, (0.3) in fact ah'm not even chargin' look, (0.5) a pound and ten pence for all the five of 'em. (0.4) *Now 'oo* can use 'em if ah go a bit lower, (0.3) than a pound tenpence? (.) Raise an 'and? [*Many audience members raise hands.*] One, (.) two, (.) three, (.) four AH CAN ONLY DO IT FER SO MANY (.) five, six, seven, (.) eight, nine, anybody at the back? (0.3) *Ten*, (.) eleven. (0.3) Here's what ah'll do with yeh FIRST come first served, (0.4) ALL the five of 'em yeh must 'ave *fifteen* pounds' worth uh pens, (0.3) [*CLAP*] ah'll tek a pound the whole jolly lot. (. . .)

In Extract 2 the sales transaction occurs after the announcement of the selling price of 'a pound'. Both the pitcher's offer to sell ('*Now 'oo* can use 'em if ah go a bit lower, (0.3) than a pound tenpence?') and the audience members' acceptance (hand-raising) occur, again, at a point prior to and separate from the announcement of the selling price.[11] However, although the exchange-implicative actions are expressed prior to the SRP they are made well after the start of the selling routine at a point where the pitcher has already used many other resources to constitute the goods as being bargains and worth buying.[12]

Again, the pitcher's offer to sell is posed as a question which is built to solicit a hand-raising response ('Getting the Forks Up') from audience members. Thus, as in the previous extract, it is the pitcher who instigates the sale. Unlike the transaction in Extract 1, however, the pitcher's offer to sell is not formulated to obtain an explicit intent to buy from audience members; rather, the item 'use' in the phrase ''oo can use 'em' establishes those hand-raising actions more as being a display of interest in the goods. However, the question ''oo can use 'em if 'ah go a bit lower than a pound tenpence?' can generate buying-implicative responses. It is not the 'use' of any goods that is being asked about but rather those particular goods the pitcher is selling at that particular price range. An affirmative response thus implicates audience members at least in the possibility of their prospective ownership of those particular goods.

If the offer to sell is somewhat equivocal the suggestion of what the exact selling price which these goods will be sold for is less so. An offer to go 'a bit lower than a pound tenpence' is designedly less equivocal than an offer merely to go 'cheaper than two quid'. A 'bit lower' does not promise the possibility of much of a further price reduction and since final selling price announcements are often given in terms of 'even money' audience members in this case may project that the final price will be £1. Furthermore, in these types of cases the pitcher is utilizing the 'exponential decay' character of the series of decremental possible selling prices which he could charge but will not be charging for the goods. This provides audience members with the materials to infer a likely exact price of those goods (see Pinch and Clark, 1986). The fact that many of the hand-raising members of the audience can be seen already to have the 'correct' money in their hands shows not only their interest in the goods, and their intent to purchase them, but also their ability to predict the selling price.

The audience members' hand-raising actions can again be taken to be unequivocal expressions. However, in this case they are as much an expression of interest in those goods as an expression of intent to buy those goods, although, as we have seen, and as it transpires in this case, even expressions of interest have a purchasing-implicative and purchasing-obligating component.

The pitcher's selling price of 'one pound' is warrantably a 'bit lower' than one pound and tenpence. Thus the pitcher has fulfilled his side of the sales 'contract'. The pitcher has again attended to his own offer to sell as being an accountable action, yet, unlike the case in the previous extract he has not had to forestall any inferences concerning deception. Because, as we shall see below, the pitcher is using the purchasing-implicative responsiveness of audience members to try to achieve more sales it is not necessary for him to produce a price reduction which is built to be less than that anticipated by audience members.

As in Extract 1 the pitcher requests a particular form of response by audience members to mark their interest ('raise an 'and'). Again, as in the previous extract, the pitcher reaffirms the hand-raising actions by pointing to those members who have raised a hand; he also reconstitutes their actions into speech as he points out each of the punters in turn ('one', 'two', 'three', etc.). However, it is recurrently the case (as it is in the sale denoted in Extract 2) that the pitcher counts more hands than have actually been raised. By this action the pitcher demonstrates his concern with encouraging other people to buy as well as ensuring that those who have raised their hands do so. Thus, the pitcher attends to responsiveness and buying as having an imitative basis. Audience members and passers-by upon seeing others expressing an intent to make a purchase may be persuaded to do so themselves. Whilst most audience members who have raised their hands can be observed to purchase the goods, in this particular sequence they are not the only audience members who do so. This strategy seems to work by using the display of 'interest' in the goods as a means to elicit even more sales at the SRP.

'Bagging Out'

This widely used routine which tends to be favoured for the sale of slightly more expensive goods shares many of the features that we have examined above. In this type of routine, however, after the audience members have expressed an interest in the goods by raising their hands they are now provided with bags (or wrapping paper, and the like) to hold the goods being sold. This occurs before the announcement of the selling price. In Extract 3 the pitcher is attempting to sell four different perfumes in a set for £3:

Extract 3

P: (. . .) now 'oo can use (.) *all* the four of 'em, (0.7) fer the purposes of the advertisement, (0.9) theh've got tuh be cleared cheaply an' quickly. (0.3) 'oo can use *all* the four of 'em, (0.5) twenty-three pounds w'th, (0.4) at *less* than three fifty raise an 'arm? [*Many audience members raise hands.*] (0.8) Anybody else? (0.5) now as – (0.3) [*To PC →*] Now listen Rick, [←] (0.5) the *first eighteen people* wi' their 'and in the air, (.) will yuh please step forward. (. . .) now look [*To PC →*] (0.6) give *every* one o' these people wi' their 'and in the air a carrier. [←] (0.4) Ah'm givin' out *eighteen* carriers an' *that's it*. (. . .)

Again, as in the previous extract, the pitcher's initial offer to sell is posed as a question designed to elicit an interest in the perfume. The action of the pitcher in distributing carrier bags to hold the goods builds on this expressed interest. This can be seen to be a way in which the pitcher attempts retrospectively to convert this display of interest (hand-raising) into having been an expression of intent to purchase the perfume. The taking of a bag by audience members more markedly implies them as having accepted ownership of the goods. The audience's acceptance of the bags is formulated as being unproblematic. Rather than asking the audience members to accept the bags the pitcher merely instructs a pitch-crew (PC) member to distribute them to those members of the audience who have raised their hands. Furthermore, the handing over and acceptance of these bags visibly shows the existence of 'willing' buyers. As in the previous routine the imitative basis of buying is used by the pitcher to attempt to attract more buyers.

The point at which the audience members' expression of interest is first made occurs earlier in the sales routine than in the previous extract. In other words, it is displaced even further away from the

SRP. This allows the pitcher incrementally to manage to constitute that interest as a commitment, and furthermore, to exploit to greater effect the imitative basis of buying. In this routine, as in the previous one examined, the pitcher warrantably keeps to his side of the sales contract. The perfumes are sold at a price of £3 which is likely to be taken by audience members to be sufficiently 'less than three fifty'. Thus again the pitcher does not attempt to forestall possible objections concerning deception.

In this particular version of the Bagging Out routine, a 'rick' is used in order to help stimulate other audience members to raise hands. A rick is a confederate of the pitcher who poses incognito in the audience as an audience member. Because the rick is the first to raise a hand, and does so in an exceptionally enthusiastic fashion, the pitcher is able to guarantee that at least one member of the 'audience' will display an interest/intent in making a purchase. Upon seeing this apparent 'audience' member with his hand in the air, other audience members may be (and often are) convinced to do the same themselves. Again the imitative basis of responsiveness and buying is being exploited, although now in a more marked fashion.

The 'Proviso'

Another regularly used method by which audience members' commitments to purchase are managed is called the Proviso. This routine is usually reserved for selling more expensive goods – those priced at over £5. The routine gets its name from the pitcher's initial solicitation of interest from audience members which is posited as being provisional upon the pitcher fulfilling his/her own side of the exchange-implicative commitment (for example, 'Providing I make the goods cheaper than £x ...'). In the following version of the Proviso the pitcher is selling a set of towels. The exact selling price of the goods transpires to be £9.95. For the purposes of the analysis we have split the routine into four sections.

The 'Hook'

Extract 4(i)
P: (...) an' ah'll *put it* tuh yuh like this, (0.9) *providin'* this morning, (0.7) that I make *any* set that's caught yer eye, (0.7) a *lot* less than Marks an' Spencers' price of twenty pound, (0.8) this *morning*, (0.5) [CLAP] providing I *make* them a *hell of a lot less* than *twelve* quid a set, (0.6) an' *when ah say* a LOT less, (0.6) *ah* DON'T mean fifty pence or a *pound* or two, (0.8) *I mean* a HELL *of a lot* less than twelve quid, (0.5) [CLAP] is there *any lady* or gentleman listenin' tuh me at the moment, (0.7) who *fancies* a set of these, (0.8) *if I* make them a *lot*, (0.4) cheaper? (0.3) Now if yuh do, (0.5) don't show me any money. (0.3) I 'aven't *asked* yuh fer any money. (0.7) If yuh've *seen* a set yuh like, (0.4) [CLAP] can yih just show me a sign here please? [*Many audience members raise hands.*]

P: *You* 'ave darlin', (0.5) *you* 'ave madam *you* 'ave sir *you* 'ave sir, (0.6) *you* have you have you have an' *so* have you. (0.3) Well *everybody* has now *just* a second, (. . .)

As in the Bagging Out routine the offer to sell is formulated to solicit an expression of interest in the goods rather than an intent to purchase, and this interest is expressed before the final selling price is known. However, in the Proviso this offer is managed incrementally in two stages. First, the pitcher solicits the interest by asking, 'Who fancies a set . . .?' Then he formulates the offer in even more equivocal terms: 'if yuh've seen a set yuh like . . . show me a sign'. This second formulation still suggests an interest in the towels but shifts the emphasis by asking for a response from those audience members who have merely 'seen' a set (they fancy). In Extract 4(i), immediately after the pitcher has asked the audience members, 'Who fancies a set?', he states, 'Now if yuh do, don't show me any money.' By refusing (displays of) money at this stage audience members are led to infer that the pitcher is not attempting so much to sell the towels as conducting a census of opinion about them.

If the offer to sell is phrased somewhat equivocally the exact amount of the price reduction that will be made, though still unstated, is made more specific. The pitcher provides a variety of materials which are built to suggest, and hint at, the actual amount of the price reduction that will be made. First, he states that the selling price will be 'a lot less than Marks an' Spencers' price of twenty pound'. Second, he gives more specific information when he announces that the towels will be 'a hell of a lot less than twelve quid a set'. Finally, he elaborates on what he means by 'a hell of a lot less' when he says 'ah don't mean fifty pence or a pound or two' (less than £12).

Having obtained the audience responsiveness the pitcher then attempts to convert the audience's expressed interest into having been an intent to purchase. He does this in a similar way to the Bagging Out routine, but in this case that intent to purchase is rendered as a more markedly ineluctable obligation upon those hand-raising audience members to purchase the goods. Rather than handing out a bag to those audience members who have raised their hands, the pitcher actually hands out the goods themselves. This is carried out in two stages. In the first stage, the pitcher hands out the goods to only one of those members who have raised their hands. This excerpt follows on from the previous extract:

Getting rid of the first set

Extract 4(ii)
[A *is one of the audience members who has raised a hand.*]
P: (. . .) now just a second, (0.7) darlin' can ah speak tuh you?

A: Yes.

P: Ah won't embarrass yuh, (0.3) just a minute love, (0.5) which colour duh yuh like best?

A: [*Points to a set of towels.*]

P: Yuh like the *Bergundy* now just a minute, (0.5) ah'm *gonna ask* this lady, (.) *one* question, (0.7) then ah'll serve, (.) everybody. (0.3) Now they've gone just come in a little bit at the front 'ere (0.4) thank yuh very much. *Darlin'*, (0.7) *would you say* at *twelve quid* that was *fair* value for your money? (1.0)

A: Aye.

P: Yes? (0.5) If I make them a lot cheaper, (.) yuh won't get annoyed will yuh? (0.8) [*Audience member makes a small shake of head.*]

P: 'Cos if yih swear at me ah'll bloody swear back. (0.4) Ah know all the words. (0.5) Listen, (0.6) ah'm gonna *put* those into a bag ah hope yer all watchin' this, (0.7) ah'm gonna *give* them tuh yuh *now*, (0.4) but yuh've got a very *nice* surprise in store for yuh (.) OK darlin'? (0.5)

P: Don't look so bloody worried.

A: [*Nervous laugh.*]

[*The goods are then handed over to the audience member.*]

The handing over of the goods to the individual audience member differs from the handing out of the carriers in the Bagging Out routine in that it is preceded by a lengthy, prefatory, exchange between the pitcher and that audience member. In Bagging Out the acceptance of the bags was treated as being unproblematic – the pitcher just instructed his pitch crew member to 'give everyone o' these people . . . a carrier', whereas in this extract the pitcher can be seen to be prospectively managing the audience member's acceptance of the goods. He does this by asking her a series of questions. Affirmative responses to these questions successively, and progressively, implicate her into having little choice other than to accept the goods, which she does.

Having established verbal contact with the audience member he asks which colour of the towels on display she prefers. A response made with reference to one of the colours of the towel sets on display implies that audience member as having expressed not merely an interest in the towels *per se* (that is, that she ' "fancies" a set') but a *preference* for a particular coloured set. The pitcher then asks: 'Would you say at twelve quid that was fair value for your money?' The affirmative response now expresses not only a colour preference for one particular set of towels on display but also a *price preference* from the audience member. The affirmative response solicited by the next question, 'If I make them a lot cheaper, yuh won't get annoyed will yuh?', imputes a purchasing decision as having already been made by that audience member. The affirmative response to the previous question can be seen to have been worked in such a manner as to act as a constraint on the type of answer that the audience member could appropriately give to the final question. To admit that she would get annoyed if he 'made them a lot cheaper' would contradict her acknowledgment that at the price of 'twelve quid' they were fair value for money. Finally the pitcher states that he is going to wrap the goods and hand them over. Of course, the fact that the goods are now wrapped draws further attention to their status as goods which have already been purchased.

By this method the pitcher is able to display to the other hand-raising audience members that one of the members who had raised a hand and expressed an 'interest' in the goods is willing to accept them and, moreover, is willing to do so before being told their selling price. As the pitcher says, 'ah hope yer all watchin' this'. Although the audience member has not actually made an explicit commitment to purchase the goods, the pitcher, by getting her to take possession of the goods, has managed to place her into having made a commitment which more markedly indicates that audience member having demonstrated an intent to purchase than a hand-raising action and the taking of an empty carrier bag. The success of this strategy for the audience members in general depends on the ability of the pitcher to be able to persuade the 'punter' to accept the goods. Of course to ensure this the pitcher may use a 'rick', or more likely in this type of routine a 'div' – a punter chosen on the basis of an inferred meek and suggestible personality. That is, a member of the audience who, will, in all likelihood, respond appropriately when 'put on the spot'.[13]

By dealing in the first place with only one of the hand-raising members of the audience the pitcher attends to both the increased difficulty in getting even an implied commitment to purchase from audience members, as well as the general reluctance of audience members to commit themselves to a purchasing decision in these types of sales routines. If one member of the audience can be persuaded to take the goods then it should be easier to get others to follow suit. By getting one hand-raising audience member to be publicly available as having made an implied commitment to purchase the goods the pitcher is able to provide those other hand-raising audience members with the materials by which a similar commitment from them can be posited as being expected, appropriate, and 'likewise' unproblematic.[14]

Getting rid of the other sets

The second stage in this incremental process of converting the audience responsiveness (that is, 'interest' in the goods) into being a purchasing-implicative commitment involves persuading other audience members who have raised their hands that they too should accept the wrapped goods. How the pitcher achieves this can be seen in the next sequence. Again this follows on immediately from the previous extract:

Extract 4(iii)
P: (. . .) *that* lady's got the first set now listen (   ) just a minute, (0.5) there's *one* gone, (0.6) ah'd like tuh make it intuh *twenty*. (0.7) For the *people* who *can't* decide, (0.8) *I'm* gonna do it *for yuh*. (0.7) At the *next* price I stop at, (0.5) theh *cost* more money, (0.5) seven or eight *years* ago. (0.6) Ah'm *showin'* yuh, (.) the *best*. (0.4) Yih can't buy *better*. (0.5) Theh *cost* twenty, (0.6) ah've just been offered *twelve*. (0.4) *Another* hint, (0.5) [*CLAP*] ah *won'* even charge yuh, (0.3) *ten* pound a set, (0.7) I am *still* coming cheaper, (0.7) an' they've *all* got that *money back* guarantee. (0.6) In other words yuh *can't* lose. (0.7) Ah'll say that *once* more tuh let the penny drop. (0.5) [*CLAP*] At less than *a tenna*, (0.4) a *set* tuhday, (0.4) who else wants a set now let me see – *everybody* ah thought so. (0.3) What colour'd yuh like darlin'?
[*The pitcher then hands out the towel bales to the punters.*]

The salience of persuading one audience member to take the wrapped goods can now be seen. The pitcher is able retrospectively to constitute this action as having been a purchasing decision. This is implied when he states that 'there's one gone', and 'ah've just been offered twelve'. This latter phrase also inverts the instigation of the commitment – it suggests that the offer was initiated by the audience member, rather than having been managed by the pitcher. The mention of the 'offer' of 'twelve' occurs in a second series of decremental price reductions which are designed to be a clearer indication of what the eventual selling price will be. Now instead of the selling price being projected as going to be a 'hell of a lot less than twelve quid', and that 'hell of a lot less' not being 'fifty pence or a pound or two', the pitcher states that he will sell the towels at 'less than a tenna'. By seemingly reducing the price (from her 'offer' of £12) after she already has the towels in her possession the pitcher breaks the normative expectation that sellers will sell goods at the highest possible price they can get for them and that buyers do not get price reductions after they have already 'bought' the goods. The pitcher has thus been able to exploit that audience member's acceptance of the goods in order to elicit similar purchasing-implicative commitments from the audience at large. The wrapped towels are handed out to another fifteen members of the audience. We can also notice that the pitcher works further to mitigate the reservations that audience members may have in accepting the goods before knowing their selling price. By announcing a 'money back guarantee' the pitcher posits the audience's acceptance of the goods as being of lesser consequence – that they can always return the goods if they are dissatisfied. Though, as we shall see, this works to the pitcher's advantage as it then places the onus on the punters to return goods and obtain their money back from the pitcher.

The 'Bat'

As in all pitching routines the final stage of the Proviso is reached when the selling price (the 'Bat') is announced at the SRP and where the pitcher (and/or the pitch crew) collects the money from those audience members who have goods in their possession:

Extract 4(iv)

P: (. . .) *This* is the price, (0.6) for the *two* bath the two hand there's *twenty* pounds' worth there, (0.8) mine's a *silly* price but it's *marvellous* value for yih money. (0.4) *Not* twenty, (0.3) [*CLAP*] ah want *nine ninety-five* a set. (.) OK? (. . .)

The pitcher's earlier indication that the selling price will be 'less than a tenna' is met by an announcement of a selling price of £9.95 – a reduction of 5p. We take it that it is again the case that the pitcher has exploited the audience's anticipation that the selling price would be lower than that which ensues. The phrase 'at less than a tenna' works in a similar fashion to the phrase 'cheaper than two quid' which we examined in the first extract in this chapter. 'Less than a tenna' projects a more substantial reduction than 5p, partly because all the other announced price reductions have been in pounds. Also the projected price reduction from £12 stated in the first of the two price-decrease sequences (the 'Hook') suggests a more substantial price reduction than that which ensues. The phrase used to project the price reduction from £12, that is, 'ah don't mean fifty pence or a pound or two' suggests a reduction greater than £2.05.

The pitcher attends to the audience's anticipation of a greater price reduction than 5p by presenting the selling price not in contrast with the previous price of £10, nor in contrast with the next previously mentioned price of £12, but instead with the largest price mentioned in that selling-price series: £20. The reduction from £20 to £9.95 seems to be built to confirm that punters are still getting a bargain – even if it is not quite as 'big' a bargain as they expected.

In these routines it is almost always the case that those members of the audience who have the goods in their possession actually do purchase them. Thus it would seem that the Proviso is a highly successful technique for obtaining mass sales. Of course, there are always some members of the public who have accepted goods and who do not subsequently purchase them (that is, who 'jebb out' of the sale). That there may also be one or two who have accepted the goods in order to walk away without paying when the price is announced is well known to pitchers. Towards the end of a sale the pitch crew often move to the back of the audience to ensure that everyone does pay for the goods in their possession. However, it appears that the success rate of the Proviso routine is taken by pitchers not only to outweigh the small amount of failures that may accrue, but also to have a higher likelihood of eliciting a larger number of sales for this price range of goods than if the purchase decision had been left solely in the hands of the audience. The success of the Proviso seems to depend upon audience members regarding responsiveness and purchasing-implicative commitments as being accountable actions; and more-over, upon the types of purchasing commitments they make (hand-raising, accepting a bag, accepting the goods) not being taken to be equivalents. Each action displays a more ineluctable commitment to purchase. The onus is on the punters not to buy (that is, to return goods already in their possession) rather than to make a purchasing decision.

The advantages to the pitcher of instigating the sale and making his or her commitment equivocal and incremental can now be seen. Price information and buyers' responses from different stages of the sale can be managed by the pitcher so as to work in his or her favour. In this case commitments are displaced and managed throughout virtually the whole sales routine.

Other similar routines
Finally, we should note that there are even more complicated routines which are used for goods of much higher prices and which also share the above features – for reasons of space we cannot document these here. Such routines, and in particular fraudulent practices known as the 'Mock Auction', 'Ram', 'Run Out', or 'the System' work by the pitcher placing audience members under an even more ineluctable obligation to buy – in the handing over of *money* by an audience member *before* the goods are handed over and *before* the final price is announced. Whilst in principle audience members can 'jebb out' from an intent expressed by a hand-raising action, by the taking of a bag, and by the taking of the goods themselves, it is much harder to do anything once the pitcher has the punter's money in his or her possession. Such fraudulent practices exhibit many of the features we have described above, though in an even more marked fashion.

Discussion

The constraining and enabling features of the norms of economic exchange
In the sales strategies we have examined in this chapter we have attempted to show how the norms which underpin sales transactions

can be brought to bear and exploited in such a way as to enhance the pitcher's prospect of sales success. The pitcher's accomplishment has been to make the audience members' responsiveness to an offer to sell comprise a more and more ineluctable obligation to buy. The element of control we have documented is effectuated by the manner in which the pitcher is able to exploit the normative properties inherent in the act of doing economic exchange. The two central norms are the following:

For the buyer. The buyer has a duty to accept and pay for the goods that he or she has indicated an intent to purchase.

For the seller. The seller has a duty to sell those goods in which a buyer has indicated an intent to purchase at the particular selling price implicated in the offer to sell.

These normative features are reciprocally binding on the parties to the exchange and 'constrain' the manner in which that exchange can be conducted and are used to facilitate an orderly sales transaction, as well as providing a strategic means whereby the participants (and in particular the pitcher) can attempt to manage the exchange. It is not only the pitcher who can exploit these norms to his or her advantage. The audience members co-participate in the sale and presumably from their point of view they are exploiting the norms to their advantage. Indeed we have often heard audience members express satisfaction with the bargains they have been obliged to purchase, though some pitchers would say that this is a 'rationalization' on the part of the punters.

Norms are central parts of both the micro- and the macro-analysis of social organization. In macro-sociology norms are usually seen mainly as constraints on action, whilst in much of micro-sociology they have been posited as having predominantly an enabling quality. Like Giddens (for example, 1976) we see norms as having both constraining and enabling qualities. Our analysis of the interaction between pitchers and audience members confirms this point and shows that both sides to the sales transaction attend to and attempt to exploit this duality. Norms carry with them rights, duties, obligations and the prospect of sanctions if they are not fulfilled and our study of the normative features of economic exchange demonstrates that participants attend to their constraining character as rendering their actions accountable. However, the manner in which these norms are interactionally constituted – how the pitcher is able to displace constituent features of economic exchange from the moment of exchange as well as invert the regular means by which economic exchange occurs – provides the central means which enables that exchange to be effected.

Social control and relationships of power

Our analysis of pitching routines has shown how a pitcher's control over the purchasing decision of audience members is made more effective by the use of the resources we have documented. We do not want to suggest that audience members are 'cultural dopes' in this process (although it is certainly the case that their comparative lack of familiarity with this type of sales transaction gives the pitcher a clear advantage). At every stage many audience members actively co-participate in these sales transactions – presumably they do so in the expectation that it is they who are getting the 'good deal'. However, pitchers have crucial resources which act in their favour.

One crucial resource stems from the pitchers' greater control of the interaction vis-à-vis that of the audience. The pitcher's whole sales strategy is built upon the premise that goods do not sell themselves and that some sort of discursive intervention between product and purchaser is crucial to sales success. For the pitcher that intervention is primarily managed in and through the use of speech – pitchers are 'patter merchants'. The achievement of the pitcher in having gathered a crowd (the 'edge' – see Clark and Pinch, 1986) to listen to his or her routine is what effectuates the inversion of the normal sequencing of sales transactions and enables the pitcher to instigate and manage the sale in a particular manner. More crucially, as we have seen, the pitcher can set up the conditions by which he is able to exploit the indexical features of language in order to manage the sale. The initial offer to sell which forms the basis of the audience members' purchasing-implicative commitments can be phrased equivocally both in regard to price and in regard to its buying implicativeness. Furthermore, the pitchers by virtue of being the initiators of the sales transaction are able to request and/or manage particular *unequivocal* forms of audience response – hand-raising, taking a bag, taking the goods, and so on. The relatively unequivocal and symbolic nature of the audience members' responsiveness works to the advantage of pitchers as we have seen. People either raise their hands or they do not.

Also, pitchers in being the initiators of the sales transaction and audience responsiveness have crucial advantages in being able to render individual audience members' actions back into speech in a next, subsequent turn at talk. This means that pitchers can not only draw attention to those actions for the benefit of the rest of the audience, but also, as we have seen, they can reconstitute those actions in a way which makes more available their buying implicativeness.

Our claim is that we have demonstrated that in the context of buying from pitchers on markets a 'power relationship' is the outcome of interaction: the result of the capability of one side, or one participant, in the act of economic exchange to manage successfully to control the other side or participants to do things by effectively limiting the range of options open to them. Indeed, much of the control of the punters is effected by the punters controlling themselves, that is, in fulfilling the obligations implied by their purchasing-implicative expressions; they are not forced or physically coerced into making purchases. It is not any 'external attributes' (for example, class, gender, or age) which the pitcher or audience members may or may not share, nor their subject position (pitcher as 'seller' versus audience member as 'buyer'), nor indeed aspects 'inherent' in the goods themselves (for example, their quality) or their selling price which preordains, guarantees, or determines that sales success. Rather, we would claim, that it is the manner in which economic exchange can be managed by the pitcher which is the central feature of how this interactional project can be effected, social control accomplished, and how this type of power relation can be constituted.

Markets, social relationships, and economic laws
It might be argued that the location for our study is somewhat unusual and that as a consequence social interactional processes are not constitutive of other sales situations and markets such as commodity markets, stock markets, and financial markets. Of course, we see this as a matter for empirical investigation. However, we take encouragement from the fact that, for instance, buying and selling on financial markets appears to be taken by members themselves as being a specialist skill, which is acknowledged by the huge salaries that successful dealers on financial markets can attract. Indeed, the recent public attention in Britain given to the huge salaries earned by buyers and sellers on financial markets in the City of London indicates the salience of our approach. If 'market forces' are independent from social skills then it has to be explained why such special dealers are needed and why they are so highly rewarded.

The data we have presented in this paper form only a small subset of a much wider corpus which we have collected in the course of our research into the rhetorical skills of market traders, and in particular pitchers. Pitching a product is taken by us to exhibit in a particular context-specific form the fundamental discursive social processes which underlie all selling, sales promotion, and advertising. We have attempted to document the interactional skills of the pitcher and members' own methods for conducting and accomplishing economic exchange by studying selling *in situ* – as it actually occurs.[15] The increasing interventions between product and purchaser made by manufacturers, retailers, advertisers, and salespeople in general are, we would claim, better understood within the sociological study of interaction than within economics. In other words, we have treated selling as an interactional accomplishment rather than as a pre-ordained economic act.

Given these concerns, our work has not only addressed the macro–micro issue as it has arisen in sociology. The more important task for us has been to show how sociological analysis *per se* provides a better account of selling and salesmanship than is available in economics (Pinch and Clark, 1986). Of course, our research does have implications for the level of aggregation appropriate to the study of economic behaviour. We would claim that any formulation of economic rules and systematic economic practices should only be obtained as a second-order analysis derived from members' own economic orientations. Furthermore, that social phenomena take on the character of being the effect of preconstituted laws – and economic laws at that – is, we believe, in itself essentially a social phenomenon.[16] Micro-sociology has much to offer macro- and indeed micro-economics.

Notes

The analysis reported here includes part of the findings of a research project funded by the Nuffield Trust during 1985–6. We are grateful to Richard Wrightson, David Holmes, and the Audiovisual Centre, York University, for technical advice and assistance.

1. At present the corpus predominantly consists of approximately eighty hours of audio-visual recordings of pitching routines from approximately seventy pitchers on markets throughout England, as well as one market in the Netherlands. In addition we have conducted both formal and informal interviews with pitchers, other market traders, and members of the public. One of the authors (Clark) earned his living for three months by working as a pitcher.

2. A general overview of the selling methods used by pitchers is contained in Pinch and Clark (1986); for a more detailed examination of how pitchers attract passers-by and build an audience, see Clark and Pinch (1986).

3. These are features to which Giddens (e.g. 1976) has drawn attention. We would agree with Brewer (see Chapter 6 below) that there does not appear to be anything particularly distinctive about this aspect of Giddens' theory of structuration and that similar conceptions of norms are to be found within ethnomethodology and interpretativist sociology.

4. The sequences examined in this chapter, whilst being actual, empirical sales sequences, have been chosen for their prototypical character. They each represent sales practices which are common to and characterize the vast majority of pitching routines.

5. We have endeavoured to represent talk in a textual form so that the reader can capture some of its rhythm, pace, and 'feel'. We have used a transcription process which is a much simplified version of that which was developed by Gail Jefferson and is used by conversation analysts (see e.g. Sacks, Schegloff and Jefferson (1974)):

Identities
 P: Pitcher
 PC: Pitch-crew member (an assistant of the pitcher)
 A: Individual audience member
 As: Audience as a group

Pauses and gaps in the extracts
 (0.4) Represents pauses within a speaker's talk, or between speakership exchanges. The number within the brackets is a rough approximation of time elapsed in seconds and tenths of seconds.
 (.) A micro-pause, a pause which is estimated to have been less than 0.3 second in duration.
 ( ) Brackets with space indicate speech which was inaudible or could not otherwise be transcribed.

Intonation and prosodic variations
 , = Slight upward ('incompleted sentence') intonation ⎤ of a prior
 . = Downward ('sentence complete') intonation ⎬ segment of
 ? = Upward ('questioning') intonation ⎦ speech.
Speech Speech printed in italics is that which has been taken to have been stressed and emphasized.
 SPEECH Speech printed in small capitals is that which has been taken to have been shouted.

6. This sequence was recorded when the halfpenny coin was still legal tender.

7. In some everyday cases the obligations of sellers are evident before the sale transaction commences. Thus it is unusual to change the price marked on goods in shops in the presence of buyers, even though they may have no particular interest in purchasing those goods.

8. Indeed, pitchers rarely give the small change back to punters. Nor are they often asked for it.

9. Such sales are often constituted in terms of punters taking a 'gamble'. This helps the audience infer that they have a chance of getting a big price reduction. The gambling element also helps forestall possible objections concerning deception – after all, the punters were taking a risk.

10. Indeed, it would not work as a mass selling strategy because, as we have shown, it crucially depends upon using the majority of the audience who have already purchased the goods as a resource against the two new punters.

The SRP is analogous to the Transition Relevance Place delineated by Sacks, Schegloff and Jefferson (1974) as a means used by interactants to co-ordinate orderly speakership exchange.

11. Pitchers work with a fixed, preconstituted selling price, which rarely, if ever, is made available to the audience prior to the SRP. Additionally, in our corpus on no occasion was the selling price marked on the goods themselves. Therefore, in the sequences which follow the reader should bear in mind that members of the public are largely unaware of what the exact selling price will be.

12. For an analysis of some of these resources see Pinch and Clark (1986).

13. In this extract a 'rick' was not used.

14. One pitcher characterized this practice as 'using a sprat to catch a mackerel'.

15. Despite the obvious importance of selling as an activity it has almost totally been ignored by sociologists. For a review of what little literature there is and for an analysis of high-street shop sales see Prus (1986).

16. Some of the means whereby economists have been able to achieve their position as the pre-eminent social scientists are documented in McCloskey (1985) and Mulkay, Pinch and Ashmore (1987).

References

Brewer, J.D. (1987) 'Micro-sociology and the "Duality of Structure": Former Fascists "Doing" Life History'. Chapter 6 below.

Clark, C. and Pinch, T.J. (1986) 'Getting an "Edge": How Market Pitchers Manufacture an Audience of Consumers'. Presented to the conference 'Erving Goffman: An Interdisciplinary Appreciation', York University, 8–11 July.

Drew, P. (1986) 'Po-faced Receipts of Teases: A Connection between Humour and Criticism', *Sociolinguistics* (special issue), 15, 140–63.

Giddens, A. (1976) *New Rules of Sociological Method*. London: Hutchinson.

Jefferson, G. (1984) 'On the Organisation of Laughter in Talk about Troubles', pp. 346–69 in J.M. Atkinson and J. Heritage (eds), *Structures of Social Action: Studies in Conversation Analysis*. Cambridge: Cambridge University Press.

McCloskey, D. (1985) *The Rhetoric of Economics*. Wisconsin: University of Wisconsin Press.

Mulkay, M.J. (1986) 'A Sociology of Humour'. York University (mimeo).

Mulkay, M., Pinch, T. and Ashmore, M. (1987) 'Colonising the Mind: Dilemmas in the Application of Social Science', *Social Studies of Science*, 17: 20–34.

Pinch, T.J. and Clark, C. (1986) 'The Hard Sell: "Patter Merchanting" and the Strategic (Re)production and Local Management of Economic Reasoning in the Sales Routines of Market Pitchers', *Sociology*, 20: 169–91.

Prus, R. (1986) 'It's on "Sale"!: Vendor Perspectives on the Bargain', *Canadian Review of Sociology and Anthropology*, 23: 72–96.

Sacks, H. (1974) 'An Analysis of the Course of a Joke's Telling in Conversation', in R. Bauman and J. Sherger (eds), *Explorations in the Ethnography of Speaking*. Cambridge: Cambridge University Press.

Sacks, H., Schegloff, E.A. and Jefferson, G. (1974) 'A Simplest Systematics for the Organization of Turn-taking in Conversation', *Language*, 50(4): 696–735.

6
MICRO-SOCIOLOGY AND THE 'DUALITY OF STRUCTURE'

As noted earlier, the 'duality of structure' is one of the key concepts in Giddens' theory of structuration. While many other attempts to overcome the dualism of agency and structure exist, most maintain an analytical separation between the polarities and often argue that one is the bedrock or cause of the other. What is characteristic of Giddens' notion of the 'duality of structure' is that it presents a view of structure as a recursive phenomenon, simultaneously shaping and being shaped by human conduct. 'Agency' and 'structure' are not analytically separable, for structure is at one and the same time both the outcome of intentional human conduct and a medium which influences how conduct occurs.

This idea that structure is Janus-faced, or in Giddens' terms a duality, has proved to be controversial. This recursive quality is said to be incapable of being demonstrated in research; it is accused of not giving enough ontological status to the pre-existence of social forms; of an overemphasis on voluntarism and an underemphasis on the constraints on agency; and of having only weak links with other key notions in the theory of structuration, such as time–space and the unintended consequences of human action.

In this chapter, Brewer supports Giddens' view of structure by the use of qualitative data from unstructured interviews with fifteen former members of the British Union of Fascists, where they looked back on their membership and the reasons behind it. In ethnomethodological terms the former Fascists were 'doing' life history. This 'accomplishment' is shown to be a recursive achievement in Giddens' sense and demonstrates the duality that is said to exist in this view of structure. The former Fascists were 'knowledgeable agents' in Giddens' terms, but the accomplishment of their life history provides empirical evidence of how real is the constraint embedded in this recursive achievement. Moreover, because the former Fascists were looking back at their membership from a much later and particular spatial-temporal location and had to take contemporary views about Fascism and Fascists into consideration, their accomplishment demonstrates how time and space can be used by agents as dynamic elements in structuration, and how structuration occurs across time and space. The unintended consequences of past actions, and the former Fascists' awareness of what effect these actions had on the current opinions about Fascism and Fascists, also became vital resources in the accomplishment of their life history. This shows how the phenomenon of unintended consequences can coexist with the 'duality of structure' and the 'knowledgeability' of agents.

The property of 'recursiveness' is vitally at issue in this analysis. The substantive criticism is that, using the structuration concept, it would appear the former Fascists 'win either way'. Their recounting of their past involvement is either oriented to new thinking and therefore confirms the space–time effect, making them 'rational', or it is not, making them consistent (and 'rational'). The conceptualization of individuals and the constraints applying to them diverge strongly in Giddens and ethnomethodology. In this case, the debate is over whether the life histories were a realistic account of their reflexive monitoring, or lies. Their notion of 'crisis' is important here, with an issue being the extent to which the researcher 'reproduces' culture. Is the accomplishment of a life history an indexical achievement? Those who see structuration as a theoretical advance need to show how it adds to our understanding of the relatively stable features of social life *and* how it spells out the connections between what happens in individual actions and (the assumed) existent structures. Ethnomethodologists would see a need to treat phenomena exclusively as collaborative accomplishments. In that approach, intersubjectivity is emphasized. The 'collective' emphasis plausibly captures the partial and jigsaw puzzle-like quality of many decisions and actions, but it is manifestly at the expense of the role accorded the individual. When the individual is strategically located (as in the case of having been a member of a somewhat obscure political group) this may be misleading. To take another case, one might consider how helpful the intersubjective emphasis is in considering judicial decision-making. Here, strategically located social actors insist their sentencing decisions are independent and individual. The variability of sentences for similar offences inclines one to agree. While this implies advantage to Giddens, there are still the widely repeated reservations about the empirical applicability of his theory. In this chapter, Brewer highlights the empirical 'testability' of Giddens' theory, and whether the development structure notion should be separated from structuration theory as a whole.

Micro-sociology and the 'duality of structure'

Former Fascists 'doing' life history

John D. Brewer

There are a number of antinomies which recur, in one form or another, in a variety of disciplines. These include individualism versus collectivism, nominalism versus realism, object versus subject, mind versus matter, materialism versus idealism, micro versus macro, and agency versus structure. Although there are many specific differences between these terms, they seem to revolve around two basic questions. The first is whether human action can be explained in terms of concrete factors related to individuals and the situations they face, or in terms of some feature outside the individual, such as culture or social structure. The second question is whether we are to determine the answer to the first by studying individuals in concrete and small-scale situations or by focusing on the abstractions said to transcend individuals. The effect of the second question is to bind empirical research closely to the theoretical issues of the first.

Even though there have recently been attempts to resolve the contradictions in some of these antinomies, most of these syntheses still see the polarities as analytically distinct. This affects the nature of research. For example, the 'aggregation hypothesis', to use Knorr-Cetina's term (1981: 25), which argues that 'macro' or 'structural' phenomena are aggregations and repetitions of 'micro' episodes and actions (for an example of which see Collins, 1981), still sees 'structure' as separate from and different to 'agency' (Giddens, 1984: 141). Indeed, in Archer's outline of what she calls Blau's morphogenesis approach she argues that 'agency' and 'structure' are dualisms which need to be analytically separated irrespective of ontological reality (1982). Research in these instances is directed towards examining how micro-episodes are repeated in larger scale to form macro or structural phenomena (examples of which are discussed by Archer, 1982: 476; Collins, 1981: 985).[1]

What is characteristic of the 'representation hypothesis', as Knorr-Cetina describes it (1981: 30), is that it presents 'agency' and 'structure', or 'micro' and 'macro' phenomena, as recursively intertwined so that they are inseparable analytically and ontologically. Social reality is composed of micro-episodes of social interaction which have structural qualities endogamous to them. Maynard and Wilson refer to this idea as 'reflexive determination' (1980: 292–5), while Giddens describes it as structuration (1976, 1979, 1981, 1983, 1984) and Bhaskar as transformation (1979, 1983). However Maynard and Wilson do not detail how structural properties emerge from this reflexive relationship.[2] In contrast, what Smith calls the 'structuration–transformation' model (1983)[3] does attempt this more difficult problem. This model asserts that the intentionality of actors becomes objectified to affect the future intentionality of actors. Agency transforms or structures itself through this objectification. According to Smith, the key to this idea is that future practices are determined not only by the agency of actors but by previous practices within which past agency is structured (1983: 13). Research in this instance has the more problematic task of demonstrating how structuration or transformation occurs in micro-episodes of social interaction, which requires that the reflexivity and recursiveness of this relationship are made tangible and concrete.

The aim of this paper is to assess Giddens' concept of the 'duality of structure', which links agency and structure, by using qualitative data from interviews with fifteen former members of the British Union of Fascists (BUF) where they looked back on the reasons for their membership. Although Giddens' concept has proved to be controversial, the data support his arguments. The former Fascists were, in ethnomethodological terms, 'doing' life history, and this accomplishment is shown to be a recursive achievement in Giddens' sense and demonstrates the duality that is said to exist in this view of structure. The data also relate to Giddens' view of power. There are two dominant approaches to the concept of power: that of those such as Weber and the pluralists, like Dahl, who see power as a capacity of the individual, referring to power as an actor's capability to achieve desired ends or interests over which there is disagreement or conflict; and that of those such as Parsons and Foucault, who see power as a capacity of the collectivity. Giddens' intent in the theory of structuration is to overcome this dualism. While he defines power as the capacity to achieve outcomes (1984: 257), this capacity is seen to be reproduced in interaction and helps to structure or bind time–space (also see Giddens, 1981: 49ff). This argument involves a number of propositions which Giddens has expounded several times (1977: 347–8, 1981: 49, 1984: 14). The first is the claim that power is linked to agency: inasmuch as Giddens sees agency as the capability to act, which involves the capacity to decide to have acted otherwise, power is presupposed by agency because it provides the resources by which actors are capable of doing otherwise. Secondly, as Giddens portrays it, this power imposes constraints on the conduct of others: the agency of each person works as a sanction on the conduct of others by restricting their capacity to do otherwise. However, characteristic of structuration theory as a whole, constraints are perceived by Giddens to be simultaneously an enablement to agency as well as a sanction. At this point his notion of 'the dialectic of control' (1981: 63) becomes relevant: even the most oppressed individual has the capability of turning resources back against the powerful because of the enabling nature of constraints. This enablement can take the form of the simple acts which Goffman calls 'secondary adjustments', where, for example, the internee of a 'total institution' might mutter under his or her breath when responding to a command in order to reserve some personal autonomy or to seek status from fellow internees. The enablements can also be more profound, as is the case with the former Fascists.

The recursive relationship between constraint and enablement is an expression of the 'duality of structure' and links power with agency and structure. In seeking to verify Giddens' view of the recursive relationship between agency and structure, the data therefore also demonstrate how Giddens' conceptualization of power can be empirically linked to agency and structure. But in addition to providing an empirical test of Giddens' controversial view of the 'duality of structure', the chapter explores other issues which the concept raises. The data will be used to contend that this recursive view is not new and that it is consistent with an ethnomethodological and Schutzian framework. Giddens' originality therefore lies in other areas of the theory of structuration. First it is necessary to outline Giddens' arguments.

The 'duality of structure' and the theory of structuration

The theory of structuration argues that there is a duality between society and knowledgeable human agents. Giddens argues that this is a conceptual divide which is not successfully bridged in previous attempts at synthesis, such as Parsons' idea of voluntarism or in interpretative sociology (1976: 23–43, 1984: xxi). This duality occurs because knowledgeable agents are seen as reproducing in action the structural properties of society, allowing social life to be reproduced over time–space. It is this reproduction or structuration over time–space to which the theory of structuration is addressed (the theory is summarized in Giddens, 1983, 1984: 281–4). The account of agency which Giddens presents in his theory emphasizes that actors are knowledgeable and able reflexively to monitor their actions and the situations in which they act. They are also able to report discursively on the reasons for their actions, although not the motives.[4] But agency itself is not defined as action to realize one's intentions (as it is in Schutz, who defines social action as the operationalization of a mental project), for there are unintended actions. Nor is it the ability to give act-descriptions, for there are unacknowledged and unrecognized actions. Agency for Giddens is merely the capability of knowledgeable agents to act (1984: 9). In terms of the theory of structuration, the most important feature of this capability is that the resultant agency is said to have structural properties embedded in it.

The meaning Giddens gives to the term structure is more controversial, for he equates it with 'structuring properties' (1984: 16–17): it refers to those structuring properties like institutional practices, rules, and resources[5] which bind time–space. Structure thus describes binding properties in time–space, not the end result, which Giddens refers to as a system (1984: 17) and which in lay terms is referred to as the social structure or society. Giddens claims that human agency has these 'structuring properties' ('structure' in Giddens' sense) embedded in it. Therefore the rules and resources ('structuring properties', 'structure') drawn upon in the production and reproduction of social action are at the same time also the means of system reproduction. So in reproducing action we reproduce the system. As Giddens says, agency is constitutive of the system (1984: 19). This argument is extended by means of an analogy with rules to show that action which is constitutive of the system is simultaneously regulated by it (1984: 19–21). The rules governing penalty taking in Association football, for example, are constitutive of the game but simultaneously impose constraints on how and when penalty kicks are taken which are themselves constitutive of the game (Giddens discusses the rules governing checkmate in chess, 1984: 19). Likewise, agency is constitutive of social life but it is also controlled and regulated in this constitution, and these sanctions are constitutive of agency. That is to say, the relationship between the 'constructionist' character of agency, to use Thomason's term (1982), and the constraining nature of society is 'recursive'. This is a favoured word in Giddens' vocabulary and he uses it to emphasize that there is no disjuncture between what Thomason calls 'constructionism' and 'realism' (1982): the systemic and structuring properties of social life are constructed by human agency but the constraints imposed by the very thing that is so created are a fundamental ingredient of the construction and a medium through which construction takes place. Thus, as Giddens says, structure is at one and the same time both the outcome of knowledgeable human conduct and the medium which influences how conduct occurs (1984: 25, passim).

These arguments culminate in Giddens' concept of the 'duality of structure'. He sees this as the key idea in the theory of structuration (Giddens, 1982: 26, 1984: 16), for it theorizes the bridge between human agency and the social system which makes structuration of social life over time–space possible. The concept denotes that there is no longer a dualism (analytical or ontological) between human agency and the social system. They are aspects of the same Janus-face, or in Giddens' terms they form a duality. It is this concept which sustains his arguments that agency has structuring properties in its very nature and that these properties, while embodying past agency, also act as a constraint on subsequent human conduct. Two points are noteworthy here. First, Giddens does not equate systemic or structuring properties with constraint, a view he attributes to functionalism, for social structures are also a facilitation and enablement to agency. This is because 'structure', in Giddens' sense, provides the rules, resources, and institutional practices (which embody past agency) within which knowledgeable human agents currently act. Thus 'structure' is simultaneously both an enablement to action and a constraint upon it. Secondly, because of this element of constraint, Giddens does not equate social structures with people's reification of the social system, a view he attributes to ethnomethodology. He believes that as a result of this constraining quality, social structures have a stronger ontological status than simply people's sense that there is a social structure.[6]

Social research and the critique of the 'duality of structure'

The concept of the 'duality of structure' has proved to be controversial. Issues of research feature strongly in the critique of the concept, although for most of the time the debate remains heavily theoretical and epistemological. Occasionally, however, empirical research is called upon to adjudicate the theoretical issues raised by the concept. Some critics contend that research demonstrates the fallibility of Giddens' theory, while Giddens uncharacteristically calls upon research to support his arguments. Other critics argue that Giddens' work simply does not lend itself to empirical test. One of the most important criticisms of this sort is the claim that the recursive and reflexive nature of the relationship between 'agency' and 'structure' is difficult to operationalize and apply in concrete situations (Smith, 1983: 3), although there has been research which attempts to apply structuration theory as a whole (Smith, 1983). This research is different from those studies others have carried out which, while not intending to apply the theory, is taken by Giddens as empirical verification of his ideas (1984: 281–354).

Critics have often made reference to research in order to attack one of the main features of the concept: namely Giddens' view of structure as both enabling and constraining. In criticizing Smith's application of the theory of structuration to beef production, Bhaskar sought to distinguish his own transformation model from Giddens' structuration theory. In so doing he criticized Giddens' work for not giving enough significance to constraint and therefore not giving sufficient ontological status to the pre-existence of social forms (1983: 85). Many people have made a similar claim. Some have done so with a view to providing a slightly more deterministic account of the relationship between human agency and the social structure (for example Archer, 1982: 461; Carlstein, 1981: 52–3; Manicas, 1980), while others argue from the standpoint of an analytical antipathy to voluntarism (for example Callinicos, 1985; Carling, 1985: 111; Isaac, 1983; Layder, 1981, 1985). The issue under dispute is whether Giddens' account of constraint overemphasizes voluntarism and makes the constraints on agency too weak. Two claims are implied here: that Giddens' account fails to capture the power of the constraint operating on agency; and that unless 'structure' is conceptualized as analytically separate from 'agency', the constraining nature of social structures will never be captured. The second claim (which presupposes the first) refers to an epistemological disagreement, but the first (which does not necessarily entail the second) is the more serious for any assessment of Giddens' conceptualization; and it is more open to empirical examination.[7]

Other criticisms refer to the concept's disjuncture with other concepts in the theory of structuration, especially to the notions of time–space and of the unintended consequences of human conduct. Shotter (1983) describes time as the 'forgotten dimension' in Giddens' work, although Archer was more correct when she criticized Giddens for having too static a view of time (1982). By this Archer means that Giddens does not successfully demonstrate how structuration occurs across time. Again two claims seem presupposed here. The first is Giddens' failure to show how patterns of social life are reproduced across time–space as a result of past human agency and come to simultaneously constrain future agency. The second is a failure to show how time–space, and senses thereof, become variables to be reproduced by human agency and are themselves used in subsequent agency.[8] These criticisms also raise issues of research, for while Giddens might not have provided empirical demonstrations of this, his ideas are able to be put to the test in research. This is also the case with the claim that Giddens does not demonstrate the dynamic role of the unintended consequences of human conduct in structuration. It is feasible for research to show how the unintended consequences of human action are reproduced over time and themselves become a constraint and enablement to future agency.[9]

The former Fascists

Between 1973 and 1976 the author undertook a series of interviews over several meetings with fifteen former members of the BUF. The data from the interviews have been used to explore many issues about Sir Oswald Mosley's peculiar brand of Fascism (Brewer, 1981, 1984a, 1984b). The interviews were partly designed to elicit the respondents' account of why they joined the movement and this aspect of the data has been used to give a sociological account of the membership of the movement (Brewer, 1980, 1984a: part 1, 1984c). In this respect the former Fascists were, in ethnomethodological terms, 'doing' life history as an ordinary practical accomplishment, or, as Hadden and Lester (1978) put it, they were 'talking identity' (also see Atkinson, 1985). All such biographical accounts are retrospective and influenced by the passage of time and by what Schutz calls attentional modifications. Garfinkel's study of Agnes' account of her life history shows the accomplishment to be indexical and closely tied to the situations of the accounting (1967: 116–85). The life histories of the former Fascists are unusual because they are more retrospective than most and more indexically conditioned by the time–space differences between their membership and the occasions of their account. The awareness among the Fascists of this time–space difference, and the change in meaning which being a Fascist has undergone as a result of it, is a fundamental feature of their accomplishment of a life history and has to be made central to any analysis.

The former Fascists were what Giddens calls 'knowledgeable agents' and their accomplishment of a life history can be usefully applied to his concept of the 'duality of structure' to both empirically verify his view of the recursive relationship between 'agency' and 'structure' and provide empirical evidence to engage in debate with critics of the concept. As a summary, what lies at the heart of this is the awareness among the former Fascists of the changed meaning which Fascism now has and the modern implications of being a former Fascist. These changes in meaning are the unintended consequence of past human agency, primarily by Fascists. This agency has become objectified over time–space into common-sense knowledge (what Giddens calls mutual knowledge), which now contains pejorative typifications and idealizations of Fascism and Fascists. These typifications have also become reproduced into a whole range of common-sense rules of thumb, recipes, formulae, and institutional practices towards the treatment of Fascists. While these objectified typifications and practices embody past agency, they also function to constrain the former Fascists in the accomplishment of a life history. These constraints simultaneously become a feature of and enable-

ment to the accomplishment. This leads to the reproduction or structuration over time–space of the very common-sense world the former
Fascists drew on in the accomplishment of their life histories.

The accomplishment of a life history

First it is necessary to outline the nature of the former Fascists'
accomplishment (for greater detail see Brewer, 1984c). When looking back on their membership former members of the BUF are
consciously aware of the holocaust, genocide, and brutality now
associated with Fascism. As one remarked, 'There was nothing
wrong with Fascism at the time. German beating up of Jews, the
horrors of Nazism, gave Fascism a bad name.' Political scientists have
complained that as a political label Fascism has been so misused that
it has lost its original meaning. But whether in political rhetoric,
humour, song, folk mythology, or everyday language, 'Fascism' is a
term of denigration and abuse. It has become associated with violence, hatred, racism, persecution, and atrocity. Interviews conducted for the original research with respondents who were not
members of the BUF give us access to their common-sense typifications of Fascism. They remarked: 'To me Fascism, anti-Semitism,
anti-colour are all part of the same thing'; 'Mosley was a waste of
time. British people, like all those with British traditions, would not
stand for dictatorship. It is not bred in them like Germans'; 'supporting the BUF would be like supporting Germany'. These unfavourable typifications not only pervade those who lived through the
period, but have been transmitted to younger generations through
the processes by which common-sense knowledge is learnt. Interviews with a group of fifth-formers in a small rural comprehensive
school threw up the following descriptions of Fascism. Fascism was
seen as: 'torture'; 'it means cruel and vicious'; 'torture and death';
'the word means to me the death of millions of Jews'; 'it means the
bad and ruthless people of Germany'.

The typifications of Fascists as types of people share these characteristics. Fascists are often seen as psychopaths, authoritarian personalities, rabid anti-Semites, cranks, and freaks who were attracted by
the discipline, the appeal of the cosh and castor oil, and by the
excitement of weapons, flag-waving and gang camaraderie. The interviews with non-members contained the following remarks about
Fascists: 'They were brash young men – bully types'; 'not very well
versed in parliamentary democracy'; 'hangers-on and strong-arm
thugs'; 'the majority came from people who wanted a scrap'. To one
schoolchild a Fascist was 'a person who said one thing and meant
another'. Other schoolchildren said that a Fascist was 'a wicked and

cruel man'; 'a man who wanted to rule the world'; 'he wanted to cause war'; 'he was clever and cunning – an evil man who enjoyed power and would go to any lengths to get it'; 'he was mad'; 'he was mad, he wanted to kill people for nothing, like the Jews'. One could go on but it is clear that the common-sense typifications which appear in common-sense knowledge associate Fascism and Fascists with evil, dictatorship, murder, brutality, hatred, irrationality, madness, power mania, ruthlessness, and, above all, with death and war.

These common-sense typifications do not just remain as thought categories but become embodied, as Schutz indicated, in action. For example, they become rendered or, as Knorr-Cetina says, represented in a whole range of recipes, formulae, rules of thumb, and institutional practices for the treatment of, behaviour towards and assessment of Fascism and Fascists. These institutional practices include, for example, the unfavourable media and film portrayal of Fascism and Fascists. Such fictional portrayals are valid indicators because they are not an invention *ex nihilo* but are generated from within common-sense knowledge. The typifications are also reflected in such institutional practices as the internment of Fascists during the Second World War, preventing them from joining the armed forces, banning the wearing of the Fascist uniform, not encouraging ex-members of the BUF who did fight in the war to join British Legion branches, and throwing them out when their membership of the BUF is discovered. They are also reflected, for example, in the practice of political parties using connections with Mosley to discredit the candidature of ex-members now standing for other parties. As one former Fascist remarked: 'As my wife and I are now respectable socialist councillors we would not wish to draw attention to ourselves in this connection. When I fought for the Labour Party in 1964 the Liberals used my connection with the Mosley lot in a leaflet and it has been used in local elections. I have no idea how the information got to these people. You can use my services in any way that will not give me troublesome explanations to make.'

This remark is indicative of how aware ex-Fascists are of the modern connotations of their membership. One member was keen to emphasize that 'Fascism could be divided into elements, the "toughs" and the "genuines" – the toughs, Hitler, and the genuines, Mosley and Mussolini. There was nothing wrong with Fascism at the time.' The views of the fifteen are perhaps best summed up in the words of one former member, who at the time of his interview was a Conservative councillor in Birmingham: 'Fascism is only a dirty word because of public misunderstanding.' In asking the former Fascists to look back on their membership and the reasons lying behind it, they were forced to confront these typifications and the practices associated with them. The statements of the former members all express an unhappy dialectic between their varying biographical situations, which were seen as leading them towards the BUF, and the pejorative typifications and practices which now surround Fascism and Fascists. In this way they became concerned to present themselves as rational beings in face of the irrationality commonsensically associated with their membership and support. This required them to set their actions as supporters and members of the BUF into a rational sequence of means–ends. This was achieved through the notion of crisis: they presented their personal biographies as involving a tremendous crisis which made their membership of the BUF a rational and pragmatic decision.

The connection between their support for the BUF and the perception of a crisis was mentioned by all respondents. As one thought, 'We lived in an age of crisis and selfless efforts were needed to save our country. The BUF came into being because of a social and economic crisis.' Another said, 'In a sense Britain was in acute danger. To me it seemed that the BUF was determined to act as a modern Saint George.' The BUF's prospective parliamentary candidate for Evesham expressed this theme as follows. 'Yes my support was connected with a crisis which I summed up as "all is finished". I was aware of the many lick-spitting pawns ready to follow the history of the annihilated empires.' On looking back at his membership as a young Catholic schoolboy in Birmingham, one said, 'Mosley saw the crisis facing the nation in dark times . . . he had seen the way in which the existing parties had proved unable to cope with the great crisis.' However, their views on what Britain needed to be saved from varied dramatically. The dangers included poverty, unemployment, bad housing, agricultural decline, the threat to the empire, international finance, usury, Jews, communism, political ineptitude and the 'old gang' of outdated politicians. The nature of the crisis varies because although the perception of a crisis is common, the nature of that crisis is determined by the member's personal biographical situation.

The respondents' emphasis on crisis presents Fascism as the last chance, the only means of hope for themselves and for Britain. Their unique biographical situation led them to commonsensically perceive Britain to be in a state of severe crisis which only the BUF could solve. In view of the common-sense typifications now surrounding Fascism, they saw their biographical situation as one which made their membership of the BUF a rational and pragmatic decision. No emotion, blood lust, pride, hatred, irrationality, power mania, or madness entered their decision; it was a rational sequence of means–ends. One respondent spoke of the selfless sacrifices that he was aware his decision to join would impose.

I did not join before 1938 because I had felt immature on the thousand and one philosophies and meanings of life. My readings had not been completed and I was not prepared to fully sacrifice the good way of life for one which I knew would change things for the rest of my life ... my support was connected with a crisis ... strong and constructive decisions stem from the agony not the peace of mind.

A year earlier he expressed this notion in a similar way.

I joined only after I had spent many months giving profound thought to the new role which I was prepared to play in life and which meant completely sacrificing the old way of social living, popularity and acceptance by all those following selfish endeavours.

For him, therefore, there was reason in being a Fascist.[10] In this way the theme of crisis seems to represent what Phillipson and Cicourel call a 'basic rule' (see Phillipson, 1972: 148). That is, a basic resource or process which people employ in their accomplishment and construction of everyday practical activities. In this instance, the theme of crisis comprised the interpretative process used by the respondents to make sense of their membership of the BUF and to sustain its rationality.

The 'duality of structure' embedded in doing life history

As Giddens notes, to offer an account of one's actions is both to explicate the reasons for them and to supply the normative grounds whereby they may be justified (1984: 30). This was what the former Fascists were doing in emphasizing the theme of crisis in the account of their life history. It was the means by which they normatively justified their actions in view of the pejorative typifications and practices associated with Fascism and Fascists. As knowledgeable agents the former Fascists were able to monitor reflexively their actions across time–space and display this monitoring when discursively elaborating upon their actions. In this regard they were able to monitor reflexively the unintended consequences of past conduct by Fascists, including themselves, and monitor how this past agency had become transformed and reproduced into a series of pejorative common-sense typifications and idealizations, and into a number of rules, recipes, formulae, and institutional practices which are predicated on these typifications. The theme of crisis was the outcome of this reflexive monitoring and simultaneously the medium by which the monitoring was discursively expressed.

This process relates to the concept of the 'duality of structure', and the debate surrounding it, in a number of ways. First, it demonstrates that there is no inconsistency between Giddens' emphasis on the knowledgeability of actors and the idea that action can have unintended consequences. The former Fascists were able to monitor reflexively their action in a knowledgeable manner and incorporate it with their awareness of the unintended consequences of the past agency of Fascists. Secondly, time and space themselves were variables in this reflexive monitoring. This is meant in a stronger sense than merely that the former Fascists were accounting for and monitoring their past agency from a later and different time–space location. It is meant in the sense that the former Fascists were aware of how time–space differences altered the connotations of their past agency and that they made these time–space differences the essential feature of their discursive accounts. That is, time–space, and senses thereof, were being used by the former Fascists as dynamic elements in the accomplishment of a life history. Thirdly, and above all, this accomplishment shows how the recursive relationship between human agency and social structure can be made tangible and concrete. The common-sense typifications of Fascists as 'killers', 'mad', 'power crazy', 'irrational', and so on, and the rules, recipes, formulae, and institutional practices predicated on them, represent the objectification of the past human agency of Fascists. This objectification results in 'structure' in Giddens' sense, in that the common-sense typifications become embodied as rules, recipes, formulae, and institutional practices for the behaviour towards and assessment of Fascists. This objectification reflects and reinforces the typifications. More important, 'structure' in this sense is itself recursively related to the Fascists' agency.

We can begin to demonstrate this by reference to Garfinkel and Cicourel's equivalent for the Schutzian term 'typification', which is 'oral dictionary' and 'descriptive vocabulary' (see Cicourel, 1972: 56–8, 61). Garfinkel and Cicourel have argued that descriptive vocabularies and oral dictionaries are used by members of the common-sense world to handle bodies of information and activities, and that the vocabulary itself becomes a constituent part of the experience or activity being described by it (Cicourel, 1972: 61). That is, descriptive vocabularies are reflexive: they index the experience but at the same time the experience acquires elements of the descriptive vocabulary as part of the generative and transformative process the experience undergoes when it is being handled. This is also a characteristic of the common-sense typifications of Fascists. For those who are a party to this common-sense knowledge, such vocabulary as 'mad', 'power crazy', 'irrational' and so on, and the behaviour it presupposes, are a constituent part of the experiences of Fascism and Fascists which it describes, and come to influence descriptions of future encounters and experiences of Fascism or Fascists.

This objectification of past agency into a series of pejorative typifications, vocabularies, and practices constitutes a constraint upon former Fascists when they accomplish life history.[11] They are forced to confront and challenge them directly in order to show their membership was a rational sequence of means–ends. This was achieved through the notion of crisis. But simultaneously the constraints embedded in this objectification are a medium through which the accomplishment of the life history is organized. The constraints become an enablement because they provide both the experiences which the former Fascists had to confront and take into account, and the principle by which the life history is organized as a practical achievement. The constraints therefore functioned as a resource, a strategic tool, which the former Fascists drew on in 'doing' their life histories. Thus this accomplishment involves both the creative and knowledgeable qualities of human agency and the constraining nature of structuring properties like common-sense rules, recipes, formulae, and institutional practices. Accordingly, if 'structure' is employed in Giddens' sense as binding or structuring properties, like rules, resources, and institutional practices, and if 'structure' becomes embodied in the rules, resources, and institutional practices that both govern and reflect other people's knowledgeability of, treatment of, views about, vocabulary for, practice towards and typifications of Fascism and Fascists, then the 'agency' involved in the former Fascists 'doing' life history simultaneously evinces 'structure'.

This accomplishment of life history, which manifests the 'duality of structure', also leads to structuration over time–space. By transforming elements of the institutional practices towards and the common-sense typifications of Fascists into the theme of crisis, the former members of the BUF reproduced the very characteristics of the wider common-sense world they drew on in their accomplishment. They did so in two ways. First, by negatively invoking these common-sense typifications, and the practices embodying them, as a constraint, the former Fascists helped to create both the facticity of these typifications and practices and the sense that they are real and deterministic (see Giddens, 1984: 330ff, where he discusses similar research). Secondly, as an unintended consequence of this negative invocation, the former BUF members reproduced the view that Fascists are 'crazy', 'irrational', 'mad' and so on. Their view that Britain was in such a state of crisis and under threat from world communism, Zionism or whatever, seems to reinforce, from everyone's point of view but their own, the common-sense typifications of Fascists as 'mad' and 'crazy' and so on. Therefore they help to reproduce the very rules, recipes, formulae, and institutional practices towards Fascists which are predicated on these common-sense typifications.[12] That is, 'structure', in Giddens' sense, is reproduced over time–

space. One further point can be stressed. Inasmuch as these typifications and practices are the unintended consequence of past agency by Fascists and they get reproduced partly in an unintended fashion, the notion of the unintended consequences of action can be empirically seen to be a dynamic element in structuration over time–space.

The data relate to the debate about power in several ways. It is a commonplace in many conceptualizations of power that power does not just adhere to people or institutions, but also to ideas, knowledge, and beliefs. This is as true for common-sense knowledge as for more rational and scientific ideas. Schutz continually implies that common-sense knowledge possesses power, while Berger and Luckmann directly address this when they argue that power in society includes the power to produce (and reproduce) social reality; and the employment and transmission of common-sense knowledge is a major process by which they see this (re)production being achieved (1979: 137). It is less of a commonplace to argue that power is an essential component of all agency and does not need observable conflict or clashes of interest in order to be manifest. Giddens' theory of structuration contends that power is inextricably a part of all action because, when agency is defined in Giddens' terms as the capability of agents to have acted otherwise, power provides agents with the resources – material and mental – by which they are capable of acting otherwise. The constraints imposed on others as a result of this capability are, however, not experienced by them as simply forms of domination requiring submission, but also as an enablement to their subsequent agency. Accordingly, power is also an integral part of the concept of the 'duality of structure', by which agency is linked to structure. This is because Giddens perceives relations of domination and autonomy, which are characteristic of power differences, to be reproduced in interaction and as having the effect of binding subsequent interaction across time–space.

The qualitative data presented here show that the common-sense knowledge surrounding former Fascists possessed power over the former members of the BUF, which was experienced by them as a constraint when they accomplished their life histories. However, they did not blindly submit to the power embedded in these common-sense typifications, but used them as a strategic resource to organize both the accomplishment of their life history as a practical achievement and its discursive formulation. The power of common-sense knowledge was experienced as a constraint and as an enablement, confirming Giddens' arguments about the 'dialectic of control'. 'Power' was therefore itself reproduced in interaction and came to influence the subsequent interaction of the Fascists across time–space. The case of the former Fascists demonstrates, then, that power is linked with agency and reproduced in interaction, as well as illustrating how power is experienced by people and used by them at the level of their micro-interactions.

The ethnomethodological and phenomenological backdrop to the 'duality of structure'

It is not the intention of this chapter to assess whether Giddens' concept of structure is ontologically correct, only to demonstrate empirically that what he calls structure does have a Janus aspect which can be seen operating in micro-episodes of social life. However, an issue which this focus does raise is how innovative this recursive conceptualization is. The data presented here, in fact, can illustrate how Giddens' emphasis on the recursive relationship between 'agency' and 'structure', which is the chief distinguishing feature of the 'duality of structure', is anticipated in the work of Schutz. In distinguishing his arguments from interpretative sociology, Giddens provides a misleading view, for he implies that interpretative sociology sees society as simply the creation of the individual (1984: xxi), without this construction imposing any form of constraint on subsequent agency (1984: 2; also see Manicas, 1980: 68). While he recognizes there are exceptions to this within interpretative sociology, the exceptions go without comment or elaboration (1984: 2). This view that interpretative sociology underscores constraint and structure is commonly held (for an overview of the criticism see Armstrong, 1979). There is some justification for it because the empirical research of early ethnomethodologists failed to specify the constraint imposed on members in the act of doing everyday life (a classic example is Leiter, 1976), and thus was unable to grasp how this constraint is itself an embodiment of human agency. This is epitomized in Garfinkel's claim that ethnomethodology suspends belief in society as an objective reality except as it appears, and is accomplished in and through the everyday activities of members themselves (discussed by Psathas, 1980: 6). There is no suggestion in this claim that these accomplishments are recursive or constraining. On the other hand, there are passages in Garfinkel's early work where he comes close to discussing recursiveness and constraint, especially in his outline of indexicality and reflexivity, which are concepts which presuppose these qualities. These are not points missed by those contemporary ethnomethodologists who have become interested in the concept of structure (for example see Maynard and Wilson, 1980: 298–9).

In contrast, the work of Schutz contains an earlier and more explicit account of the recursive relationship between society and human agency. The basis of this is Schutz' notion of 'factual reality'. Because common-sense knowledge is a public knowledge composed of shared typifications, recipes, idealizations, and other schemes of experience which members assume to be common, the common-sense world takes on a certain 'standardized sameness' (compare Collins, 1981: 989) and thus constitutes itself vis-à-vis the individual as a 'factual reality' (for an overview, see Brewer, 1984d). This is what Gellner meant when he said that people think in holistic terms. For Schutz the factual, objective, and external character of the common-sense world is seen to reside in the members' use of seemingly anonymous, factual, and abstract thought and speech categories, and in the assumptions members thereby make about the 'interchangeability of stances' and the 'reciprocity of perspectives' in the common-sense world (see Rogers, 1981: 139–43). Garfinkel's breaching experiments illustrate that these are assumptions which members of everyday life make (1967: 55ff). All these are familiar arguments and recur, in one form or another, in Garfinkel and Cicourel. On this basis it seems possible to refute the claim made by O'Keefe (1979; also Psathas, 1980) that there is a disjuncture between the versions of ethnomethodology in Cicourel and Garfinkel. This difference is said to lie in the fact that Cicourel offers a Schutzian account focusing on the cognitive processes and interpretative procedures that are embedded in action and which lie behind the emergence and use of 'basic' and 'surface' rules in society, while Garfinkel is said to be less Schutzian in his emphasis on the accomplishment of facticity through conversational practices and methods (O'Keefe, 1979: 193). Irrespective of whether this is an accurate assessment of their work there is no incompatibility between them. As Schutz makes clear in his account of language (1982), such features of talk are an integral part of practical common-sense reasoning. He points out that it is through language use and the employment of anonymous and abstract speech categories that members partly develop a sense of the social structure or 'factual reality'. The case of the former Fascists shows that the cognitive processes and interpretative procedures which Cicourel emphasizes, such as typifications and their embodiment in action, are fundamentally linked to the accomplishment of talking identity, which itself helps to regenerate the facticity of the common-sense world.

However, the essential feature of these arguments in phenomenology and ethnomethodology is that the factual character of the social world does not, as Giddens believes (1984: 25), constitute itself as a reification. For Schutz the factual world has a stronger ontological basis than merely people's sense that there is a social structure. He makes clear that anonymous thought and speech categories become objectified in action and come to impose constraints upon action. Cicourel, who is most closely identified with the notion of members' sense of social structure, also discussed how this sense leads to constraints (1972: 62, 1981; compare with Garfinkel, 1967: 76ff). According to Schutz this constraint lies in the fact that typifications and other cognitive processes and interpretative procedures are constituted from and applied through experience and action, while these experiences and actions come to embody the typifications used to apprehend them, thus constraining future descriptions and categorizations of experiences and actions (see Natanson, 1970; Rogers, 1981: 139). He emphasizes that common-sense typifications and the practices which embody them become 'givens' which are utilized or confronted by human agents. So they become what Giddens calls 'structural constraints' (1984: 176). This constraining quality was referred to by Schutz when he said that the world of experience is a typified and pre-constituted world: the common-sense world is apprehended through the employment of typifications which pervade common-sense knowledge whose use simultaneously endows the common-sense world with coherence, facticity, and anonymity. This facticity, although it embodies agency, comes to constrain agency. Thus it is that Schutz emphasizes that the *Lebenswelt* has a dialectic character, partly given to us and partly constructed by us on the basis of the givens and our biographical situation. This conceptualization has been referred to as Schutz' 'dual vision' (Gorman, 1976), and is what Giddens means by recursiveness. The objectively given world and the subjectively constructed world are experienced simultaneously, so that the typifications employed in subjectively constructing the world reproduce at one and the same time the anonymity and factual character of the world (emphasized by Berger and Luckmann, 1979).[13]

Arguments like these in Schutz, and to a lesser extent in Garfinkel and Cicourel, constitute a backdrop against which Giddens developed his concept of the 'duality of structure'. Therefore Giddens' innovativeness tends to lie in other areas of the theory of structuration. He himself thinks it is found in his incorporation of unintended consequences with the reflexive character of agency;[14] and there is some justification for arguing that interpretative sociology has ignored the phenomenon of unintended consequences.

Conclusion

It can be argued that it is no surprise that the ex-BUF members talk about their pasts in the way described, and that any theory of human action that could not accommodate what they have to say is inadequate. Two criticisms are implied by this view. First, if all theories of human action could and need to account for the Fascists' discourse, the arguments in this chapter cannot be an empirical test of Giddens' theory as a whole for it is not placed against competing theories and explanations. However, the intentions of the chapter have not been that ambitious. More modestly the arguments do show that what the Fascists had to say about their pasts is consistent with Giddens' concept of the 'duality of structure', and is therefore inconsistent with the critics of the concept who claim that it is untestable in empirical research and does not in concrete situations link with other concepts in the theory of structuration. None the less the data also indicate that their discourse can be accounted for by using the work of Schutz and Garfinkel, which does allow one to say that at least Giddens' concept of the 'duality of structure' can be subsumed within other theories.[15] Secondly, if it is the case that the Fascists could be expected to recast their biography, the arguments here become immune to falsification. However, former Fascists who have to live with their past involvements have a variety of options. They can simply remain hidden and avoid having to reveal and hence recast their past; admit shame, express sorrow, and claim they deserve whatever pejorative evaluation they are given; take pleasure and pride in the evaluation; or, as was the case here, try to confront the evaluation by placing their involvement in a rational sequence of means–ends.[16] The first choice precludes research, but it is feasible for groups of self-selected Fascist respondents to contain those who have taken any of the remaining options. Accordingly, the nature and content of the former Fascists' discourse about their past is problematic and is not to be expected and taken for granted.

There are two levels to the account that is offered here. At one level, the empirical data explore the attempt by former members of the BUF to look back at Fascism and the reasons for their membership. On another level the data present their attempt to do life history as a practical, everyday accomplishment. It is on this plane that the data illustrate the structural component that exists at the level of people's micro-experiences and actions. The accomplishment of this life history was a knowledgeable, reflexive, and creative act of agency on the part of the former Fascists, yet was simultaneously organized and enabled by a component which confronted them as something external and constraining, but which embedded, in an unintended fashion, past human agency.

However, two caveats need to be mentioned. Whether or not we call this component 'structure', as Giddens does, depends on the epistemological preferences that influence our definition of the term. The case of the former Fascists does not provide empirical evidence to enter that debate. Moreover, it seems that the case study is particularly apposite to Giddens' view of the 'duality of structure'. The former Fascists are untypical in several ways. Not everyone engages in the same retrospective recounting of their past, although it is done frequently in certain situations, such as interviews and encounters with strangers. But not everyone who does this has time–space differences that impose such a constraint. This tends only to be the case with stigmatized groups like Fascists. Finally the Fascist respondents on which this study is based were a self-selected group who wished to directly confront these time–space differences. Thus, neither are Fascists typical of all those who engage in retrospective recounting of their biography, nor are these particular respondents representative of all former members of the BUF. Therefore the chapter remains neutral on the question whether the data 'prove' that recursive duality is a universal feature which is empirically demonstrable in other areas.

Notes

The author thanks Roy Wallis and Steven Yearley for comments on an earlier draft, and Barry Hindess, Wes Sharrock, Robert Dingwall, Christie Davies and Karin Knorr-Cetina for a lively discussion on Giddens' work at the Surrey conference.

1. This analytical separation is also true of what Knorr-Cetina calls the 'hypothesis of unintended consequences', which argues that 'macro' and 'structural' phenomena emerge as an unintended consequence of micro-episodes (1981: 27). Only if this relationship between society and agency is conceptualized as a recursive one, as it is, for example, in Giddens, does this analytical separation break down. I disagree with Knorr-Cetina when she describes Giddens' structuration theory as an example of the 'hypothesis of unintended consequences'. I see it as coming within what she calls the 'representation hypothesis'.

2. Maynard and Wilson do suggest that people make the social structure seem real in and through their talk, which is not necessarily to claim that social structures emerge in and through our talk. Using the work of Sacks they argue that people talk as if there are structures (1980: 299, 304). Schutz also showed how the facticity of the social world is partly created and reinforced through language (1982; also see Atkinson, 1982; Collins, 1981: 1000), but he emphasized that society has a stronger ontological status than merely people's sense that society is real. This will be returned to further below.

3. Bhaskar, however, is keen to distinguish his work from that of Giddens (see Bhaskar, 1983).

4. According to Giddens, reasons are the grounds given for the action, while motives are what prompts the action. Reasons can be discursively accounted but motives cannot (1984: 2–6).

5. Giddens does not define institutions as organizations but as enduring patterns of behaviour which exist across time–space (1984: 24). He defines rules in a way which is similar to Schutz's notion of recipe: rules are simply formulae to be followed in order to achieve an end result (1984: 20–1). However, they have a 'constitutive' and 'regulative' aspect (for a similar conception of rules, see Hund, 1982).

6. This is a criticism which can be made against Maynard and Wilson (1980), who do not mention constraint in their outline of 'reflexive determination'.

7. Some people make the reverse claim that Giddens puts too much emphasis on constraint (see Dallmayr, 1982).

8. Compare this with Collins, who considers time one of only three genuine macro-variables (1981: 989ff).

9. However, Giddens does discuss Willis' work on 'the lads' (1977), in which Giddens uses Willis' ethnography to show how the lads' behaviour in school helped to reproduce, in an unintended manner, the wider working-class culture which they drew on in being lads (1984: 298–304). Giddens does not emphasize that the agency of the lads leads in an unintended manner to low teacher expectation of lads, which acts both as a form of constraint on the lads' behaviour in school and as an enablement. It is an enablement because it produces the climate, system of rules and institutional framework within which they can realize being lads vis-à-vis 'ear 'oles' and teachers. The constraints imposed by teachers' expectations become a means by which lads distinguish themselves from others, which in turn is an enablement to being a lad.

10. This account of the Fascists' accomplishment is a second-order construct in both Schutz' and Giddens' sense, but it has been constructed from face-to-face interviews with the subjects of the investigation. In this way it satisfies what Schutz calls the postulate of adequacy, which is the process by which Schutz sees second-order constructs being phenomenologically validated. The postulate requires that the construct be understandable to the actors and be expressed in terms used by them in their common-sense knowledge. The lengthy quotations presented in the text have been necessary to demonstrate that the account has been expressed in the terms the former Fascists used themselves. The quotations have also been deliberately chosen to offer a selection from various meetings with the former members of the BUF in which the crisis model was discussed with them and repeated by them in their own terms. In this way the account is a construct of the actual common-sense first-order constructs used by the former Fascists in their everyday life. The question whether the respondents were lying can be posed. The issue of whether the statements of the former members can be taken as a reliable indicator of what happened at the time of their membership is irrelevant to the analysis. It would be so only if the intention was to engage in oral history. With the approach adopted here, the issue is whether their statements can be taken as a reliable external indicator of their glance back at their membership. Given that the author did not share the same life-world as the Fascists, in a spatial, temporal, or political sense, it was impossible to engage in the meaning-construction-through-interpretation process which Schutz says ego can undertake to understand alter from ego's point of view. Therefore, the analysis is forced to rely on the veracity of their statements alone. However, the bias from *ex post facto* rationalization is not a problem, for the point of the study is to show that they did confront the pejorative typifications of Fascism and this bias is itself a resource which the analysis attempts to study.

11. These common-sense typifications and the practices which embody them are constraints in two of the three senses that Giddens gives the term constraint (1984: 174–9). They are structural constraints in that while they still derive from the situated nature of social action they confront Fascists as givens and thus constrain and bind their agency (1984: 176). They are also negative sanctions in that they have a punitive element embedded in them (1984: 176).

12. Further empirical research could easily establish this reproduction by asking non-members their views of the Fascists' emphasis on this dark foreboding crisis. Unfortunately the original interviews did not do this, so this claim is not being

supported by empirical evidence. It is also important to note the role of the researcher in this reproduction. The interviewer helped reproduce the common-sense world by asking them their reasons for joining, thus imposing on them in the interview situation the very constraints which they had to confront. Usually this 'interviewer effect' is seen as a form of bias, but for interpretative sociology it confirms the indexical nature of the accomplishment of life history and the need to treat phenomena as collaborative accomplishments.

13. Schutz therefore does have a conception of society as 'real' and 'deterministic'. This has been a source of criticism and many have claimed that Schutz's social phenomenology is socially over-deterministic (for example, Gorman, 1976; Thomason, 1982; for an overview, see Brewer, 1984c). However, the case of the former Fascists shows that this so-called over-determinism is an accurate reflection of empirical reality.

14. This view is contained in a personal communication to the author and repeated elsewhere (see Giddens, 1983).

15. To say that two ideas are consistent is not necessarily to say that they are closely related or identical. With this in mind it is also possible to argue that the 'duality of structure' is implicit in the equilibrium feedback mechanism in economics, where decisions by agents about supply and demand come to have a constraining quality on the subsequent agency of consumers and producers, while simultaneously reproducing 'the market' in which these decisions were made.

16. It can be claimed that the 'rationality' of the Fascists is assured either way: either they recast their biography in such a way that it appears rational, or they do not, thus making their beliefs and discourse consistent, which can be taken to be one feature of rationality. I think the Fascists saw the rationality of their acts and their account of them lying in other areas than consistency. Even so this is not a problem for the explanation, for it only serves to show how the meaning of the term 'rationality' is indexical and contingent and how 'rationality' is itself a practical accomplishment of people.

References

Archer, M. (1982) 'Morphogenesis versus Structuration', *British Journal of Sociology*, 33.

Armstrong, E.G. (1979) 'Phenomenologophobia', *Human Studies*, 2.

Atkinson, J.M. (1982) 'Understanding Formality: The Categorization and Production of "Formal Interaction"', *British Journal of Sociology*, 33.

Atkinson, P. (1985) 'Talk and Identity: Some Convergences in Micro Sociology', in H.J. Helle and S.N. Eisenstadt (eds), *Micro-sociological Theory*. London: Sage.

Berger, P. and Luckmann, T. (1979) *The Social Construction of Reality*. Harmondsworth, Middx: Penguin.

Bhaskar, R. (1979), *The Possibility of Naturalism*, Brighton: Harvester Press.

Bhaskar, R. (1983) 'Beef, Structure and Place: Notes from a Critical Naturalist Perspective', *Journal for the Theory of Social Behaviour*, 13.

Brewer, J.D. (1980) 'The BUF: Some Tentative Conclusions on its Membership', in S. Larsen, B. Hagtvet and J. Myklebust (eds), *Who Were the Fascists?* Bergen: Norwegian Universities Press.

Brewer, J.D. (1981) 'The BUF in Birmingham', *West Midland Studies*, 14.

Brewer, J.D. (1984a) *Mosley's Men: The BUF in the West Midlands*. Aldershot: Gower.

Brewer, J.D. (1984b) 'The BUF and Anti-Semitism in Birmingham', *Midland History*, 9.

Brewer, J.D. (1984c) 'Looking Back at Fascism: A Phenomenological Analysis of BUF Membership', *Sociological Review*, 32.

Brewer, J.D. (1984d) 'Competing Understandings of Common Sense Understanding: A Brief Comment on "Common Sense Racism"', *British Journal of Sociology*, 35.

Callinicos, A. (1985) 'Anthony Giddens – A Contemporary Critique', *Theory and Society*, 14

Carling, A. (1985) 'Rational Choice Marxism'. Department of Interdisciplinary Human Studies, University of Bradford (mimeo).

Carlstein, T. (1981) 'The Sociology of Structuration in Time and Space: A Time-Geographic Assessment of Giddens' Theory', *Swedish Geographical Yearbook*. Lund: Lund University Press.

Cicourel, A. (1972) *Cognitive Sociology*. Harmondsworth, Middx: Penguin.

Cicourel, A. (1981) 'Notes on the Integration of Micro–macro Levels of Analysis', in K. Knorr-Cetina and A. Cicourel (eds), *Advances in Social Theory and Methodology*. London: Routledge & Kegan Paul.

Collins, R. (1981) 'On the Micro Foundations of Macro Sociology', *American Journal of Sociology*, 86.

Dallmayr, F. (1982) 'Rejoinder to Giddens', in A. Giddens, *Profiles and Critiques in Social Theory*. London: Macmillan.

Garfinkel, H. (1967) *Studies in Ethnomethodology*. Englewood Cliffs, NJ: Prentice-Hall.

Giddens, A. (1976) *New Rules of Sociological Method*. London: Hutchinson.

Giddens, A. (1977) *Studies in Social and Political Theory*. London: Hutchinson.

Giddens, A. (1979) *Central Problems in Social Theory*. London: Macmillan.

Giddens, A. (1981) *A Contemporary Critique of Historical Materialism*. London: Macmillan.

Giddens, A. (1982) 'Response to Dallmayr', in A. Giddens, *Profiles and Critiques in Social Theory*. London: Macmillan.

Giddens, A. (1983) 'Comments on the Theory of Structuration', *Journal for the Theory of Social Behaviour*, 13.

Giddens, A. (1984) *The Constitution of Society*. Cambridge: Polity.

Gorman, R. (1976) *The Dual Vision*. London: Routledge & Kegan Paul.

Hadden, S. and Lester, M. (1978) 'Talking Identity: The Production of "Self" in Interaction', *Human Studies*, 1.

Hund, J. (1982) 'Are Social Facts Real?' *British Journal of Sociology*, 33.

Isaac, J. (1983) 'Realism and Social Scientific Theories', *Journal for the Theory of Social Behaviour*, 13.

Knorr-Cetina, K. (1981) 'Introduction: The Micro-sociological Challenge of Macro-sociology – Towards a Reconstruction of Social Theory and Methodology', in K. Knorr-Cetina and A. Cicourel (eds), *Advances in Social Theory and Methodology: Toward an Integration of Micro- and Macro-sociologies*. London: Routledge & Kegan Paul.

Layder, D. (1981) *Structure, Interaction and Social Theory*. London: Routledge & Kegan Paul.

Layder, D. (1985) 'Power, Structure and Agency', *Journal for the Theory of Social Behaviour*, 15.

Leiter, K. (1976) 'Teachers' Use of Background Knowledge to Interpret Test Scores', *Sociology of Education*, 49.

Manicas, P. (1980) 'The Concept of Social Structure', *Journal for the Theory of Social Behaviour*, 10.

Maynard, D.W. and Wilson, T. (1980) 'On the Reification of Social Structure', in S. McNall and G. Howe (eds), *Current Perspectives in Social Theory*, vol. 1. Greenwich: JAI.

Natanson, M. (1970) 'Phenomenology and Typification', *Social Research*, 37.

O'Keefe, D. (1979) 'Ethnomethodology', *Journal for the Theory of Social Behaviour*, 9.

Phillipson, M. (1972) 'Phenomenological Philosophy and Sociology', in P. Filmer, M. Phillipson, D. Silverman and D. Walsh (eds), *New Directions in Social Theory*. London: Collier-Macmillan.

Psathas, G. (1980) 'Approaches to the Study of Everyday Life', *Human Studies*, 3.

Rogers, M. (1981) 'Taken for Grantedness', in S. McNall and G. Howe (eds), *Current Perspectives in Social Theory*, vol. 2. Greenwich: JAI.

Schutz, A. (1982) *Life Forms and Meaning Structures*. London: Routledge & Kegan Paul.

Shotter, J. (1983) '"Duality of Structure" and "Intentionality" in an Ecological Psychology', *Journal for the Theory of Social Behaviour*, 13.

Smith, C.W. (1983) 'The Duality of Structures, Structuration and the Intentionality of Human Action', *Journal for the Theory of Social Behaviour*, 13.

Thomason, B. (1982) *Making Sense of Reification*. London: Macmillan.

Willis, P. (1977) *Learning to Labour*. Farnborough: Saxon House.

7
INDIVIDUAL AND SOCIAL CONNECTIONS

The theoretical significance of recursiveness suggests that it is important to be able to establish interrelations within sets and sources of data. Q-analysis is a methodology that has been developed over the last decade and which is based on the theory of set mathematics. It is concerned with defining the interrelationships within a data set and offers the advantage that its holistic approach allows complex situations to be represented. A matrix is required in which the elements of one set are described by a second set of descriptions. A simple incidence matrix is evolved by deciding which element or 'simplex' in the first set has each of the descriptors in the second. From this binary relationship the connectivity between the simplices in the first set is defined. If the matrix is in non-binary form an appropriate slicing parameter is required. The first part of the analysis is the derivation of a shared-face matrix in which the connectivity with each simplex in the set and every other is calculated. From this the output of the q-connected components arises, that is, at each q-value, which simplices are q-connected.

These techniques are illustrated from two different data sets. In the first, q-factor weightings were studied in a matrix representing 183 patients and their ratings on each of 140 psychiatric symptoms. This analysis showed that the identified groups of patients and symptoms had clinical and diagnostic meaning. The second data set was a matrix of 250 Japanese companies and their shareholders. The groupings of companies and shareholders were found to throw new light on the formation of enterprise groups in Japan. Further questions are raised about how hierarchy is manifest in such data, and the relationship of hierarchy found in a mathematical sense to hierarchy in an ontological sense. Arguably, Q-analysis maps a model for the idea of reality itself, and this is considered along with the distinction between this and other forms of cluster analysis.

Individual and social connections
A perspective from the Q-analysis method

John Scott and Peter Cowley

The problem of relating the 'micro' and 'macro' levels in social research has generally been seen as the problem of constructing concepts of organized and collective action from concepts of individual action. Talcott Parsons, for example, tried to demonstrate the ways in which the 'social facts' described by Durkheim could be conceptualized as 'emergent properties of social action' (Parsons, 1937). The rival 'methodological individualist' position refuses to countenance such emergent properties, arguing that all social phenomena must be explained as predicates of individual action.[1] Giddens has recently proposed a convincing alternative to these opposing positions; an alternative which effectively dissolves the micro-to-macro problem. There is, argues Giddens a 'duality of structure': 'action' and 'structure' are not separate and distinct realms, but each implies and influences the other (Giddens, 1979, ch. 2).

For Giddens, 'micro' analysis merely involves a convenient focusing of attention on face-to-face interaction, and might more simply be described as situational analysis. 'Macro' analysis, on the other hand, focuses on institutional phenomena which cannot be reduced to immediate interactional terms. Each form of analysis involves a specific form of *methodological* bracketing, and should not be taken as implying an *ontological* dualism between distinct realms. The virtue of Giddens' rejection of this dualism is that it recognizes that there is a whole hierarchy of levels of analysis, of which the terms 'micro' and 'macro' pick out just two. Face-to-face situational analyses concern themselves with personal subjects and their strategic actions, and have generally failed to recognize that some of the collectivities (re)produced through their action may be regarded as collective subjects capable of strategic action. Such collective subjects have a decision-making apparatus and can act 'in their own right' in a way that is not true of those institutionalized collectivities which lack a decision-making apparatus. While business enterprises, trades unions, and departments of State, therefore, may be regarded as collective subjects, collectivities such as the working class and the British nation cannot. From this point of view the analysis of collective subjects lies 'between' that of personal subjects and that of institutionalized collectivities, and the actions of collective subjects are not easily dealt with by a sociology which is concerned only with micro- or macro-levels of analysis.

Our aim in this chapter is to discuss and illustrate a formal method of data analysis which is compatible with Giddens' perspective. It will be shown that data collected on individual units can yield information on the structure of relations among these units, and that this structure is a constraining influence upon the subsequent actions of those individual units. This will be illustrated with data from both personal subjects and collective subjects. From clinical data on psychiatric patients, for example, structures of symptoms and clusterings of patients can be discovered which have a clinical and diagnostic significance. From data on business enterprises it is possible to discover structures of intercorporate relations which constrain the possibilities that the enterprises have for the formation of coalitions and alliances, and which fundamentally influence the power relations between enterprises. The method of analysis which we have used – Q-analysis – is specifically designed for use with relational data, and it will be shown to have relevance to material as varied as national economic structures and personal mental constructs.

An outline of Q-analysis

Q-analysis has developed over the last ten years from its origins in set mathematics and algebraic topology. It is one of a range of approaches which are concerned with the 'holistic' or relational features of human data rather than with the aggregate or statistical analysis of individual attributes. The starting-point for all such relational approaches is the matrix of connections among the elements being studied, and Q-analysis aims to provide a language for describing the multidimensional geometry of this matrix.[2] The matrix consists of two sets of elements (which may be identical), and the cells show the presence or absence of a connection between the elements. Each element is regarded as a 'simplex', having a dimensionality which describes the nature of the space in which it is located. A pair of simplices connected by a single relation, for example, must be represented in one dimension. The dimensionality of a simplex is simply one less than its total number of connections, and is readily calculated from the incidence matrix. The network created by connected simplices is termed a simplicial complex, and the central concern of Q-analysis is to describe the structure of this complex. 'q' designates the dimensionality of simplices, relations, and complexes, and simplices are said to be 'q-near' and 'q-connected' to one another.

q-nearness reflects what graph theorists term the multiplicity of the line connecting two points: q-nearness is a measure of the dimensionality of the connection between two simplices. Thus, two elements with three features in common are connected by a relation of dimensionality two – they are 2-near. The initial step in Q-analysis is to construct a matrix of q-nearness from the initial incidence matrix, and it should be apparent that two such matrices can be derived from any incidence matrix. One matrix refers to the q-nearness of the first set of elements and the other to the second set, and thus each matrix is a square adjacency matrix.

Q-analysis, in its most basic form, proceeds to partition the matrices into components on the basis of their q-nearness. Elements are regarded as members of the same component at a specified level of q if they are connected by an unbroken chain of connections with that dimensionality. Thus, at $q = 2$, for example, a component will contain all those simplices which are connected to at least one other simplex by a connection of dimensionality two. It does not follow, however, that all members of the component will be linked to one another at this level: the members of a component are 'q-connected' but not necessarily 'q-near'. Two simplices (A and B), for example, may be joined by a relation of dimensionality two – they are 2-near – but they may each be joined to a third simplex (C) at dimensionality four. A, B, and C, therefore, comprise a component in which all members are 4-connected (A is connected to B at this level via its link with C). That is to say, q-connectedness takes account of direct and indirect links, while q-nearness takes account only of direct links.

A standard Q-analysis produces a structural model of nested components. A particular level of q-connectedness is chosen and the components which exist at that level are identified and listed. The level of q-connection is then reduced and the search for components is repeated: the intensely connected components of the first level are therefore regarded as embedded, or 'nested' within larger and less intensely connected components. Successive reductions of the level of q-connection, until a value of $q = 0$ is reached, will generate a complete analysis of component structure. The results can be visualized as a 'contour map' of the network of relations. The most closely linked elements form peaks in a range of hills and valleys, the size of each 'peak' increasing as the lower foothills of the range are approached. Q-analysis, therefore, generates a series of horizontal cross-sections through the multidimensional structure.

The standard Q-analysis identifies cut-off thresholds of connectedness on the basis of an absolute measure of intensity – the same cut-off point is used for all simplices – but a recent development of Q-analysis allows the use of a more sensitive measure of relative intensity. In this approach the cut-off threshold varies for each simplex, and components are identified on the basis of relations which are especially significant *from the standpoint of the simplices concerned.* It is assumed that those connections of above-average intensity for a simplex are more salient to it, and the mean connectivity of each simplex is thus used as the initial cut-off threshold: the simplex is regarded as unconnected to those other simplices with which its links are below this level of intensity. To produce a nested set of components a q-factor weighting is applied to the mean connectivities, this weighting being the same for all simplices and being progressively increased in each step of the analysis. With each increase in the weighting the components identified have a stronger level of internal connection, and their members have correspondingly weaker connections to outsiders. The relative intensity measure is, therefore, more sensitive to the existence of groups of elements which are relatively marginal to a larger component but have relatively close connections among themselves. It is sensitive, that is to say, to the subtle internal structural patterns of components.

Patients and their symptoms: a Q-analysis

Data on patients' symptoms were collected during the Leicestershire trial on electroconvulsive therapy. This was a double-blind trial examining the efficacy of ECT in a group of clinically selected patients (Brandon *et al.*, 1984). As part of the initial assessment prior to entering the trial patients were assessed on the Comprehensive Psychopathological Rating Scale (CPRS) (Asberg *et al.*, 1978). The CPRS is composed of sixty-five items broken down into a check-list of forty symptoms reported by the patient and twenty-five signs observed by the interviewer. Each item is rated on a four-point rating of 0–3 according to severity of the symptom or sign. The CPRS was completed on 139 in-patients and a matrix established such that the Y-axis was formed of the patients, and the symptoms and signs formed the X-axis. Each cell in the matrix contained a 0, 1, 2, or 3 depending on the interviewer's rating. This set of data was transformed into a binary relation for the application of Q-analysis by using a 'slicing parameter' of 2 or more, thus retaining only the most severe symptoms in the matrix.[3]

To illustrate the analysis, from the incidence matrix (Figure 7.1) a shared-face matrix is constructed with the number of q-connections between each simplex and every other (Figure 7.2). The mean q-connectivity is calculated by the formula,

$$\text{mean } q\text{-connectivity} = \frac{v}{n-1},$$

where v = the sum of the number of vertices which the simplex shares with other simplices, and n = the total number of x-simplices. The basic output from Q-analysis shows at each value of q which simplices are q-connected (Table 7.1). For each simplex a cut-off value is

Table 7.1   *Q-analysis output*

q-value	Components							
14	($X5$)							
13	($X5$)							
12	($X5$)							
11	($X5$)							
10	($X5$)							
9	($X5$)							
8	($X5$)	($X8$)						
7	($X5$)	($X8$)						
6	($X5$)	($X8$)	($X3$)	($X6$)	($X10$)			
5	($X5$)	($X8$)	($X4$)	($X6$)	($X10$)	($X4$)	($X7$)	($X9$)
4	($X5$)	($X8$)	($X4$)	($X6$)	($X10$)	($X4$)	($X7$)	($X9$)	($X1$)
3	($X5, X8, X6, X10$)		($X3$)	($X4$)	($X7$)	($X9$)	($X1$)	($X2$)
2	($X5, X8, X3, X6, X10, X4, X7, X9, X1, X2$)							
1	,,	,,	,,	,,	,,			
0	,,	,,	,,	,,	,,			

	$X1$	$X2$	$X3$	$X4$	$X5$	• • •	Xn
$Y1$	1	0	1	1	0		
$Y2$	0	0	0	1	0		
$Y3$	1	1	0	1	0		
$Y4$	0	1	1	1	1		
$Y5$	0	0	1	0	0		
•							
•							
•							
Yk							

Figure 7.1   *Incidence matrix*

X1	X2	X3	X4	X5	X6	X7	X8	X9	X10		Mean connectivity
4	2	2	—	—	—	—	—	—	—	X1	0.67
	3	2	—	—	—	—	—	—	—	X2	0.67
		6	2	—	—	—	—	—	—	X3	1.00
			5	2	—	—	—	—	—	X4	0.67
				14	3	—	3	—	3	X5	1.67
					6	2	—	—	—	X6	0.78
						5	2	—	—	X7	0.67
							9	2	—	X8	1.11
								5	2	X9	0.67
									6	X10	0.78

Figure 7.2   *A shared-face matrix*

defined as: mean q-connectivity + (mean q-connectivity * q-factor). By incremental increases in the q-factor, say by 0.25, the cut-off value is raised. In the analysis we require that the value of q that connects two simplices be greater than the cut-off values of both simplices. The increase in the q-factor weighting causes simplices that have low-intensity connections to become removed. If the pattern of q-connections is drawn as shown in the top of Figure 7.3 (p. 176), the effect of increasing the q-factor weighting is demonstrated.

The basic output of Q-analysis when applied to the matrix of 139 patients and sixty-five symptoms and signs is shown in Table 7.2. The commonest-occurring symptom is sadness, $q = 97$ with observed sadness at $q = 87$. These two become q-connected at $q = 79$. The number of q-connected separate components increases to $q = 60$ and then decreases until a single component exists at $q = 40$. By this level eleven different symptoms have come together in one component, indicating these are likely to form an important subgroup. Below $q = 35$ the number of q-connected components increases to reach a maximum of six separate components at $q = 7$. Apart from the main

Table 7.2   *Q-analysis output*

q-value	Qq-value	Components
97	1	(Sadness)
87	2	(Sadness) (Observed sadness)
79	1	(,,)
77	2	(,,) (Lassitude)
76	3	(,,) (Lassitude) (Worry)
68	2	(,,) (Worry)
67	3	(,,) (Worry) (Concentration difficulties)
61	4	(,,) (Worry) (Concentration difficulties) (Fatigue)
60	5	(,,) (Worry) (Concentration difficulties) (Fatigue) (Inner tension)
59	5	(,,) (Concentration difficulties) (Fatigue) (Inner tension) (Reduced sleep)
56	5	(,,) (Fatigue) (Inner tension) (Reduced sleep) (Indecision)
52	4	(,,) (Fatigue) (Reduced sleep) (Indecision)
51	3	(,,) (Reduced sleep) (Indecision)
49	4	(,,) (Reduced sleep) (Indecision) (Reduced appetite)
47	2	(,,) (Reduced appetite)
46	3	(,,) (Reduced appetite) (Lack of feeling)
44	2	(,,) (Lack of feeling)
40	1	(,,)
35	2	(,,) (Autonomic disturbance)
34	3	(,,) (Autonomic disturbance) (Suicidal feelings)
33	4	(,,) (Autonomic disturbance) (Pessimistic thoughts) (Reduced sexual interest)
32	3	(,,) (Autonomic disturbance) (Reduced sexual interest)
30	2	(,,) (Reduced sexual interest)
29	3	(,,) (Reduced sexual interest) (Slowness)
28	3	(,,) (Slowness) (Aches and pains)
27	2	(,,) (Aches and pains)
23	3	(,,) (Aches and pains) (Memory disturbance)
22	2	(,,) (Memory disturbance)
19	2	(,,) (Muscular tension)
18	2	(,,) (Other delusions)
17	3	(,,) (Other delusions) (Phobias)
16	5	(,,) (Other delusions) (Phobias) (Other auditory hallucinations) (Agitation)
14	4	(,,) (Phobias) (Other auditory hallucinations) (Compulsive thoughts)
13	3	(,,) (Other auditory hallucinations) (Compulsive thoughts)
12	3	(,,) (Other auditory hallucinations) (Ideas of persecution)
10	5	(,,) (Ideas of persecution) (Rituals) (Derealization) (Reduced speech)
9	3	(,,) (Hostile feelings) (Disrupted thoughts)
8	4	(,,) (Depersonalization) (Hostile feelings) (Disrupted thoughts) (Hypochondriasis)
7	6	(,,) (Hostile feelings) (Disrupted thoughts) (Hypochondriasis) (Feeling controlled) (Observed muscle tension)

6	4	(,,) (Hostile feelings) (Commenting voices) (Visual hallucinations)
5	2	(,,) (Hallucinatory behaviour, Disorientation) (Commenting voices)
4	2	(,,) (Lack of sensation) (Perplexity)
3	4	(,,) (Involuntary movements) (Perplexity) (Elation) (Pressure of speech)
2	3	(,,) (Other hallucinations) (Increased sexual interest) (Ideas of grandeur) (Elation, Pressure of speech)
1	2	(,,) (Overactivity, Distractability) (Withdrawal)
0	1	(,,) (Mannerisms, Elated mood, Hostility, Lability of response, Lack of response, Speech defects, Flight of ideas)

Simplices connected into the main component are indicated by (,,).

component, there are no components containing more than one simplex, but the large number of separate components might reflect several different groupings of symptoms. At $q = 2$, one of the components contains two simplices (elation, pressure of speech) and this may indicate a separate group of symptoms.

Figure 7.4 (p. 178) shows the emergence of subcomponents at different q-factor weightings. At q-factor $= 0.00$ there is no disconnection, but at q-factor $= 0.25$ there is a separate subcomponent composed of seven simplices. These are elation, pressure of speech, ideas of grandeur, overactivity, elated mood, flight of ideas and distractability. If the standard Q-analysis method had been applied with a q-factor weighting of 0.25 on the shared-face matrix then at $q = 0$ there would be two separate 0-connected components, and the smaller one would comprise these seven simplices. At q-factor $= 0.50$ a second subcomponent occurs made up of depersonalization, derealization and ritualistic behaviour. As the q-factor weighting is increased more subcomponents emerge and at q-factor $= 1.25$ six distinct subcomponents occur (Table 7.3). The depressive syndrome contains many of the simplices that occur in the standard analysis with the highest q-values.

The choice of names of these symptoms reflects general psychiatric usage. Even so, the symptoms in the depressive syndrome would be considered to have such melancholic significance even by non-psychiatrists. There are three syndromes associated with what might be called psychotic disorders. First a paranoid syndrome containing other delusions, ideas of persecution and auditory hallucinations occurs and, secondly, a schizophrenic syndrome with disrupted thoughts, feeling controlled, commenting voices, and hostility. It has long been accepted within psychiatry that the first three symptoms in the schizophrenic syndrome have considerable diagnostic importance in this condition. The third psychotic syndrome has been called

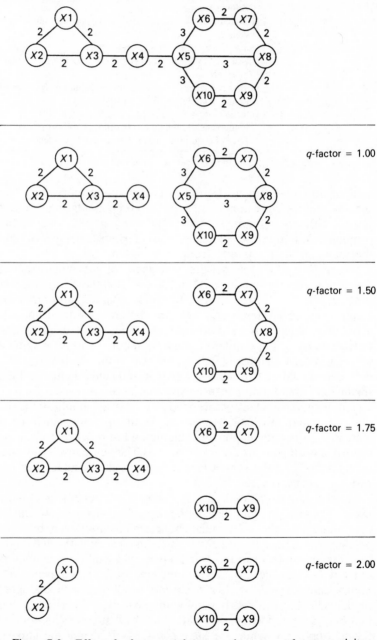

Figure 7.3   *Effect of q-factor weightings on the pattern of q-connectivity*

Table 7.3   *Subcomponent syndromes that occur at q-factor = 1.25*

Depressive syndrome	*Paranoid syndrome*
Sadness	Other delusions
Observed sadness	Ideas of persecution
Lassitude	Other auditory hallucinations
Worry	
Fatigue	*Schizophrenic syndrome*
Inner tension	Disrupted thoughts
Reduced sleep	Feeling controlled
Reduced appetite	Commenting voices
Indecision	Hostility
Lack of feeling	
Autonomic disturbance	*Manic syndrome*
Suicidal feelings	Elation
Pessimistic thoughts	Pressure of speech
	Ideas of grandeur
Unspecified psychotic syndrome	Overactivity
Other hallucinations	Elated mood
Withdrawal	Flight of ideas
	Distractability
Depersonalization syndrome	
Depersonalization	
Derealization	

'unspecified' as there are only two symptoms in it and both are too imprecise to attach a clear label to it. It is interesting to observe that in Figure 7.4 the paranoid and schizophrenic syndromes join together with visual hallucinations at q-factor = 1.00, supporting the clinical observation that there is an overlap or grey area between the paranoid disorders and schizophrenia.

If the standard Q-analysis showed separate q-connected components at $q = 0$, then the q-factor weighted analysis would show distinct components as separate subcomponents no matter how small a value the q-factor was given. This means that subcomponents in the weighted analysis that occur at low q-factor values are those that are relatively distant from the main structure. From Figure 7.4 the subcomponent that emerges at the lowest q-factor is the manic syndrome. This would indicate that in this set of data the presence of such a syndrome is not closely related to the main structure. The choice of prescribing ECT for the disorder of mania is relatively unusual and it would be expected that symptoms associated with mania would remain distinct from depressive symptoms in any breakdown of symptom groupings. In the standard analysis elation and pressure of speech form a separate component at $q = 2$, which may have given a hint that they were indicating a different syndrome, but the true nature of this has only become apparent by using the q-factor weightings. The depersonalization syndrome is the second syndrome

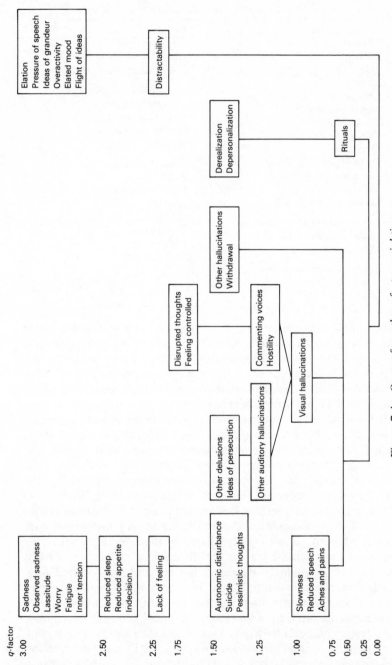

q-factor

3.00 | Sadness
      | Observed sadness
      | Lassitude
      | Worry
      | Fatigue
      | Inner tension

      | Elation
      | Pressure of speech
      | Ideas of grandeur
      | Overactivity
      | Elated mood
      | Flight of ideas

2.50 | Reduced sleep
      | Reduced appetite
      | Indecision

2.25 | Lack of feeling

1.75

1.50 | Autonomic disturbance
      | Suicide
      | Pessimistic thoughts

      | Other delusions
      | Ideas of persecution

      | Disrupted thoughts
      | Feeling controlled

      | Other hallucinations
      | Withdrawal

      | Derealization
      | Depersonalization

1.25 | Other auditory hallucinations

      | Commenting voices
      | Hostility

1.00 | Slowness
      | Reduced speech
      | Aches and pains

      | Visual hallucinations

0.75

0.50

0.25

0.00

Distractability

Rituals

Figure 7.4   Output from the q-factor weightings

to occur at the next highest q-factor. Clinically these symptoms can be difficult to determine accurately and the place of depersonalization among the classification of psychiatric disorders is confused as it can occur within other conditions as well a being an entity in its own right with a wide variety of aetiologies. So the slightly eccentric position of this syndrome is not unexpected. The remaining four syndromes all arise at a similar q-factor value suggesting that the three psychotic and the depressive syndromes had equal central importance in this group of patients.

Intercorporate connections: a Q-analysis

The data used relate to the shareholdings which 250 large Japanese enterprises maintain among themselves. The 250 largest financial and non-financial enterprises of 1980 were selected and lists of the ten largest shareholders in each enterprise were obtained.[4] The incidence matrix, therefore, was of size 250×250, with each cell showing the presence or absence of a shareholding between the enterprises. As this is the matrix of a directed graph, the initial analysis involves the construction of two undirected adjacency matrices: one for the enterprises regarded as shareholders and one for the same enterprises viewed as targets of investment. In the first case, enterprises are regarded as connected to one another if they have one or more shareholdings in common – they invest in the same range of enterprises. In the second case, enterprises are regarded as connected if they have one or more common shareholders.

The results of the standard and extended Q-analysis of the network of investing enterprises are shown in Tables 7.4 and 7.5. The largest investor in the top 250 Japanese companies is Nippon Life Insurance, with 149 participations – and thus a 'top q' value of 148 – but this has no q-connections to other enterprises until $q = 88$, at which level it is connected to Dai-Ichii Mutual Life through 89 common investments. Table 7.4 shows, at intervals of ten for the value of q, the way in which this pair of connected enterprises gradually 'grow' into a large connected component which includes 122 of the enterprises. The component remains small until the value of q reaches 30, at which point it increases in size steadily, but the main growth occurs at values of q less than 10, that is to say, most of the enterprises which have any shareholding participations at all are connected to one another at fairly low levels of intensity, and only a relatively small number of dominant investors maintain a wide spread of investments in common. The fact that just one component exists in the network suggests that there are few obstacles to any attempt by the dominant investors to mobilize support for a co-ordinated plan of action. This conclusion must be qualified, however, in the light of the evidence from Table

Table 7.4   *Japanese investors:*
growth of large component (1980)

Value[1] of q	Size of component[2]
100	–
90	1
80	2
70	2
60	2
50	3
40	6
30	11
20	19
10	32
0	122

[1] The highest value of q for any investor
was 148, but a component of size greater
than 1 did not appear until $q = 88$. The
network contained a single large
component.
[2] Components of size 1 are isolates and
are not counted in Tables 7.4–7.7.

Table 7.5   *Japanese investors: number and growth of components (1980)*

q-factor weighting	Number of components	Size of largest component
20	5	4
19	5	4
18	6	4
17	7	4
16	7	4
15	9	7
14	10	7
13	10	7
12	12	8
11	11	9
10	8	18
9	5	31
8	3	46
7	3	52
6	3	54
5	3	57
4	2	62
3	2	64
2	2	66
1	1	71
0	1	76

7.5, based on the measure of relative intensity. The table shows that the core of the large component comprises a group of 76 enterprises with significant common investments, but that this component is fragmented into subgroups with high levels of internal connectivity. At a q-factor value of 10 there are eight distinct components, the largest of which includes eighteen enterprises. The size of the remaining components at this level ranged from two to eight. These smaller components correspond to the key members of the enterprise groups widely recognized by Japanese business commentators, groups such as Mitsui, Mitsubishi, Sumitomo, and Fuyo. But the groups were not found to be all of a similar character, each having distinct patterns of connection. In the case of the Mitsubishi and Sumitomo groups, for example, the small components contain exclusively non-financial enterprises, their financial members forming part of the large component. Within the large component they are connected with a number of other large financials, though the factor-weighted analysis shows that they retain a relatively distinct identity within this component: at higher levels of relative intensity the large component fragments into its constituent enterprise groupings.

It can be concluded that the enterprise groups are real and important centres of co-ordinated investment, with the largest groups maintaining wide, but relatively weak, connections amongst their leading financial members. Any attempt to generate co-ordinated action on the part of the individual enterprises would tend to be contained within the circles of the separate business groups themselves. A certain level of loose co-ordination over general matters might be possible if organized through the leading financials, but attempts to influence the behaviour of particular enterprises could take place only *within* groups. The importance of this fragmentation is brought out clearly in the case of the Mitsui group, whose financial and industrial members emerge as a distinct component at a factor weighting of 10 and maintain a high level of internal cohesion. This high level of autonomy and cohesion would make it difficult for it to be included even in any general co-ordination of action.

This conclusion is confirmed by the results for the network of controlled companies – the investment targets – which are shown in Tables 7.6 and 7.7. In the standard Q-analysis separate components appear at $q = 4$, and the number of components multiplies rapidly to nine. The largest of the components broke up catastrophically at $q = 6$: at this level there are three components of size 5, one of size 4, and the remainder are of size 2. Although a high proportion of the top 250 are loosely q-connected through common shareholders, very few big components exist at high levels of connection. The factor-weighted analysis in Table 7.7 shows that the measure of relative intensity is

Table 7.6   *Japanese investment targets: growth of large component*

q-value	Number of components	Size of largest component
10	0	–
9	0	–
8	0	–
7	2	3
6	9	5
5	9	65
4	2	158
3	1	194
2	1	216
1	1	224
0	1	229

Table 7.7   *Japanese investment targets: number and size of components (1980)*

q-factor weighting[1]	Number of components	Size of largest component
11	2	2
10	2	4
9	5	4
8	8	8
7	9	9
6	11	10
5	9	20
4	10	59
3	5	137
2	1	217
1	1	223
0	1	224

[1] No useful subdivisions appeared at factor weightings greater than 12.

sensitive to the structures which underly this fragmentation. At factor weightings of 6 and 8 the nucleii of a number of the enterprise groups appear as separate components: the subordinate members of the Mitsubishi, Sumitomo, Toyota, and other smaller groups appear as distinct components. It appears that the group-structuring of the network of investors made itself felt in the group-structuring of the network of investment targets. The extent of any communication and co-ordination among subordinate enterprises is constrained by the structural divisions among the key controlling enterprises.

The Japanese intercorporate network, therefore, shows a high degree of weak connectivity, centred on the leading financials, but an underlying structure of strongly connected enterprise groups. The extent to which 'macro-level' phenomena can be achieved in the Japanese economy is limited by this fact. The network permits the co-ordinated action of collectively organized enterprise groups, which may pursue common investment and trading strategies; but the structure precludes the establishment of any significant degree of co-ordination *between* these groups. To the extent that such co-ordination has occurred, this must have involved the intervention of an agency from outside the network. Indeed, it has frequently been remarked that Japan's Ministry of International Trade and Industry (MITI) operates in exactly this way (Johnson, 1982).

Conclusion

This chapter began with the claim that the conventional formulation of the micro–macro problem was misleading. It was argued that the two levels are not separate and distinct realms, but that 'agency' implies 'structure'. Giddens claims that the only usefulness that the micro–macro distinction may have in social analysis is in pointing to the difference between relations of face-to-face interaction involving a high level of spatial and temporal immediacy, and relations between groups or collectivities which may be more extended over space and time (Giddens, 1979: 77).

The analysis of psychiatric data concerning individual agents showed the existence of structural phenomena – syndromes – at the individual level. It was shown that these clusters of symptoms corresponded closely to the diagnostic categories used by psychiatrists, but also suggested novel diagnostic possibilities. The analysis of Japanese enterprises also showed the existence of structural phenomena – in this case, enterprise groups – which could be seen as effective constraints upon the actions of the separate enterprises and as a constraining backcloth to attempts at intercorporate co-ordination. The validity of the analysis was confirmed by the close correspondence between the groups identified and those recognized by Japanese business commentators, yet it was suggested that these commentators have typically overstated the separation of the groups. The big groups were found to exhibit varying levels of internal integration and to have varying degrees of embeddedness in the wider network.

It could be argued, however, that as the psychiatric data were based on doctors' reports of psychiatric symptoms, the Q-analysis has merely disclosed the structure of psychiatric language and doctors' taken-for-granted assumptions about mental illness (Szasz, 1961). Similarly, the derivation of the Japanese data from business directories may be argued as having produced an analysis which tends to reproduce the categories employed by business commentators. In both cases, therefore, the relatively close correspondence between the Q-analysis and 'professional' categorizations would be unremarkable. We would not wish to counter such arguments simply by asserting the status of our data as 'brute facts'. We would argue that, while all accounts of the world are mediated through the accounts of others, the novel insights thrown up in our accounts demonstrate that *Q*-analysis has not simply reproduced the practical categorization of participants. The analyses grasped something of the real structures of the world.

Our purpose in raising these problems is to emphasize that the hierarchy of levels to which we have referred in this chapter is not to be interpreted as a direct reflection of what exists 'out there'. We do not propose to replace the ontological dualism of 'micro' and 'macro' with an ontological hierarchy of levels. The various levels of analysis to which we have referred involve a methodological bracketing on the part of the researcher; a decision to concentrate on certain features of the world and to pay less attention to others. This is what we see as the central implication of Giddens' rejection of the conventional micro–macro distinction. It has been argued in this paper that *Q*-analysis is a powerful and illuminating method for pursuing this conception of social science.

Notes

1. See the useful collection of papers in O'Neil (1973).
2. Basic sources on *Q*-analysis are Atkin (1974, 1981), and Beaumont and Gatrell (1982).
3. This 'slicing parameter' can be altered by the researcher to disclose structural gradations in the data.
4. The background and method of this project are discussed further in Scott (1986).

References

Asberg, M., Montgomery, M.A., Perris, C., Schalling, D. and Sedvall, D. (1978) 'A Comprehensive Psychopathological Rating Scale', *Acta Psychiatrica Scandinavica* (Suppl.), 271m: 5–27.
Atkin, R.H. (1974) *Mathematical Structure in Human Affairs*. London: Heinemann.
Atkin, R.H. (1981) *Multidimensional Man*. Harmondsworth, Middx: Penguin.
Beaumont, J. and Gatrell, A.C. (1982) *An Introduction to Q-analysis*. Norwich: Geo Publications.
Brandon, S., Cowley, P., McDonald, C., Neville, P., Palmer, R. and Wellstood-Eason, S. (1984) 'Electroconvulsive Therapy: Results in Depressive Illness from the Leicestershire Trial', *British Medical Journal*, 288: 22–5.
Giddens, A. (1979) *Central Problems in Social Theory*. London: Macmillan.
Johnson, C. (1982) *MITI and the Japanese Miracle*. Stanford: Stanford University Press.
O'Neil, J. (ed.) (1973) *Modes of Individualism and Collectivism*. London: Heinemann.
Parsons, T. (1937) *The Structure of Social Action*. New York: McGraw-Hill.
Scott, J. (1986) *Capitalist Property and Financial Power*. Brighton: Wheatsheaf.
Szasz, T. (1961) *The Myth of Mental Illness*. New York: Harper & Row.

8
THE 'STRUCTURATION' OF ACTION

The essence of the comparative narrative method is to reduce data by making suitable translations from narratives at the individual to the collective level. Peter Abell's chapter sketches in the method in relation to moving from statements about the action of individuals to statements about the action of collectivities. Matters for debate in this approach include recognizing when the least divisible, most abstract statement has been arrived at, and how the approach accommodates actions whose origin lies less in previous actions than in cultural or structural 'givens'. Another point is that, stripped to their skeletal features, it becomes easier to depict narratives as the same. One might argue that *West Side Story* is the same as *Romeo and Juliet*, at root. This reveals a strength of the approach. One might be undecided as to the similarity of two narratives and this approach to comparison would help where interest in both things separately was subordinate to interest in a global analysis. Further, one might be able to find systematic relationships between the nature of organization and the type of stories characteristically produced by members. Any statement about constraint of the organization must, because organizations create social worlds, be reducible to statements about individuals.

The 'structuration' of action
Inference and comparative narratives

Peter Abell

My claim in this chapter is as follows: that the theory and method of comparative narratives provides the most appropriate analytical framework within which to formulate the relationship between statements about what individuals do and forbear from doing and statements about what collectivities, comprising the individuals, do and forbear from doing. The analysis will thus build upon my theory of comparative narratives, which I have presented in detail elsewhere (Abell, 1984, 1985, 1986). I will not here, therefore, develop many of the technical details of the theory.[1]

Since what individuals do or refrain from doing can, normally, only be understood within the framework or the context in which they perform their actions,[2] my chapter will also debate the ways in which we should conceptualize and research the connection between action and context.[3] If the social sciences are to find a way of evading the simple polarity of, on the one hand, a picture of human action as driven by Durkheimian 'structural' forces and, on the other, extreme 'voluntarism' then a suitably articulated technical language is needed within which to nuance the polarity. My claim is that narrative theory can help in this direction.[4]

Since we are concerned with the action of individuals and collectivities, some initial remarks about this central concept are in order.

Actions, I will equate with those things an individual (or collectivity) does/prevents or forbears to do/prevent, either intentionally or 'unintentionally', whilst doing something else intentionally. To do something intentionally is to intentionally bring it about; similarly an actor can intentionally prevent something occurring, when, if it had not been for what the actor did (on the occasion in question) then that something would have happened. An actor may, of course, be said to do/prevent things which were not intended, whilst doing/preventing something else. An actor forbears to do or prevent (intentionally or otherwise) all those things which the actor (individual or collective) could do/prevent on the occasion in question and which the actor does not do/prevent (Abell, 1982; Porn, 1970; Von Wright, 1963).[5] In the broadest sense, actions by individuals link certain of their mental states to realized states of affairs, what Von Wright refers to as the internal and external manifestations of actions.

Although there may be (though I doubt it) a sense in which some properties of collectivities cannot, as a matter of principle, be reduced to or deduced from the properties of *and* relationships between its constituent entities (that is, so-called *emergent* properties) I will argue that this is not so, at least, as far as the predicates 'doing' and 'forbearing to do' are concerned. A concept describing collective action can always, without remainder, be translated from statements about interrelated individual actions.[6] This does not mean, of course, that the action of a collectivity (in the sense of what it brings about) is necessarily intended by any individual within the collectivity. The unintended consequences of individual actions, in a collective context, are clearly of great analytical interest. I wish, therefore, to argue quite strenuously against any concept of *emergent action*.

The advantage of addressing the logico-empirical problems associated both with the individual-to-collective inference and the structuration of individual action, from the perspective of narrative theory, will, I trust, become evident as we proceed. Essentially, it rests with the ability of the theory to handle, in a systematic fashion, the notion of *structural determination*. It does this through the agency of well-defined *homomorphic translation rules* which permit us to say of two or more structures that they are sufficiently similar to be regarded as embodying a generalization.

An informal approach to the issues

There is a robust and obvious sense in which a human collectivity (a group, a class, an organization, and so on) comprises: (a) individual humans endowed with motor energy; (b) the actions they perform (to include forbearances); (c) the context of their actions (which may or may not contain reference to the collectivity in question); (d) some indication of how these context-specific actions (that is, situated actions) are related one to another (that is, structured).[7] Put even more colloquially, a human collectivity is made up of individuals doing (or forbearing to do) things, in context, and where the actions of some (possibly all) are dependent upon the actions of others. The collectivity will perforce possess a history, since the various doings will be protracted in time. I can attach no meaning to any concept of what the collectivity itself does (or forbears to do) which transcends the content implied by the statements (a) to (d) above. Notwithstanding, a number of difficult analytical issues remain as to how a well-founded concept of collective doing (forbearance) may be arrived at. The inference (or translation rule) from a set of interdependent situated actions to such a concept will possess two aspects. First a *semantic* one, concerned with the content (meaning)[8] of the situated actions and, second, a *syntactical* one, concerned with the dependency structure connecting the actions over a specified period of time.[9] The logical question which then arises is: what form should the translation rule(s) take and how much of the *local* content and syntactical structure should be preserved in arriving at a *global* conception of action?

The concept of 'situated action' needs however some prior clarification. The ways in which actions may be declared to carry 'meaning' or content has, of course, generated much debate both in the analytical-philosophical (Danto, 1973; Davidson, 1971, 1972), and in the hermeneutic and post-hermeneutic, traditions (Gadamer, 1975; Habermas, 1970; Ricoeur, 1977). I do not wish, here, to get entrammelled in these various debates, for most of what I say will not depend crucially upon the particular interpretation one may care to adopt. I will assume, as in my earlier publications referred to above, that situated actions can be adequately described/explained/ understood by the contingent practical syllogism (Abell, 1985; Von Wright, 1971).[10] The 'situation' of an action is then captured in two ways. First, and directly, by a contingent set of descriptions, *C*; these will characteristically be expressed in natural language and may be extensive.[11] Furthermore, the interdependence of actions ((d) above) requires that set *C* may contain descriptions of other actions by the same or other actors. Second, since an action is predicated upon the *objectives* (*intentions*) and *beliefs* of the actor in question, then one might quite rightly seek the social genesis of these.[12] I will argue that this is best accomplished in terms of narratives – which I will term *socialization narratives*. The structuration of actions is now reduced to an understanding of the complex ways in which they are located in the structure of narratives, which are homomorphically translatable to each other. I should like briefly to justify this statement before developing the argument further.

An anti-philosophical aside

The polarity I referred to earlier has, of course, given train to much mischief in the social sciences. Are our actions our own, are we the originators of them, or are they in some way causally determined within us? Is there free will or is there not? Are free will and determinism in fact incompatible? The philosophical debate will, of course, continue to rage and it would be an entirely hopeless project if social scientists were required to await the final adjudication on these issues, before they could begin to construct an adequate theory linking individual actions with their (social) context. Indeed, there appears, almost, to be an inverse relationship between the theoretical development of a social-science discipline and the degree to which it takes these issues seriously. Economists, for instance, largely ignore them and possess the most impressive theoretical structures. Sociologists are in the reverse position!

I propose to sidestep the issues of free will and determinism;[13] so rather than asking whether our actions are, or are not, determined from without, I will pose the question as to whether or not our actions are, in fact, discernibly patterned, in terms of the narratives of which they are part. This patterning might refer either to various socialization narratives or, directly, to a specific narrative. *So, the issue of structuration becomes one of the degree to which there is, or is not, a detectable generalization (pattern) in the narrative(s) which may be adduced to account for the incidence of a specific type of action (or its outcome).*[14]

Such generalizations will be expressed as translation rules (homomorphisms) between the structures of comparable narratives. If a homomorphism can be detected then the action is structurally generated, if not, it is not. Homomorphisms are, thus, the very stuff of structuration.[15]

Defining a narrative

A narrative comprises (Abell, 1985, 1986): (a) a finite set of individual actors, I; (b) a finite set of situated actions, A; (c) an assignment mapping of the actors on to the actions; (d) an ordering of the actions in time; (e) a non-symmetric, reflexive, non-cyclic relation[16] L on set A; where a_iLa_j means that action a_i 'leads to' action a_j. A narrative is, thus, conveniently depicted as an a-cyclic di-graph.[17] We require also that the graph be weakly connected,[18] an intuitively sensible restriction, which formally merely requires that the relation links all parts of the narrative. There are no bits that can be broken off!

If for shorthand convenience we depicted the narrative (di-graph) as $G(A;L)$, then the analytical problems we face amount to the following:

(1) In the context of the structural determination of action (structuration) – whether a translation rule (homomorphism) can be defined between the set of narratives which generate apparently identical actions.

(2) In the context of the individual (action) collectivity inference – whether a rule can be defined which enables us to reduce a narrative to a single 'action' describing what the collectivity does (forbears to do).

In both cases we need to translate as follows:

$$G(A;L) \xrightarrow{\quad \Psi \quad} G(C;L).$$

But what properties should Ψ possess? I will discuss each case in turn. The following two sections should be read in conjunction with Appendices I and II respectively.

Narratives and the structuration of action

Consider a given narrative $G(A;L)$ constructed to account for the occurrence of a given action a_j which, in terms of the time ordering of actions, is the ultimate action of the narrative. $G(A;L)$ gives the story, in terms of connected situated actions, portraying how a_j came about. The particular action, a_j, will also embody its own intrinsic beliefs, values, and affective orientations (that is, in terms of the appropriate practical syllogism) and socialization narratives may *in principle* be constructed to account for these also.[19] Any given narrative $G(A;L)$, is, thus, in principle underwritten by a series of socialization narratives. But let us ignore these here and concentrate upon $G(A;L)$. If we accept my above interpretation of structuration (with the provisos in note 15 in full view) then the analytical question becomes: is there a translation rule between $G(A;L)$ – which generates a_j – and similar narratives $G(C;L)$ constructed to account for the occurrence of other instances of the action a_j? To the degree that there is, then a_j is a 'structurated' action – it evidences a generalized narrative pattern or structure in its social construction. So what form will the rule take? I have argued elsewhere – and in a slightly different context – that semantically the rule should comprise a mapping between the point sets A and C in $G(A;L)$ and $G(C;L)$ which creates either an equivalence or tolerance relation on set A.[20] Syntactically, the requirement is that, if any two actions in A are mapped to a single action in C then all the actions on *all* paths (that is, directed sequences of relations) running between those two actions in $G(A;L)$ must also be mapped to the selfsame action in $G(C;L)$. Rules satisfying these semantic and syntactic restrictions can be conveniently expressed as homomorphisms defined between groupoids respectively attached to $G(A;L)$ and $G(C;L)$.[21] An identical analytical technique can also be used to 'fold up' the narrative structure giving a simplified picture of the 'context' of the action in question: a_j. The narrative eventuating in a_j, that is $G(A;L)$, is homomorphically reduced to a simpler narrative – expressed more abstractly – which also accounts for the occurrence of a_j.[22]

Narratives and the individual-to-collective inference

An identical analysis technique can be used to research the individual-to-collective inference. Now the rule Ψ which translates:

$$G(A;L) \xrightarrow{\ \ \Psi\ \ } G(C;L)$$

will be one which reduces set A to a single 'collective action' C. It should be clear that since $G(A;L)$ is, by definition, weakly connected, a rule which reduces the structure to a single-point structure will have both the semantic and syntactic characteristics mentioned above.[23] The whole action set A of the di-graph $G(A;L)$ will be mapped to a single equivalence class and in so doing – since the first and last action are both mapped to C – then all those actions in between, and all paths, will be consistently mapped to C also. This observation effectively provides a necessary (though not sufficient)[24] condition for treating individual actions as contributing to a collective action. Putting it succinctly, a collectivity must possess a story (a narrative).

The implications for research

I want in the final section of this chapter to sketch the manner in which the theory of comparative narratives may be used to refocus empirical research into the linkage between what individuals and collectivities 'do' and their context (that is, 'social structural environment'). The conventional 'variable centred' method of studying the linkage between context and individual action is to search for correlations (in specified populations) between the occurrence of the actions and certain 'contextual variables'. In socialization studies the parallel activity is to search for the correlates of beliefs, values, and so on. This method is very much within the Durkheimian tradition. The correlations, with well-known provisos, are often then regarded as indicative of causal linkages. Although this step from correlation to causality has, of course, produced much philosophical debate, most research, if not explicitly at least implicitly, assumes that the regularities (or laws) we seek which connect action to context will be of this form. My contention is that this approach, whilst valuable in detecting gross patterns of correlation, is not likely to lead to the detection of fundamental regularities and to lay the empirical grounds for the development of systematic theory. The regularities – or, if you like, laws – which connect context to action can more fruitfully be construed in terms of the homomorphic mappings of structures as described above. I believe research should be refocused accordingly.

This is not to say, however, that the location of variable-centred correlations is a pointless exercise. In my view such correlations often provide clues as to the nature of the connections which need *explicating* in terms of the narrative structure which show how they are, in fact, socially generated. Let us sketch how this may be accomplished. Assume we locate a correlation between a variable C (ie. a contextual one) and a particular social occurrence O. So we have, shall we say:

Cor $(C,O) > O$.

This should then provide the impetus for the search for generalizable narratives which connect C and O. The correlation is, as it were, a prompt in this direction. We might then find, for example:

– in C α does X
– α doing X *leads to* α doing Y
– α doing y *leads to* β doing j.

.
.
.

α does O.

Therefore, in C, α does O; and generalizing across α, β etc., C becomes connected to (correlated with) O. In general, it should be clear from what I have said above that in each case the narrative structures connecting C with O will be not identical but sufficiently similar for them to be *homomorphically* translatable. If they are not, then the linkage between C and O is narratively speaking *overdetermined*. That is to say, there is more than one way of socially fabricating the linkage between C and O.

This sketch provides a role in social research for both variable-centred and narrative methods but implies a greater emphasis than has been placed before upon delineating the action mechanisms which connect doing (individual and collective) to context.

Notes

1. I will, however, footnote some details in a semi-technical manner in order to help the reader unfamiliar with the technical issues. I have attempted to make the text accessible to those readers with little or no familiarity with the formal ideas that underpin narrative theory (i.e. deontic logic, some group theory, and graph theory).

2. I will use the term 'action' to cover acts and forbearances unless the distinction needs to be drawn.

3. Now sometimes, following Giddens, called 'structuration'. It is not technically well founded in Giddens' writing, and thus open to a variety of interpretations some of which are, I suspect, much more profound than I am able to handle.

I will also throughout use the word 'context' to describe what others might refer to as 'social structure', largely because I wish to preserve the word structure to describe aspects of narrative. To use the word in both senses might cause confusion.

4. And only help. I make no ambitious claims for what follows. I suppose what we would like, eventually, to be able to do is to depict a particular action on a scale in terms of the degree to which it is 'structurally determined' as opposed to 'structurally free'. These however will, needless to say, be complex ideas. I will later give some indication of how this complexity may be addressed within the framework of narrative theory.

5. There are many problems associated with this rather simple picture of action. See Abell (1986) for an attempt to resolve some of them. It does, however, provide a sufficiently rich descriptive framework for analysing much if not all action. The picture formally is isomorphic with Von Wright's (1971) d, f, and T calculi.

6. In the sense that individual actions provide the only source of motor energy, their description is clearly necessary to an understanding of what a collectivity 'does'. The interesting question, however, is whether or not such descriptions are also sufficient. I will argue that they are.

7. It would be analytically possible to dispense with the naming of actors and view a collectivity as a set of interdependent actions which just happen to be performed by the actors in question. This may be particularly true where the actions are institutionalized as responses to role expectations (Abell, 1986, ch. 6). There seems no good reason to limit ourselves in this way at the outset, however, but rather to let such institutionalized situations stand as a special case.

8. I will prefer the phrase 'the content of action' to the phrase 'the meaning of action', though, in referring to the semantic aspects of a translation rule, the latter might appear to be more appropriate. I do, however, feel that the word 'meaning' has been given too many meanings and that the apparent parallel between linguistic acts (speech) and other acts fails in certain crucial aspects (Danto, 1973). Although I will below give a specific interpretation to the 'content' of a situated action my analysis will not depend upon it.

9. What this period should be is discussed in Abell (1986).

10. The explanation of an action thus takes the form: in a situation C the actor intended that Y *and* in situation C the actor believed that if the actor did X then Y would (be likely to) result. The actor did Y therefore the actor did X (both in C). For a more elaborate justification of the use of the practical syllogism see the references mentioned in the text.

11. As a number of observers have noted, set C is potentially infinite (cf. the role of the initial conditions in the Hempelian deductive nomological mode of explanation).

12. We may assume intentions, in turn, depend upon values and/or affects. So actions are situated in terms of the genesis of beliefs (cognitive socialization), values (normative socialization), and affects (affective socialization).

13. I will assume that if there exists a pattern of actions which bring about a particular action, the situation could have been otherwise but was, in fact, not so. Whether or not one wishes to describe this as (causal) determination seems to me not to be a crucial matter.

14. In the sense that actions generate outcomes. Structuration, in the way I am using the term, may also (through the agency of a socialization narrative) refer to accounts of the genesis of beliefs, values, and affects (see note 12) which are the constituents of an action.

15. They in practice can be formulated at different levels of abstraction (see Abell, 1986).

16. Non-symmetric in the sense that if a_i leads to a_j then a_j cannot lead to a_i; reflexive in the sense that, for logical convenience, we allow that actions partly lead to themselves; non-cyclic in the sense that if a_i leads down a path (sequence of relations) there is no way of returning to a_i.

17. A di-graph is a set of points in a plane (in this case the actions) and a directed relation (line) connecting all or some of the points.

18. Weakly connected means that there exists a path (i.e. a sequence of lines) between all pairs of points in the graph ignoring the direction of the relations.

19. One should emphasize the 'in principle' here; in practice we often take these as given as a consequence of prior socialization. But the important point is that the acquisition of beliefs, values, and affects (assuming they are not biologically determined) is best studied in terms of the narratives which generate them. That is, socialization theory should, in my view, be primarily set within a narrative framework not a variable-centred framework (see note 15).

20. The simplest case is, of course, where two (or more) narratives have identical action sets; then the semantic mapping is one to one between the actions. In general, however, this will not be the case. This being so the mapping will be sometimes one to many (expansion) and sometimes many to one (condensation). A tolerance will arise when a particular action may be translated to more than one action. For a fuller technical treatment of these issues see Abell (1986).

21. An example may be found in Abell (1985, 1986).

22. This amounts to what I have termed *abstraction* as opposed to *generalization* (the previously outlined technique). I have argued (Abell, 1986) that the homomorphic abstraction and generalization of narratives are interrelated in the context of the abstraction/generalization space.

23. This is not quite true, see Abell (1986).

24. Presumably collectivities must possess additional properties. Many connected narratives will not provide the grounds for speaking of collective action.

Appendix I   An elementary example of structuration

(For a more technical presentation see Abell, 1985, 1986.)

1   Let a_j and a^1_j be generated by the following narratives, depicted as di-graphs (a_i and c_i are action descriptions in terms of the contingent practical syllogism).

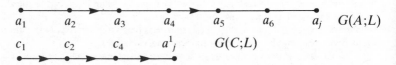

$$a_1 \qquad a_2 \qquad a_3 \qquad a_4 \qquad a_5 \qquad a_6 \qquad a_j \quad G(A;L)$$

$$c_1 \qquad c_2 \qquad c_4 \qquad a^1_j \qquad G(C;L)$$

2   For a_j and a^1_j to be *structured* there must exist a way of translating from $G(A;L)$ to $G(C;L)$ (or vice versa) which enables us to say these are essentially the same 'story' eventuating in a_j and a^1_j respectively. That is to say a well-defined rule Ψ must enable us to make the following translation:

$$G(A;L) \xrightarrow{\ \Psi\ } G(C;L).$$

3   If $G(A;L)$ and $G(C;L)$ were to be identical then there would be no problem. The two narratives have identical actions and structures. In general, however, they will only be similar. Two stories may be 'the same story' without being identical! How can we decide they are sufficiently similar to say they are essentially the same story?

4   *One* way would be to define a mapping as follows:

a_1 and $a_2 \longrightarrow c_1$

$a_3 \longrightarrow c_2$

$a_4, a_5,$ and $a_6 \longrightarrow c_3$

$a_j \longrightarrow a^1_j$

Note that (a) the actions c comprise equivalence classes on set A (semantic requirement); (b) the action c_3 embraces a_4 and a_6 and *must* therefore embrace a_5 (the syntactic requirement).

5   It is possible to express all this formally in terms of homomorphisms between the structures. When the structures are much more complex this becomes a far from simple matter.

Appendix II   An elementary example of the individual-to-collective inference

1   Let the connected series of individual actions be depicted as a di-graph as follows:

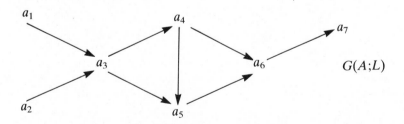

2   The problem is to reduce this to a single-point graph $G(C;L)$.

3   So all a_i ($i = 1$ to 7) are mapped to C. Note this satisfies the semantic and syntactic rule.

References

Abell, P. (1982) 'Action, Reason and Power', *Acta Sociologica*, 25(2): 133–45.

Abell, P. (1984) 'Comparative Narratives: Some Rules for the Study of Action', *Journal for the Theory of Social Behaviour*, 14(3): 309–32.

Abell, P. (1985) 'Analysing Qualitative Sequences: The Algebra of Narrative', in Michael Procter and Peter Abell (eds), *Sequence Analysis*. Aldershot: Gower.

Abell, P. (1986) *The Syntax of Social Life: The Theory and Method of Comparative Narratives*. Oxford: Oxford University Press.

Danto, A. (1973) *Analytical Philosophy of Action*. Cambridge: Cambridge University Press.

Davidson, D.C. (1971) 'Agency', in R. Binkley (ed.) *et al.*, *Agent, Action and Reason*. Toronto: Toronto University Press.

Davidson, D.C. (1972) 'Freedom to Act', in T. Honderich (ed.), *Essays on Freedom of Action*. London: Routledge & Kegan Paul.

Gadamer, H. (1975) *Truth and Method*. New York: Continuum.

Habermas, J. (1970), *Zur Logik der Sozialwissenschaften*. Frankfurt: Suhrkamp.

Porn, I. (1970) *The Logic of Power*. Oxford: Basil Blackwell.

Ricoeur, P. (1977) 'The Model of the Text: Meaningful Action Considered as a Text', in F. Dallmayr and T. McCarthy (eds), *Understanding and Social Inquiry*. Notre Dame, Ind.: Notre Dame University Press.

Von Wright, G.H. (1963) *Norm and Action*. London: Routledge & Kegan Paul.

Von Wright, G.H. (1971) *Explanation and Understanding*. London: Routledge & Kegan Paul.

Conclusion
MICRO-SOCIOLOGY AND MACRO-THEORY

Nigel G. Fielding

This book began with an assertion of the centrality of issues of power in contemporary social theory and pursued at some length Giddens' formulation of the concept of structuration as a means of expressing the recursive nature of social relations. Giddens' is by no means the only formulation, but it is perhaps the most widely known. Micro-sociology presents such formulations with an opportunity and a problem. The opportunity is to pin down in empirical reality what is essentially an elegant speculation. The problem is to choose a means to do so.

How would a concept like structuration be empirically manifest? If people are both creators and creatures of social organization how will this be apparent? We have to consider how best to establish the linkage between holistic world-view and situated fragment. The further we stray from the data, the less 'grounded' our theory, and yet there would be little point in gathering such concrete data if we could not address the 'big' issues. It is a matter reminiscent of Zelditch's comment on the entrenched division between qualitative and quantitative research in social science. The caricature of qualitative research is that it is 'soft' whereas quantitative research is 'hard'. It would be naïve to deny a distinction which researchers feel so strongly, but it would also be foolish to ignore the dilemma posed by Zelditch: 'Quantitative data are often thought of as "hard" and qualitative as "real and deep"; thus, if you prefer "hard" data you are for quantification and if you prefer "real, deep" data you are for qualitative participant observation. What to do if you prefer data that are real, deep *and* hard is not immediately apparent' (1962: 566). Put this way it is hard to imagine anyone who could not want both the security of robust data and the reach of theoretically relevant data.

It is equally apparent that we need to 'fill in' the interstitial region between the micro-sociological world about which we have highly concrete knowledge and the macro-social world whose trans-situational patterns suggest the arena in which matters of moment and power are contested. While the various contributors to this book have vigorously asserted distinctive ways of doing so, they share a conception of where such efforts must begin. In Knorr-Cetina's words, 'We are now in a new position not only to raise the question of the relation between micro- and macro-social theory and methodology, but also to point out new directions in which to search for a resolution . . . This direction will be heavily informed (but not bounded) by advances in the more microscopic approaches, for it is there that most theoretical and methodological developments have taken place . . . Paradox[ically] it is through *micro*-social approaches that we will learn most about the macro-order, for it is these approaches which through their unashamed empiricism afford us a glimpse of the reality about which we speak' (1981: 41–2). Knorr-Cetina goes on to assert that fixing at the 'microscopic' level will not give us a grasp of the whole of the matter. It is simply that its most tangible and reliable signs are manifest there.

As we have seen, the contributors agree that it is no longer plausible to subscribe to a separation between the micro and the macro. In that sense they endorse the essential idea behind the concept of structuration or notions which are akin to it. We inhabit, and are inhabited by, an enacted environment (Weick, 1964) which makes us creators and creatures of the macro-social.

Beyond this, the thrust of the argument in the book points to theoretical developments which will force future debate along new lines. While the early chapters in the book pose the theoretical issue as it stands, and the central chapters illustrate it empirically, the closing chapters, with their mathematical core, point plainly to the application of formal logic in the analysis of actions described by micro-sociological studies. It is curious, and gratifying, that the running in current work on artificial intelligence is in many cases being made by qualitative researchers, such as ethnographers and discourse analysts (Agar and Hobbs, 1985). In the design of 'expert knowledge systems', the experts have been obliged to turn to those who can best model real social action – the micro-sociologists.

References

Agar, M. and Hobbs, J. (1985) 'Growing Schemas out of Interviews', in J. Dougherty (ed.), *Directions in Cognitive Anthropology*. Urbana, Ill: University of Illinois Press.

Knorr-Cetina, K. (1981) 'The Micro-sociological Challenge of Macro-sociology: towards a reconstruction of social theory and methodology', in K. Knorr-Cetina and A.V. Cicourel (eds), *Advances in Social Theory and Methodology: Toward an Integration of Micro- and Macro-sociologies*. London: Routledge & Kegan Paul.

Weick, K. (1964) *The Social Psychology of Organizing*. New York: Appleton-Century-Crofts.

Zelditch, M. (1962) 'Some Methodological Problems of Field Studies', *American Journal of Sociology*, 67.

Index

Abell, P. 16, 17, 185, 186
accounts 35, 38, 39, 55, 107, 110, 127, 135, 136, 150, 154, 184
action 2, 3, 5, 7, 12–14, 17, 20, 21, 24, 33, 35, 38, 47, 54, 55, 62–5, 80, 82, 83, 95, 106, 112, 114, 147, 160, 183, 185, 186, 188–92
Agar, M. 86, 198
agency 3, 56–8, 60, 61, 64, 66, 76, 118, 142, 144–50, 155, 156, 158, 160, 183
aggregation hypothesis 12, 16, 32–6, 39, 144
Alexander, J. 4, 21
Anderson, B. 6
Apel, K.-O. 1
Archer, M. 3, 4, 14, 144, 149
Armstrong, E. 158
Asberg, M. 171
Atkin, R. 184
Atkinson, J. 162
Atkinson, P. 5, 150
authority 2, 75, 76, 81, 82, 90
autonomy 1, 3, 4, 14, 47, 54, 57, 75, 146, 157

Bailey, F. 45
Barley, N. 104
Barthes, R. 83
Bateson, G. 83
Beaumont, J. 184
belief, 9, 14, 78–84, 94, 95, 99, 188, 190, 191
Bellah, R. 80
Berger, P. 30, 157, 160
Berreman, G. 43, 84
Bhaskar, R. 21, 145, 149
Birdwhistell, R. 22
Birkbeck, C. 7
Bittner, E. 75, 81
Black, D. 6
Blau, P. 144
Bloomfield, L. 43
Blumer, H. 5
Bourdieu, P. 13
Brandon, S. 171
Braudel, F. 41, 42, 44, 46, 48
Brewer, J. 15, 16, 139, 142, 143, 150, 151, 159
Brewer, M. 8
Brittan, A. 32

Buckley, W. 3
bureaucracy 99–110, 112, 114
Burgess, E. 6

Callinicos, A. 149
Callon, M. 45
Carling, A. 149
Carlstein, T. 149
causal 7, 8, 10, 24, 25, 34, 47, 60, 62, 64, 66, 80, 81, 106, 110, 117, 188, 191
Chatterton, M. 2
Cicourel, A. 10, 12, 21, 23, 29, 30, 32, 34, 39, 154, 155, 159, 160
Clark, C. 15, 117, 127, 137, 139
class 10, 11, 12, 23, 33, 34, 168, 187
cluster analysis 167
collectivity 1, 3, 4, 10–12, 17, 20, 21, 34, 63, 143–5, 168, 169, 183, 185–7, 189, 191, 192
Collins, R. 9, 12, 21, 32–4
comparative narrative 16, 17, 185, 186, 191
conflict 1, 6, 89, 94
connectivity 167, 170, 171, 173, 182
constructionism 147
context 1, 2, 9, 10, 14, 15, 83–6, 88, 186, 187, 191, 192
conversational analysis 1, 10, 29, 117
Cowley, P. 16
critical theory 1
Culler, J. 82
cultural bias 85, 88
culture 2, 11, 33, 43, 81, 144

Dahl, P. 145
Dandeker, C. 4
Danto, A. 188
Davidson, D. 188
Davis, N. 6
'descriptive vocabulary' 155, 156
determinism 4, 56, 149, 156
Dewey, J. 24
dialectical 2, 4, 153, 160
dialectic of control 146
di-graph 189, 191, 194
discourse 80–6, 198
Ditomaso, N. 21
Ditton, J. 8
documentary method 64
domination 157

'double production' 20
Douglas, J. 22, 83
Drew, P. 125
duality, dualism 3, 4, 14, 15, 17, 54–6, 58, 61, 136, 142–8, 150, 154, 157, 158, 160–2, 168, 184
Durkheim, E. 40, 80, 168, 186, 191
Duster, T. 13

Eco, U. 82, 84, 91
epistemological 59, 100, 148, 149, 161
Erikson, K. 102
Esterton, A. 46
ethnomethodology 1, 5, 14, 29, 54, 56–9, 61–8, 71, 142, 143, 145, 146, 148, 150, 158, 159
Etzioni, A. 34
Evreinow, Q. 27

Fabrega, H. 84, 86
'factual reality' 159
Faris, J. 84, 86
Fielding, J. 7
Fielding, N. 7
Fine, G. 81
Fleck, L. 28, 29
Foucault, M. 46, 145
Frake, C. 29
France, A. 40
free will 188
functionalism, neo-functionalism 1, 3, 34, 36, 113, 148

Gadamer, H. 188
Garfinkel, H. 4, 29, 30, 62, 83, 150, 155, 158, 160, 161
Gatrell, A. 184
Geertz, C. 80
Geiger, T. 80
Gellner, E. 159
gestalt 60
Giddens, A. 1–4, 9, 14–16, 21, 32, 34, 35, 57, 81, 82, 118, 136, 139, 142–50, 154–7, 159–62, 168, 169, 183, 184, 192, 197
Gilbert, M. 9
Gilbertson, D. 102
Glaser, B. 8
Glassner, B. 7
Goffman, E. 22, 25, 27–9, 83, 84, 146
Gorman, R. 160
Gouldner, A. 100
Greimas, A. 85
grounded theory 8
Gumpertz, J. 29, 43
Gurwitsch, A. 24

Habermas, J. 1, 188
Hadden, S. 150
Hall, A. 87
Harré, R. 9, 21, 32, 34–6
head terms 84, 86, 88, 91
hermeneutics 1, 188
hierarchy, hierarchical 6, 75, 88, 90, 117, 167
Hindess, B. 5
Hobbes, T. 45
Hobbs, J. 198
Holdaway, S. 2
holism, holistic 2, 7, 16, 159, 167, 169, 197
homology 105
homomorphism 17, 187, 189–92
humanism 5
Husserl, E. 4
Hymes, D. 29
hypothesis of unintended consequences 32, 34–6, 38, 39, 162

idealism, idealist 5, 59, 144
ideology 6, 11, 80, 81, 85
indexical 33, 80, 103, 110, 124, 137, 143, 150, 158
individualist 5, 11, 12, 20, 21, 25, 62, 63, 144
induction 7, 8, 101
instantiation 4, 43, 71
instrumentalist 22
interactionism 1, 4, 14, 15, 26, 54, 56, 71, 100, 101
intersubjectivity 11, 143
introspection 9
Isaac, J. 149

James, H. 5
Jefferson, G. 124
Johnson, C. 183
Johnson, G. 5

Knorr-Cetina, K. 9, 13, 14, 20, 21, 32, 37, 45, 46, 54, 144, 152, 198
Kurzweil, E. 84

Laing, R. 46
Latour, B. 45, 46
law 14, 82, 191
Law, J. 46
Layder, D. 149
Leiter, K. 158
Lemert, C. 24, 81, 84, 86
Lester, M. 150
Levinson, S. 83
Lévi-Strauss, C. 36, 83

life-world, *Lebenswelt* 15, 22, 99, 160
Lockwood, D. 3
loose-belief analysis 78, 83, 85, 86, 95
Luckman, T. 30, 157, 160
Lukes, S. 3

MacCannell, D. 86
MacCannell, J. 86
McKinney, J. 25
macro-scale, macro-social 1, 9, 10, 12,
    13, 16, 20, 21, 32, 33–5, 38, 39, 41, 46,
    48, 54, 120, 136, 197, 198
mandate 80, 81, 85, 86, 88
Manicas, P. 149, 158
Manning, P. 14, 78–81, 84, 86, 99, 101
Marxian, Marxist 1, 22, 34, 40, 100, 113
materialism 144
matrix 167, 169–71, 173, 175, 179
Mayhew, B. 21, 34
Maynard, D. 145, 158
Mead, G. 4, 5, 24
meaning 1, 2, 7, 17, 25–8, 43, 80–6, 91,
    102–5, 113, 188
Mehan, H. 30
Merton, R. 34
methodological individualism 23–5, 72,
    168
methodological situationalism 12, 20–5
micro-economics 117, 139
micro-social, micro-sociology 1, 2, 5, 9,
    10, 12–15, 20–3, 28, 30, 32–6, 38, 39,
    41, 45–8, 54, 117, 120, 136, 139, 197,
    198
Miller, R. 25
morphogenesis 3, 4, 144
motive 106, 113
Mulkay, M. 124, 125

narrative 16, 17, 188–92
Natanson, M. 160
Needham, R. 80, 84
network analysis 16
nominalism, nominalist 5, 144
nomological 1
normative 119, 120, 135, 136, 154

objectification 107, 111, 118, 145, 150,
    155, 156, 160
objective, objectivity 11, 58, 66, 67, 110,
    113
Ofverbeck, P. 95
O'Keefe, D. 159
O'Neill, J. 23, 46, 184
ontology, ontological 22, 34, 38, 62, 66,
    142, 144, 148, 149, 158, 159, 167, 168,
    184

'oral dictionary' 155
order 6
organic 6
Ostberg, G. 95

paradigm 6, 83, 85, 86, 88, 90, 91
Park, R. 6
Parsons, T. 6, 21, 145, 146, 168
Patterson, W. 87
Peirce, C. 82
Perrow, C. 94
perspectival 67, 104, 106
phenomenology 2, 4, 7, 100, 107, 113,
    158, 159
Phillipson, M. 154
Picou, J. 5
Pinch, T. 15, 117, 127, 137, 139
pluralism 145
Porn, I. 186
positivist 9
power 1–3, 12, 15, 16, 33, 40, 41, 44–8,
    54, 75, 78–82, 99, 100, 117, 118, 120,
    137, 138, 145, 146, 157, 158, 169, 197
process 3, 8, 15, 80, 111, 112
Psathas, G. 84, 158, 159
Punch, M. 101

Q-analysis 16, 167, 169–75, 177, 179,
    181, 183, 184
qualitative 7–12, 17, 100, 101, 142, 145,
    157, 197, 198
quantitative 8, 9, 11
Quine, W. 31

realism 5, 9, 144, 147
reciprocity 26
recursive, recursiveness 4, 15, 20, 142–8,
    150, 155, 158, 160, 162, 167, 197
reductionism 5, 9, 11, 22, 23
reflexive, reflexivity 2, 31, 105, 108, 145,
    146, 148, 154, 155, 158, 160
reification 41, 148, 159
representation hypothesis 20, 21, 32, 35,
    40, 144, 162
representations 13, 41, 44–6, 106, 114
Restivo, S. 46
Ricoeur, P. 188
Robey, D. 84
Rock, P. 15, 99, 112, 117
Rogers, M. 159, 160
role 13, 81, 86
Ross, E. 6
rule, rules 2, 3, 5, 15, 30, 31, 41, 76, 81–
    4, 105, 117, 139, 147, 148, 150, 154,
    155, 158, 160, 162, 167, 197
Rydnert, B. 95

Sacks, H. 29, 62, 125
Saussure, F. 81
Schegloff, E. 29
Schutz, A. 24, 26, 39, 80, 83, 146, 147, 150, 152, 155, 157–61
Scott, J. 16, 184
Scott, W. 95
Scull, A. 6
semantic 78, 80–3, 86, 91, 95
semiotics 78, 82–4, 88
Serres, M. 48
Sharrock, W. 14, 54, 78
Short, J. 95
Shotter, J. 149
Simmel, G. 21, 24, 26
slicing parameter 167, 171, 184
Smith, C. 145, 148, 149
social institution 1
social reality 1, 5, 39, 99, 144, 145
social reproduction 35
social setting 14, 64, 66, 67, 74, 76
social structuralism 34
social system 1, 3, 13, 35
space 4, 9, 15, 33, 44, 106, 142, 143, 145, 146, 148–51, 154–7, 162, 183
Spitzer, S. 6
Starr, P. 94
status 81, 82
Strauss, A. 8
structural constraints 160, 186
structuralist 4, 5, 21, 36, 84, 100, 113
structuration 1–4, 14–16, 20, 35, 81, 95, 139, 142, 143, 145–9, 151, 156, 157, 160, 161, 185, 187–90, 197, 198
structure 1–5, 7, 10–16, 20, 29–31, 33–6, 38–40, 44, 54–8, 60–2, 64–8, 74–6, 78–81, 83, 95, 99, 100, 104, 105, 108, 111, 114, 118, 142, 144–50, 154–6, 158–62, 168, 169, 183, 185, 188–90, 192, 194, 195
structuring properties 147
subjective, subjectivity 7, 8, 11, 12, 25–7, 58, 61, 66, 67
symbol, symbolic 13, 80–2, 99, 101, 109, 110, 114, 137
synoptic 66–9
syntactical 82
Szasz, T. 183

teleology 105
Thomason, B. 147
Thompson, M. 85
time 4, 9, 15, 33–5, 106, 114, 115, 142, 143, 145, 148–51, 154–7, 162, 183
Tolstoy, L. 46, 47
transformation 85, 145, 155
translation 5, 187–90
Turner, S. 5
Tyler, S. 83

unintended consequences 142, 143, 147, 149, 150, 154–7, 160

validity 55
van Maanen, J. 101
variable-centred method 191, 192
Voegelin, E. 40
voluntarism 4, 56, 142, 146, 149, 186
Von Wright, G. 186, 188

Wallerstein, I. 36
Wardell, M. 5
Warriner, C. 24
Watkins, W. 23
Watson, R. 14, 54, 70, 77
Weber, M. 12, 24–6, 145
Wedgewood, C. 36, 37, 40, 46
Weick, K. 84, 85, 101, 198
Whyte, W. 105
Wieder, D. 30
Wildavsky, A. 85
Williams, R. 8, 46
Williams, R.A. 87
Willis, P. 163
Wilson, T. 145, 158
Wirth, L. 21
Wittgenstein, L. 30, 43
Wood, H. 30
Woolgar, S. 46
world-view 2, 7, 106, 116, 197
Wuthnow, R. 11

Zelditch, M. 197
Zenzen, M. 46
Zimmerman, D. 30
Znaniecki, F. 7